"I only went out for a walk,
and finally concluded
to stay out until sundown,
for going out, I found,
was really going in."

— John Muir

ALPINE SIERRA TRAILBLAZER
Where To Hike, Ski, Bike, Fish, Drive From Tahoe to Yosemite

fourth edition, first printing
text by Jerry Sprout
photography, production, design by Janine Sprout

Still for Carrie and Jerry, Lea and Al

ISBN 0-9670072-6-7
Library of Congress Catalog Card Number: 99-90115

Diamond Valley Company, Publisher
89 Lower Manzanita Drive
Markleeville, CA 96120

Thanks to Paula Pennington, Jimmy Dunn, Suzanne and John Barr, Heather Barr, Kate and Richard Harvey, Joan Wright, Greg Hayes, Jack and Sandy Lewin, the Rob Moser family, Heidi Hopkins, Patty and John Brissenden, Cynthia, Michael, Thomas and Sara Emmaline Sagues, Matthew and Amy Sagues, Tim Pemberton, Edie Paulson, Elsa Kendall, Tim and Jan Gillespie, Georgia and Vic Sagues, Carol Mallory, Jim Rowley, Nicole Rowley, Gary and Barbara Howard, Judy Farnsworth, Linda Kearney, John Manzolati, Margaret Daniels, Mina Wood, and Chris at the Markleeville Post Office, Ellen and Sam Scott, Joe Stroud, Chet Carlisle, Marge and Jerry Purdy, Carolyn Spratt, Edwin O. Hagstrom, Nick Hartzell, Allie Bornstein, Karen and Bill Marshall, Mark and Vicki Hyde, Steve Martin, Paul Hallings.

Dick Edwards and Ellen Martin, Alpine County Museum; Teresa and June, Alpine Chamber and Forest Service; Sara Slolm and Mark Kinbrough, Tahoe Rim Trail Association; Judy Warren, Horse Feathers; Camille and Elliot, Mono Basin Visitors Center; Cadie, White Mountain Ranger District; Claudia Welsh, Ansel Adams Gallery; Sarah, Mono Inn; The Ruddens at Markleeville Store; Dave Kirby, Woodfords Station; Donna, Sierra Pines; Gina and Ruggero Gigli, Villa Gigli; South Lake Tahoe Chamber of Commerce; Everyone at the Alpine County Library; Jeff and Erika, Bridgeport Ranger District; Donna, Carson Valley Historical Society; Mono County Historical Society; Carson City Visitors Bureau; Gary and staff, Carson City Ranger District; Staff of the El Dorado Interpretive Association; Shelton Johnson, Ben and numerous rangers at Yosemite National Park; Rob, Jane, and Dennis, Tioga Gas Mart; Ron and the Kit Carson Mountain Men; Paul et. al. at Bear Valley Adventure Company; Staff at League to Save Lake Tahoe and Sierra Nevada Alliance; Pat Wright, Yosemite Association; Shiela, Lake Tahoe Visitor Center; Paul and Gloria, Family Mountain Shuttle; Laurie at Mono County Visitor Informantion.

Proofreader: Greg Hayes

COVER: MARKLEEVILLE PEAK FROM CHARITY VALLEY

*Alpine Trailblazer is
dedicated to preserving
the irreplaceable bounty
that nature has bestowed
upon these unspoiled
California mountain
communities.*

LEMBERT DOME, YOSEMITE NATIONAL PARK

ALPINE SIERRA
Trailblazer

WHERE TO
HIKE, SKI, BIKE, FISH, DRIVE
FROM TAHOE TO YOSEMITE

JERRY AND JANINE SPROUT

DIAMOND VALLEY COMPANY

MARKLEEVILLE, CALIFORNIA

PUBLISHERS

TABLE OF CONTENTS

The Sierra Nevada forms the eastern border of California, 200 miles from the Pacific, a 400-mile wall of peaks averaging 70 miles wide and more than two miles high. An impenetrable barrier to the Spaniards who named it "Range of Snow" in 1776, the Sierra today has the world's longest system of interconnected mountain trails.

On its west side, the range rises gently to its crest over a distance of 50 to 65 miles, up from near sea-level valleys that span the midsection of California. From its crest toward the east is a different story: the Sierra Nevada drops abruptly in 5,000- to 7,000-foot escarpments into the valleys of the Great Basin high desert.

Because of the Sierra's geographic and topographic features, a trip across the width of the range from the Great Valley to the Great Basin is one through widely diverse ecosystems—from streamside woodland to yellow pine belt, through mixed conifers and subalpine belt, over the treeless crest,

BAGLEY VALLEY

through the Jeffrey and piñon pine belts, and into the sage lands of high desert. In this 60- to 80-mile, west-to-east trip, climactic and biological features vary equivalent to that of a north-south range from northern Mexico to the fringes of the American Arctic.

Of the nine Sierran automobile passes, six are within or bordering Alpine County—Echo, Carson, Luther, Ebbetts, Monitor, and Sonora. The highest and most-southern pass, Tioga through Yosemite, is a two-hour drive. Alpine is the trans-Sierra gateway partly due to topography. Glacial and volcanic features folded together here, making for anomalous breaks in the range of peaks. But Alpine was also the historical route choice due to rich gold and silver deposits in the Mother Lode, Comstock

SAND HARBOR, HOPE VALLEY

MONO LAKE, SONORA PASS, EBBETTS PASS

Lode, and several eastern Sierra strikes, that beckoned emigrants and entrepreneurs by the tens of thousands from 1850 through the early 1900s.

The Sierran wall gets taller as you go from north to south, with peaks averaging around 7,000 feet in the northern region, elevating to nearly 11,000 feet around Tahoe and the Alpine Sierra. From Tuolumne Meadows in Yosemite south, summits are 12,000- to 13,000-feet and up. Generally, the range is more arid as you go south, with the exception of "the Pineapple Express," winter storms from the South Pacific hitting the California coast.

The Golden Gate, the mouth of the San Francisco Bay, is a break in the Coastal Range west of Alpine that acts as a door for Pacific storms that drop rain and snow, increasing in volume as air rises, to a maximum downpour at an elevation of 6,500 feet on the west slope. In the hundred-odd years since records have been kept, the greatest snowfall was recorded at Tamarack Lake in Alpine County, a depth of 73.5 feet. Storms are mostly spent as they cross the Sierran Crest, with some 20 inches of rain on the east slope at 5,500 feet, compared to almost quadruple that amount at the same elevation on the west side. Thus, the aridity of the Great Basin combines with Pacific storms, sun with water, providing Alpine with optimum conditions for mountain flora and fauna.

What the Pacific bequeaths, the Sierra only partially returns. From high-mountain origins, rivers such as the American, Mokelumne, and Tuolumne flow westerly to the ocean, on the way providing irrigation to farms that supply the nation with its fruits and vegetables, and San Francisco with its drinking water. Much of the melted snow, however, flows east of the crest, in the Walker, Carson, and Truckee rivers, headed to a system of east Sierra lakes and finally to the alkaline sinks of the Great Basin. The Alpine Sierra is the origin of the Upper Truckee River, which is Lake Tahoe's largest single source.

JIMMY DUNN

FORESTDALE DIVIDE

Alpine was made a county in 1864, when silver deposits were discovered in the area. Until that time, most of Alpine was thought to be part of the Nevada Territory. Wishing to avoid losing more riches to Nevada, the California Legislature resurveyed the State's eastern border, getting the land officially into the Golden State. It then created Alpine County by biting off chunks of the high country from five existing counties—Amador, El Dorado, Tuolumne, Calavaras and Mono. The result of this geographic pastiche is a county uniquely diverse in its scenery and natural features.

The name "Alpine" was chosen because Scandinavian miners and others who had been to Europe thought the region's grassy river valleys with surrounding forests and snow-capped peaks were much like the Alps. Alpine is also apt because the Pacific Crest Trail runs through the center of the county, and much of it is above the treeline, the very definition of "alpine." You might also call this "Alpine" because of Snowshoe Thompson, Alpine County's mountain expressman. In 1854 he fashioned the first downhill skis in America and as mail carrier crossed the Sierra for a decade before the railroad was completed. Snowshoe Thompson put on displays of downhill derring-do, perhaps setting then land speed records, and later engaged in competitions that were the origins of alpine skiing.

Alpine County is 775 square-miles, 95 percent of it public land. Its population of about 1,200 is by far the smallest in the state, and far fewer than the number of cows, deer and a number of other resident mammals. The county has more campsites than homes, even factoring in the major ski resorts at Kirkwood and Bear Valley. All highways are official scenic routes, and traffic control consists of a blinking yellow light at Woodfords.

CATHEDRAL LAKES, YOSEMITE NATIONAL PARK

TRAIL TO LAKE MARGARET

At the northern edge of the county is the Tahoe Basin, the ring of mountains that holds what many feel is the world's most beautifiul lake. Known for its glizty casinos and world-class ski resorts, Tahoe also boasts hundreds of miles of wilderness trails and unsurpassed rides for mountain bikers.

The southern end of Alpine County blends with the Sierra at Sonora Pass, the gateway to the Yosemite high country. Most people are familiar with the treasures of Yosemite Valley, but far fewer visit the fabulous trails around Tuolumne Meadows, with its paths leading north and south. From Tuolumne you can day hike to Yosemite Falls and to views of Half Dome and the valley.

In this book you will find 88 trailheads in the Alpine Sierra around Hope Valley and Markleeville—and extending to all of Tahoe and the Tuolumne high country of Yosemite National Park. These trails lead to several wilderness areas— Carson-Iceberg, Mokelumne, Desolation, Emigrant, Mt. Rose, Hoover, Ansel Adams—as well as three National Forests: Toiyabe, Stanislaus and El Dorado.

Hikes explore major rivers, dozens of creeks, and peaks, and more than 60 high-mountain lakes. Topography includes polished granite, volcanic plugs, slate-topped peaks, mountain meadows, hot springs, alpine ridges, and sage-belt piñon forests. With its mountain passes and Forest Service spur roads that go north and south, Alpine gives access to the interior of the Sierra toward all points on the compass.

LOCAL DRIVE TIMES

MARKLEEVILLE TO:

Hope Valley	20 minutes	Tahoe:	
Grover Hot Springs	10 minutes	South Lake Tahoe	40 minutes
Gardnerville/Minden	30 minutes	Stateline Tahoe	1 hour
Kirkwood	50 minutes	Incline Village	1.5 hours
Ebbetts Pass	35 minutes	Tahoe City	1.5 hours
Bear Valley	1.25 hours	Emerald Bay	1 hour
Brigdeport	1.5 hours		
Yosemite:			
Tioga Entrance	2 hours		
Yosemite Falls trail	2.5 hours		

THE PASSES:

Echo Summit (7,382') Hwy. 50, South Tahoe to Sacramento
Luther Pass (7,740') Hwy. 89, Hope Valley to South Tahoe
Carson Pass (8,573') Hwy. 88, Hope Valley to Sacramento/Stockton
Kingsbury Grade (7,334') Hwy. 207, Tahoe to Carson Valley
Monitor Pass (8,314') Hwy. 89, Markleeville to Hwy. 395 (closed in winter)
Ebbetts Pass (8,730') Hwy. 4, Markleeville to Stockton (closed in winter)
Sonora Pass (9,628') Hwy. 108, Bridgeport to Stockton (closed in winter)
Tioga Pass (9,945') Hwy. 120, Yosemite east entrance (closed in winter)

COURTESY ALPINE COUNTY MUSEUM AND HISTORICAL SOCIETY

WOODFORDS

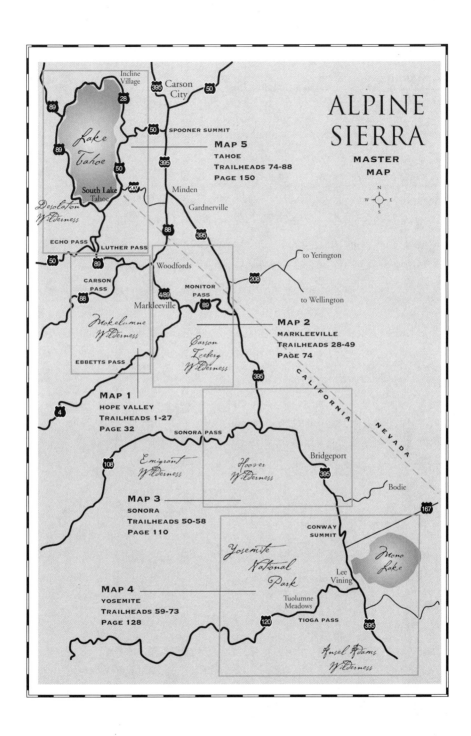

Incline Village
Carson City
395 50

SPOONER SUMMIT

ALPINE SIERRA
MASTER MAP

MAP 5
TAHOE
TRAILHEADS 74-88
PAGE 150

N
W E
S

Lake Tahoe
South Lake Tahoe
Minden
Gardnerville

Desolation Wilderness

ECHO PASS LUTHER PASS
Woodfords
to Yerington

CARSON PASS
MONITOR PASS
to Wellington

Markleeville

Mokelumne Wilderness

MAP 2
MARKLEEVILLE
TRAILHEADS 28-49
PAGE 74

Carson Iceberg Wilderness

EBBETTS PASS

CALIFORNIA

NEVADA

MAP 1
HOPE VALLEY
TRAILHEADS 1-27
PAGE 32

SONORA PASS

Emigrant Wilderness

Hoover Wilderness

Bridgeport

Bodie

MAP 3
SONORA
TRAILHEADS 50-58
PAGE 110

CONWAY SUMMIT

Mono Lake

Yosemite National Park

Lee Vining

MAP 4
YOSEMITE
TRAILHEADS 59-73
PAGE 128

Tuolumne Meadows

TIOGA PASS

Ansel Adams Wilderness

STRATEGIES FOR VISITING THE SIERRA

Alpine Sierra Trailblazer can be used for a lifetime's worth of outdoor exploring—or for a single pass through the region in a rental car. Think about how long you have and the type of time you want to have, and then choose from one of the following strategies. See *Resource Links* for selected accommodations and campgrounds.

1. THE ALPINE DAY TRIPPER — All of the hikes can be (and have been) accomplished as day trips from the Markleeville-Hope Valley area. In some cases it will be a long summer day, with 3- to 5-hours of scenic driving time. Most of the trailheads are within 30 to 45 minutes. You can enjoy the close-by, diverse hikes in the quieter areas of Alpine County for a day or two. Then spend all day exploring the farther reaches of Yosemite and North Lake Tahoe. This type of visit works well for people who want to stay in one place, and have a week or less to visit. The Markleeville-Hope Valley area is much less populated than Lake Tahoe and sees far fewer visitors than Yosemite. *Downside:* To see the farthest reaches, you will spend more time driving, albeit scenic.

2. THE SIERRA SAMPLER— Divide your trip up into three segments and then stay one-third of your time in: North or South Lake Tahoe; Markleeville-Hope Valley; and Bridgeport-Tuolumne. You can pick and choose among the hikes in each region, and get to know each—keeping notes for return visits. You will spend less time driving, and be able to enjoy sunrise and sunsets outside of the car. This strategy is best if you have a week or more and want to get a thorough introduction to the Sierra. Visitors who are driving through may select this option. *Downside:* You will do more sleeping around.

3. THE BASE CAMPER — Pick a region and stay in the area for your whole visit. You will get to know each place better and can dedicate full days to some of the more adventurous hikes. Each region still covers a lot of ground, and you will find plenty to do. This plan will work best for people with shorter times to visit, and for those who will be repeat visitors to the Sierra. *Downside:* There's a lot of beauty that will have to wait for your next trip.

KEY TO READING TRAILHEAD DESCRIPTIONS

23. TRAILHEAD NAME   ACTIVITIES BANNER

What's Best:
Park:
Maps:

HIKE:
BIKE, SKI, FISH:
Be Aware: More Stuff:

(SAMPLE)

"23." Trailhead Number: These correspond to numbers shown on the five Trailhead Maps. There are 88 trailheads. Numbers begin on Map 1, Hope Valley, and get larger as you go south. Trailhead numbers that are close together numerically are usually close geographically. Exception: The Tahoe excursions, which are north of Hope Valley, are last in the sequence (Map 5, Trailheads 74-88).

Trailhead Name: This is where you park to begin hikes and other activities. Some trailheads offer a single activity, such as hiking. Other trailheads include multiple activities, such as hiking, skiing, and fishing.

Activities Banner: Each trailhead is suitable for one or more of the following activities.
 HIKE = Day hikes, treks, and strolls
 BIKE = Mountain and road biking
 SKI = Cross country skiing and snowshoeing
 FISH = Lake, stream, and river fishing

What's Best: Notes what is special about this trailhead and what in general to expect.

Park: Gives directions to the primary parking spot. The parking spot is noted on the trailhead maps. A single trailhead may have additional (nearby) parking spots for other activities.

Map(s): Lists U.S. Geological Survey 7.5-minute topographical quadrangle map(s) for this trailhead. The region described is covered by 65 USGS quads. But don't despair, since most hikes in this book can be done without a map. Maps are recommended for backcountry hiking. In addition, the *Resource Links* section in the back of the book gives advice and sources for other trail maps for the different regions and wilderness areas.

HIKE:

The first paragraph gives hike destinations, length of hike in miles to the nearest .25-mile. (Miles off-trail, if any, is in parentheses.) All distances are ROUND TRIP, unless otherwise noted for car-shuttle (point-to-point) hikes. Elevation gains of 100 feet or more are also given.

The second paragraph gives brief directions to each hike destination. The first mention of a **Hike Destination** is boldfaced. Closest destinations come first, followed by those places farther along the same trail. The hikes are described in the same order they are listed in the first Hike paragraph. You can pick out the length of hike that seems appealing, and then scan down in the hike descriptions to read about it.

Be Aware: Lets you know about hazards, peculiarities, and special regulations.

More Stuff: Gives other hikes and add-ons to primary hikes. These suggestions will appeal mostly to repeat visitors and those wishing to explore the more out-of-the-way places. Also included will be ideas for backpackers.

BIKE: SKI: FISH:

Below the hiking directions are the descriptions for the other recreational activities offered at this trailhead. Directions to begin these activities are given seperately—unless they are already mentioned in the hike descriptions. For instance, a hike in summer may be a cross-country ski route in the winter, or be part of a biking route.

CACULATING HIKE TIMES

Hikers in average condition will cover about 2 mph, including stops. Groups and slower-movers will make about 1.5 mph, or less. Well-conditioned hikers can cover 3-to-3.5 mph. Everyone should add about 30 minutes for each 800 feet of elevation gain. Also add 60 minutes to all-day hikes, for a margin of error.

To check your rate of speed: 65 average-length steps per minute, equals about 2 mph; 80 steps per minute is about 2.5 mph; 95 average steps per minute comes to about 3 mph.

Recommendation: Before beginning a hike, calculate the number of hours a hike will take to make sure you don't run out of daylight. (Divide the hike's length by your rate of speed. Then add 30 minutes for each 800 feet of elevaton. Then throw in an hour for all-day hikes, and you have the total hiking time.)

TRAILHEAD DIRECTORY

HIKE: Day hikes and longer treks **SKI:** Cross-country skiing and snowshoeing
BIKE: Mountain and road bike trips **FISH:** Lake, stream, and river fishing

TH = Trailhead

HOPE VALLEY
TRAILHEADS 1-27, MAP 1

MARKLEEVILLE
TRAILHEADS 28-49, MAP 2

SONORA
TRAILHEADS 50-58, MAP 3

YOSEMITE
TRAILHEADS 59–73, MAP 4

TAHOE
TRAILHEADS 74–88, MAP 5

Best Of
THE
ALPINE SIERRA

Twenty Lakes Basin

WHAT DO YOU WANT TO DO TODAY?

HIKING—

TOUGH PEAKS

Round Top Peak, TH4, page 39

Raymond Peak, TH19, page 57

Silver Peak, TH37, page 85

Highland Peak, TH41, page 92

Dicks Peak, TH76, page 154

Pyramid Peak, TH87, page 172

EASY PEAKS

Elephants Back, TH4, page 39

Leviathan Peak, TH48, page 103

Lembert Dome, TH67, page 139

Mount Watkins, TH70, page 142

Castle Rock, TH86, page 171

BIG VIEW PEAKS THAT STAND ALONE

Hawkins Peak, TH21, page 61

Big Sam, TH52, page 114

Sonora Peak, TH53, page 115

Clouds Rest, TH69, page 141

Mount Hoffman, TH71, page 143

TAHOE RIM PEAKS

Waterhouse Peak, TH1, page 33

Stevens Peak, TH2 or TH3, page 34

Jobs Sister, TH25, page 66

Freel Peak, TH25, page 66

Mount Tallac, TH76, page 154

Snow Valley Peak, TH84, page 168

Genoa Peak, TH86, page 171

PEAKS WORTH THE CLIMB BUT FEW DO

Markleeville Peak, TH16, page 52

Reynolds Peak, TH19, page 57

Cary Peak, TH23, page 64

Thompson Peak, TH26, page 68

Tryon Peak, TH41, page 92

Mt. Baldy, TH81, page 165

VIEWING PLATFORMS

Caples Creek Buttes, TH7, page 43

Thunder Ridge, TH11, page 46

Sorensen's Cliffs, TH22, page 63

East Carson vista, TH30, page 80

Thornburg Canyon, TH32, page 32

Dump Canyon, TH48, page 104

Emerald Overlook, TH77, page 156

LAKES WITH FEWER VISITORS

Shealor Lakes, TH9, page 45

Grouse Lake, TH18, page 56

Bull Lake, TH41, page 56

Bull Run Lake, TH45, page 98

Emma Lake, TH54, page 116

Oneida Lake, TH60, page 130

East Peak Lake, TH86, page 172

LAKES WITH GREAT VIEWS

Winnemucca Lake, TH4, page 38

Raymond Lake, TH19, page 57

Granite Lake, TH18, page 56

Anna Lake, TH54, page 110

Summit Lake, TH59, page 129

Spillway Lake, TH63, page 134

Young Lakes, TH67, page 139

Cathedral Lakes, TH68, page 140

Susie Lake, TH76, page 154

LAKES TUCKED IN HIGH MOUNTAINS

Crater Lake, TH2, page 34

Fourth of July Lake, TH4, page 38

Raymond Lake, TH19, page 57

Par Value Lakes, TH57, page 121

Hoover Lakes, TH59 page 129

Granite Lakes, TH64, page 136

East Peak Lake, TH86, page 171

BEST FOR FALL COLORS—

Scott Lake, TH1, page 33

Charity Valley, TH16, page 52

Sorensen's Cliffs, TH22, page 62

Willow Creek, TH24, page 65

Monitor Pass, TH48, page 103

Green Creek, TH57, page 121

General Creek, TH79, page 160

Spooner Lake, TH84, page 168

BEST FOR WILDFLOWERS—

EARLY SEASON, LOWER ELEVATION

East Carson vista, TH30, page 78

Pleasant Valley, TH31, page 78

Grover Hot Springs, TH33, page 81

Bagley Valley, TH47, page 104

Slinkard Valley, TH49, page 105

SUMMER, MID-ELEVATION

Lake Margaret, TH6, page 42

Indian Valley, TH19, page 58

Freel Meadows, TH26, page 68

Pacific Valley, TH44, page 98

Buckeye Creek, TH55, page 118

Page Meadow, TH80, page 163

SUMMER HIGH ELEVATION

Carson Pass, TH4, page 38

Devils Corral, TH18, page 56

Ebbetts Pass, TH40-41, page 90

Burt Canyon, TH54, page 116

Vogelsang, TH65, page 137

Mount Tallac, TH76, page 154

FISHING—

LARGER LAKES TO DRIVE TO

AND FISH FROM A CRAFT

Silver Lake, TH10, page 45

Lake Alpine, TH45, page 98

Virginia Lakes, TH59, page 129

Saddlebag Lake, TH62, page 133

Fallen Leaf Lake, TH76, page 153

Echo Lakes, TH87, page 172

—and Lake Tahoe, page 151

SMALLER LAKES TO DRIVE TO

AND FLOAT TUBE

Woods Lake, TH14, page 50

Red Lake, TH15, page 52

Tamarack Lake, TH19, page 58

Burnside Lake, TH21, page 60

Kinney Reservoir, TH40, page 90

Green Lake, TH57, page 120

SMALL LAKES TO FLY-FISH

A SHORT HIKE FROM THE CAR

Crater Lake, TH2, page 36

Granite Lake, TH18, page 57

Kinney Lake, TH40, page 92

Cooney Lake, TH59, page 130

FLY-FISHING STREAMS AND RIVERS

CLOSE TO THE CAR

Silver Fork of the
American, TH8, page 44

West Carson River, TH20, page 59

East Carson River, TH34, page 83

Mokelumne River, TH43, page 97

Walker River, TH51, page 114

Hope Valley

TOWARD SORENSEN'S CLIFFS WITH BIJOU, THE BEST DOG A GUY EVER HAD

TRAILHEAD PREVIEWS

Hope Valley has always been a crossroads. In the 1840s, Kit Carson and Fremont's Expedition were led through here by Washoe guides. In the 1850s, the Emigrant Trail through Hope Valley was one of the world's main thoroughfares, the yearly route for 50,000 wagons to the California Gold Rush. In the decade that followed, during the even-richer Comstock Lode in Virginia City, the valley was also the corridor for eastbound silver seekers.

The Pony Express riders came through here too, after mounting fresh horses at a station in Woodfords. During the winter months up until the late 1860s, Snowshoe Thompson, the Norwegian emigrant who carried mail across the Sierra on homemade skis, was the only means of transportation through the Sierra. His route took him from the Carson Valley, up Woodfords Canyon into Hope Valley, over Luther Pass, and, finally, up Echo Summit and down to Placerville.

About a decade into the Comstock boom, the railroad route was completed over Donner Pass, some 60 miles away on the north side of Lake Tahoe. Local silver strikes continued to draw thousands through Hope Valley's high country until the 1870s, after which time it became off-the-beaten-path for most travelers. Little has changed since then. Only a few scars on granite from wagon wheels and the carvings on aspen by Basque sheepherders echo the valley's past. Today, Hope Valley is center-stage for a region that has retained its pristine nature due in part to the efforts of the Friends of Hope Valley,

WEST CARSON RIVER, HOPE VALLEY

Sierra Nevada Alliance, and Trust for Public Land—groups that have worked to promote conservation of scenic resources. Travelers are not passing through these days, but coming to recreate and enjoy nature's priceless bounty.

The area is virtually all public land, including portions of the El Dorado and Toiyabe national forests and the Mokelumne Wilderness. In the western reaches of the Hope Valley region are two large lakes, Caples and Silver, and dozens of smaller ones. West of the crest at Carson Pass are examples of glacial erratics—big rocks sitting alone, left behind by melting glaciers—and views toward

the Sacramento Valley and a sense of the Pacific beyond. Through these granite fissures fall the headwaters of the American River. North and south of the Carson Pass are lakes and peaks of the Sierran Crest, an area that sees deep winter snow and a summer of wildflowers. The Truckee River, Tahoe's main tributary, has its origins in Meiss Meadow, and the Pacific Crest Trail crosses Highway 88 at the pass.

East of the pass is the high meadow region, where a ring of peaks collect snow and send streams into Hope, Faith and Charity valleys. Blue Lakes lie above these valleys. This region was the site of several mining towns,

CARSON PASS NORTH, WINNEMUCCA LAKE

HOPE VALLEY

now vanished, that were home for years to thousands of miners and the business-men who fed off of them. The West Carson River forms here, meandering at first and then cascading through rugged Woodfords Canyon.

On the north side of Hope Valley is the Tahoe Rim, with the huge peaks of the Carson Range rising above mixed-conifer forests—Red Lake, Stevens, Waterhouse, Freel, and Jobs Sister. From the tops of the eastern peaks are vistas contrasting Lake Tahoe with the high desert of the Great Basin. Virtually every tree to be found in the Sierra Nevada grows within a ten-mile radius of Hope Valley, includ-ing a profusion of aspen that set autumn ablaze with color. National forest lands between wilderness areas have roads that can be used as tracks by mountain bikers and cross-country skiers, as well as for access by fishermen, hikers, and horsemen.

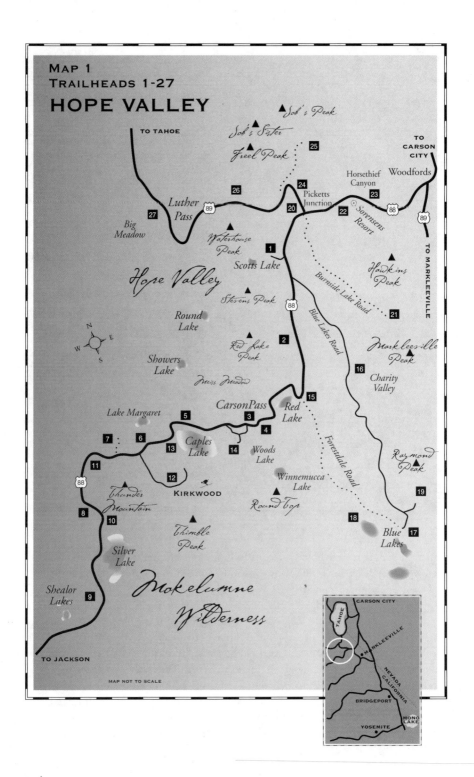

MAP 1
TRAILHEADS 1-27

HOPE VALLEY

TO TAHOE

▲ Job's Peak

▲ Job's Sister

▲ Freel Peak

25

TO CARSON CITY

Horsethief Canyon

Woodfords

26

24 Picketts Junction

23

Luther Pass

89

20

22 Sorensens Resort

88

89

27

Big Meadow

1

▲ Waterhouse Peak

Scotts Lake

TO MARKLEEVILLE

Hope Valley

▲ Hawkins Peak

Burnside Lake Road

▲ Stevens Peak

88

Round Lake

Blue Lakes Road

2

21

Showers Lake

▲ Red Lake Peak

Markleeville Peak

16

Charity Valley

Moss Meadow

CarsonPass

3

15

Red Lake

Lake Margaret

5

4

7

6

13

Caples Lake

14

Woods Lake

Forestdale Road

▲ Raymond Peak

11

88

12

▲ Thunder Mountain

KIRKWOOD

Winnemucca Lake

19

8

10

▲ Thimble Peak

Round Top

18

Blue Lakes

17

Silver Lake

Shealor Lakes

9

Mokelumne Wilderness

TO JACKSON

MAP NOT TO SCALE

N W E S

CARSON CITY

TAHOE

MARKLEEVILLE

NEVADA CALIFORNIA

BRIDGEPORT

MONO LAKE

YOSEMITE

T R A I L H E A D S

TH = TRAILHEAD, FS = FOREST SERVICE ROAD, NUMBERED

All hiking distances in parentheses are ROUND TRIP, unless noted for car shuttles. Elevation gains of 100 feet or more are noted. Maps listed are USGS topographical, 7.5 series. See Resource Links for recommendations for other optional trail maps.

1.   SCOTTS LAKE   HIKE, BIKE, SKI, FISH

WHAT'S BEST: Take a group hike to enjoy fall color, or drive in during summer months and take a pleasant tree-lovers stroll. Park nearby to scale Waterhouse Peak for a postcard shot of Lake Tahoe.

PARK: For Scotts Lake and Big Meadow hikes: Turn right, or north, on unmarked Scotts Lake road, 1.5 mi., west of Picketts Jct. on Hwy. 88. Drive in about .5-mi. on FS079, veering right, and park at locked gate. At 7,100 ft. During summer months, the gate is unlocked and 4WD vehicles can continue on FS079 to the lake. *For Waterhouse Peak:* Head north, toward Tahoe, on Hwy. 89 from Picketts Jct. Park at the first turnout on left when you reach Luther Pass. **Maps:** Freel Peak, Echo Lake

HIKE: Hope Valley to Scotts Lake, 5.5 mi., 800 ft.; Scotts Lake to Big Meadow 4.5 mi., 450 ft.; Waterhouse Peak, 4.5 mi. (all off-trail), 1,875 ft.

The walk to **Scotts Lake** is best for the spring and fall, when the gate is locked. The switchbacking, wide road will accommodate groups as it traverses through colorful aspen. The lake is set in a forested bowl, prettiest when water is high in the spring and summer. To continue from **Scotts Lake to Big Meadow**—one of the better hikes out of Hope Valley—stay to the right at the lake. The easy-walking trail follows a crease between Waterhouse Peak and the shoulder of Stevens Peak, alongside some giant red fir as well as a mixed bag of alpine conifers. Willow and aspen add generous dollops of fall color. *More Stuff:* This trail makes for an excellent car-shuttle hike; park a second vehicle as noted for TH27, Big Meadow, page 69.

Before attempting the off-trail scamper to **Waterhouse Peak**, check out the route from near Picketts Junction. You want to switchback up the mountain's forested shoulder that is prominent from this angle, and then veer right when you are three-quarters of the way to the top. From the parking area, walk Old Highway 89 for a short distance toward Hope Valley and then cut right at the true saddle—before the road starts to drop. Switchback up through the conifers, making sure to stay south of rocky areas that crop up if you get too much to the Tahoe side of the peak.

You'll pop out of the trees at the top and get some fine views westward of Hope Valley from a ridgeline. Go right up the ridgeline on an easy ramp to the shaded summit at 9,475 feet—with its big-time view of Lake Tahoe.

BIKE: **Scotts Lake Road** is part of a network of Forest Service roads below Waterhouse and Stevens peaks, a recommended riding-around spot.

SKI: The highway turnout is good parking for **Hope Valley** moonlight skiing in the flats. During the day, ski up the road to **Scotts Lake**, an infrequently used track. You can also glide down into **Hope Valley from Luther Pass** by using the parking for the Waterhouse Peak hike—or doing an out and back from the parking described in TH20, page 58. This glide is on the **Snowshoe Thompson Trail**, an old section of Old Highway 89. *Local Lore:* The trail was a small portion of the trans-Sierra trek used by Alpine's intrepid mountain man who delivered mail across the wintry crest to Placerville in the 1850s, before telegraphs and railroads were established.

FISH: Some fishermen come in by horseback to fly-fish for rainbows and browns in **Scotts Lake**.

2.   **CRATER LAKE**   HIKE, BIKE, SKI, FISH

WHAT'S BEST: Splashes of fall color accent 360-degree alpine views in an old mining district. This spectacular cirque lake has high scenic value, but sees far fewer visitors than nearby Carson Pass.

PARK: Turn north on Crater Lake Rd., FS091, 2.25 mi. west of Blue Lakes Road on Hwy. 88. The road is paved for a short distance before a cattle guard. Although you can 4-wheel most all the way to the lake, hikers will want to park after about .75-mi., at the junction with a road that departs from the right. At 7,600 ft. *Note:* You'll pass two other minor roads on the highway on the right after passing Blue Lakes Rd.; the first goes to Alpine Mine, and the second connects with Crater Lake Rd. **Map:** Carson Pass

HIKE: **Crater Lake, 4 mi., 900 ft.; Stevens Peak, 7.5 mi. (3 mi. off-trail), 2,400 ft. *Note:* Subtract the distance you drive from the hiking distances.**

To reach **Crater Lake**—an aquamarine pool beneath the steep walls of Red Lake Peak—walk up the road on its long switchbacks and take a fork to the left after about .75-mile. (The right fork loops back to the highway.) The wide road then makes a couple more long curves and reaches another junction that is about 1.25 miles from the highway; take the left fork, the one that does not cross the creek. (The right fork winds up to Alhambra Mine.) The route has a final steep section that should halt all drivers. The lake has been made larger by a cowboy dam at its eastern spillway. Walk around the lakeshore to get the full impact of this dramatic setting.

To reach **Stevens Peak**, take the right fork off the road, which crosses the creek that falls from Crater Lake. From this crossing you can see the road climbing steeply toward Alhambra Mine. (A second mine, Alpine, is .25-mile to the north of Alhambra.) After climbing 200 feet and crossing another creek, depart the road. Pick a route to your left and steeply upward. The lower part of this trek is the toughest. Stay westerly, picking your way up the creek's basin. You'll reach the long, open saddle between Red Lake and Stevens peaks. At the saddle is a trail that switchbacks up Stevens—to your right. Rocks have been cleared to make a cozy nest at the barren top, at 10,061 feet. *Local Lore:* The first recorded sighting of then-unnamed Lake Tahoe was said to have been made from this peak, by Fremont's Expedition of the early 1840s. Captain Fremont and his scout, Kit Carson were led by local Washoes. *Be Aware:* Abandoned mines are a danger to hikers; watch your step. Experienced hikers can eyeball their way to the top of Stevens Peak, but a topo map is recommended. Make sure to equip your pack.

BIKE: Park at Highway 88 and take **Crater Lake Road, FS091**. Take a leg-burning pedal to Crater Lake and then backtrack to the **right-forking road to Alhambra and**

Alpine Mines, as described in the hiking section. Near the bottom of the ride, about .75-mile from the highway, you can branch to your left and take a different route down. This quality ride is not on the radar for most mountain riders.

SKI: Finding where to park can be hard due to plow berms, but **Crater Lake Road** is little-used and offers great downhill runs through junipers and aspen. Follow the road to the lake and ski open slopes on the downhill run. Southern exposure can make for sticky snow.

FISH: You can drive to within .25-mile of **Crater Lake** or follow hiking instructions. Mostly brook trout inhabit these waters.

3. CARSON PASS NORTH   HIKE, SKI, FISH

WHAT'S BEST: Wildflowers and fall color await on this *Sound-of-Music* landscape. Take the Pacific Crest Trail into one of the Sierra's showpieces.

PARK: At Carson Pass, Hwy. 88, on north side of road just west of pass. A federal fee area. At 8,500 ft. *For the Big Meadow car-shuttle*, leave second car at Big Meadow, TH27. **Maps:** Carson Pass, Caples Lake, Echo Lakes (car-shuttle only)

HIKE: Meiss Pond, 2.5 mi., 350 ft.; Meiss Meadow, 5.5 mi., 800 ft.; Red Lake Peak, 4.75 mi. (some easy off-trail), 1,500 ft.; Meiss Lake, 8.5 mi., 900 ft.; Big Meadow car-shuttle, 8 mi., 900 ft.; Showers Lake, 10.25 mi., 1,300 ft.

All trails start northward on the Pacific Crest Trail. You begin on a westward contour, through aspen and junipers with views of Caples Lake. The trail then turns north and drops into and across a drainage, before switchbacking up to top out at **Meiss Pond**. From this vantage you'll see Tahoe to the north as well as the crags of Round Top Peak to the south. **To Red Lake Peak,** take an unmarked trail just north of pond, heading to your right up the west slope of Red Lake Peak. Diagonal steadily upward toward the saddle between Red Lake and Stevens peaks. (The trail continues to Stevens Peak, less than 2 miles away, which gives a two-peak option for more energetic hikers.) From the saddle, head to your right and make your way up the north slope of Red Lake Peak. *Be Aware:* At the very top, you'll need to use your hands for the last, difficult 40 feet or so to make the volcanic knob at the top, at 10,063 feet. Don't try it if you feel uncomfortable. Dramatic views are to be found just below the peak.

More Stuff: From Meiss Pond, you can also veer left, or eastward and walk the top of Meiss Ridge—plainly visible. Stay on the ridgeline to capture views from 9,500 feet. The going is easy, but don't try to drop off the escarpments to either side. Seasoned trekkers can follow the ridge as it descends northward to Showers Lake. About .75-

mile from the lake you'll reach a sketchy trail junction, where you have an option of continuing north to Showers or dropping down steeply to the right and reaching the PCT in Meiss Meadow, which is almost a mile from the junction. The ridge is part of the Sierran Crest.

To **Meiss Meadow,** and the remaining hikes, continue on trail from Meiss Pond. It's fairly level for a short distance, through a green, flower-dotted expanse. You then drop down several hundred feet and come to the cabin and corral in Meiss Meadow. The stream in the meadow is the headwater of the Upper Truckee River, Tahoe's main tributary. Just north of the corral, the trail forks, with the Tahoe Rim Trail taking off to the right. **Meiss Lake** is about .75-mile north of this fork—between the two trails. You can take either the PCT or Rim Trail toward the lake and then cut over when you get abreast of it. *Be Aware:* You want to avoid walking straight at the lake through the marshlands to avoid mucking up the meadow as well as your shoes.

For the **Big Meadow car-shuttle** veer right on the Tahoe Rim Trail, at the junction north of the cabin. The first mile is northerly through undulating topography, reaching the forested confines of Round Lake. From Round Lake, head toward Big Meadow, staying on the main trail.

To reach **Showers Lake,** stay on the west side of Meiss Meadow and stay on the left-forking Pacific Crest Trail. The trail will climb north and west. The lake is a beauty, with huge granite monoliths forming portions of the shore. *Be Aware:*

Big Meadow Trail, Carson Pass North

Since Showers Lake is in a different drainage, it's easy to lose your way if you venture off-trail.

SKI: The schuss into **Meiss Meadow** is fantastic and you'll find good skiing on shoulders of Red Lake Peak and Meiss Ridge. The ski through to **Big Meadow and Luther Pass** is recommended for experienced skiers on days with good visibility, but be prepared to take your skis off and post-hole the last steep mile through trees to the car at the Big Meadow parking area.

FISH: **Meiss Lake**, the source of the Upper Truckee River, has cutthroat and some brook trout. The same species will be found at **Showers Lake**, a backpackers' choice.

4. CARSON PASS SOUTH   HIKE, SKI, FISH

WHAT'S BEST: Wildflowers abound at knockout peaks and lakes, offering hiking and backpacking for all experience levels. The lakes south of the pass are among the most beautiful—and popular—in the Alpine Sierra.

PARK: At Carson Pass on Hwy. 88, near the information center and Snowshoe Thompson Monument. This is a fee area in summer and Sno-Park in winter. At 8,500 ft. *For Red Lake car-shuttle*, park second car at Red Lake, TH15. *For Devils Ladder*, take the Red Lake Overlook Rd., which is less than .25-mi. east of Carson Pass; drive in and park in the turnaround area. **Maps:** Caples Lake, Carson Pass

HIKE: Frog Lake, 2 mi., 300 ft.; Forestdale lakelet loop, 8.5 mi. (4 mi. difficult off-trail), 1,800 ft.; Carson Pass to Red Lake car-shuttle, 7.25 mi. (1.5 mi. off-trail), 800 ft.; Winnemucca Lake, 5 mi., 450 ft.; Elephants Back, 6.75 mi. (2 mi. off-trail), 950 ft.; Round Top Lake, 7.25 mi., 900 ft.; Round Top Peak, 8.5 mi. (2 mi. off-trail), 1,850 ft.; Fourth of July Lake, 10 mi., 1,600 ft.; Devils Ladder, 2.75 mi., 600 ft.

All hikes begin at the El Dorado Forest Information Center, located near the trailhead. Step inside for local hiking advice, as well as gifts and interpretive tidbits. Then head up the Pacific Crest Trail, located behind the building. **Frog Lake**, overlooking Hope Valley, is just a few hops in from the trailhead, but also a worthy destination. A prime vista awaits at the lip of the lake, across the water from the trail.

For the less-traveled **Forestdale lakelet loop**, go about .25-mile south from Frog Lake and take the Pacific Crest Trail south, which is a left-bearing fork. The PCT goes around the north and then east face of Elephants Back. Then you hook south, heading toward the visible upper part of the drainage of Forestdale Creek, which holds the lakelets. To return, climb the shoulder above the lakelets, to the northwest, up to the top, which is the saddle between Round Top Peak and the Elephant. From there, you'll get the big view of Winnemucca Lake and of your route back. Contour to the north below Elephants Back, staying above the lake, until reaching the Winnemucca trail that takes you back. *Be Aware:* Only sure-footed, prepared hikers should attempt this strenuous cross-country trek. You can also backtrack on the PCT from the lakelet.

For the **Red Lake car-shuttle**, go to the Forestdale lakelet, as described above, and from there go off-trail another .25-mile to the Jeep trail (Forestdale Divide Road) that leads back to Red Lake. You will be able to see the road across the drainage from the PCT. An occasional vehicle may join you on the easy downhill leg to Red Lake, through open country dotted with lodgepole and aspen.

Winnemucca Lake is one of the darlings of the Sierra and this trailhead's primary destination. To get there, continue on the trail from Frog Lake, keeping to the right at the PCT junction. The craggy wall of Round Top rises above the granite basin that holds the lake. To top **Elephants Back**, walk up the dwarf-sage-covered slope east and north of Winnemucca—to your left as you face the lake. Sturdy kids will enjoy this peak, which gives up a big payoff for a relatively small effort. *Be Aware:* Stay back from the peak's steep east face.

Round Top Peak is that big huge thing towering south and a bit west of Winnemucca. Its top does not appear round. To climb it, take the trail that leaves from the west shore of Winnemucca, toward **Round Top Lake**. The lake is about a mile west of Winnemucca, and 400 feet above it. To scale the peak, go left when you reach the lake—leaving the main trail that continues along the north side of the lake. Make your way up the draw, toward a saddle formed by the peak on your left and The Sisters—peaks to the right that are only 200 feet lower than Round Top. Once you reach the saddle (phew!) cross through it a short distance and approach the 10,381-foot summit from the backside, the southwest. *Be Aware:* Start early for this hike. During thunder-shower conditions, normally in late summer, retreat quickly if you see clouds forming.

Fourth of July Lake is surrounded by 1,500-foot walls on three sides and a 1,000-foot drop into Summit City Creek at its spillway. The lake is less than 2 miles south of Round Top Lake, but with more than a 1,000-foot descent. Continue on the trail on the north of Round Top Lake, which curves west before beginning its steep drop downward. Be sure to visit the outlet on the south side of Fourth of July Lake, a sheer drop to Summit City Canyon.

Be Aware: Always take rain gear in the Carson Pass area. Hail can appear quickly in the summer; lightning poses a threat at higher elevations. The entire south Carson Pass region of the Mokelumne Wilderness is ideal for backpacking. It's also popular and suffers from overuse. Don't plan on fires, stay on trails, and camp away from all water sources.

Nowadays, **Devils Ladder** is an easy walk down an old section of the highway that was once the Amador-Carson Valley Wagon Road of the early 1860s. You could park a second car at Red Lake, TH15, which is the end of the old road. The ladder, near the parking area, is where the pioneers had to haul their rigs. Sharp-eyed hikers may find scars on the granite here and there, made by wagon wheels. The forested walk affords a good view of Red Lake.

SKI: The best skiing is toward **Winnemucca Lake** from Carson Pass, and then down the bowl below Round Top Peak that leads to Woods Lake. Keep your bearings. From Woods Lake, finding the eastward trail back to the pass can be confusing.

FISH: Most people walk into **Winnemucca Lake** for wildflowers and scenery. Not as many for the fishing, which is good news for fishermen. Backpack to **Fourth of July Lake** for brookies and cutthroat.

5.   SCHNEIDER COW CAMP   HIKE, BIKE, SKI

WHAT'S BEST: Alpine wildflowers and open vistas are plentiful on this family hike where volcanic meets granitic. You may not be lonesome, but this trail gets fewer hikers than nearby Carson Pass. Skiers take note during winter months.

PARK: On Hwy. 88 at Caples Lake, turn in toward the Cal Trans maintenance station. Veer left between a large building and sheds, passing the maintenance yard on unpaved FS10N13.2. Park at a primitive camping area on your left, about 1.5 mi. from the highway. At 8,300 ft. *Note:* If the gate to FS10N13.2 is locked at Cal Trans, you'll have to walk in and add 3 mi. to round-trip hiking distances. *For Meiss Meadow car-shuttle*, park second car at Carson Pass North, TH3. **Maps:** Caples Lake, Carson Pass (for car-shuttle)

HIKE: Showers Lake: via Little Round Top 9 mi., 1,100 ft.; or via Meiss Ridge, 4 mi., 1,200 ft; Schneider-Showers loop, 6.5 mi., 1,200 ft.; Schneider to Meiss Meadow car-shuttle, 6 mi., 1,500 ft.

For **all hikes** walk the last part of the road to Schneider Cow Camp, with its old barn set below a high ridge. For the circuitous route, **Showers Lake via Little Round Top**, follow the Forest Service road for a short distance and take a trail to your right. Little Round top, at 9,595 feet, will be due north. The trail climbs out of the meadow and hooks all the way around behind it. Once on the north side of Little Round Top, you'll reach a junction with the Pacific Crest Trail, where you go right and continue the last 1.75 miles to the lake.

To **Showers Lake via Meiss Ridge**, head up a trail due east from the cow camp that follows the stream drainage to the ridge more than a mile away and about 800 feet up.

CARSON PASS NORTH

Once at the ridge, go left, or north, dropping down about .75-mile to the lake. To combine these two routes to Showers Lake on a **Schneider-Showers loop**, you probably want to start out using the Meiss Ridge trail. Once at the lake, pick up the Pacific Crest Trail northbound—but make darned sure to hang a left (go west) on the trail junction back to Schneider Cow Camp. This junction is almost 2 miles from the lake, on the north shoulder of Little Round Top.

For the highly scenic **Schneider to Meiss Meadow car-shuttle**, take the trail up the stream drainage that is due east of the cow camp. After humping up to the ridge's saddle, continue east at the trail junction. This portion takes you down to the Pacific Crest Trail in the meadow. Hang a right, or south, and continue up the meadow. You'll climb to see the majestic views at Meiss Pond, and contour around to the trailhead at Carson Pass. *Note:* The saddle in the Meiss Ridge is actually the Pacific Crest.

BIKE: From **Schneider Cow Camp** you can take a 10-mile car-shuttle ride to **Strawberry Canyon** on Highway 50. The drive between the two trailheads is very long. The pedal is also difficult, to be attempted by experienced riders with maps; see *Resource Links*. The descent is more than 3,000 feet. The better bet for visiting riders is to take **FS10N13.2** into the cow camp and beyond, and then retrace your route back. The road begins its serious descent about 4 miles from Highway 88.

Ski: Schneider Cow Camp, behind a ridge, is a good cross-country basin. Park behind the Cal Trans yard and ski in FS10N13.2 to the barn and beyond. *Be Aware:* Be careful of straying—the topography here can turn craggy higher up, with avalanche danger under and on cornices.

6. LAKE MARGARET   Hike

What's Best: This hidden lake hike hosts a variety of flora, including aspen and lush-loving wildflowers. Plan on taking a swim to a rock island in the heat of summer.

Park: Look for turnout on Hwy. 88, just east of Kirkwood Cross Country Center. At 7,800 ft. **Map:** Caples Lake

Hike: Lake Margaret, 4.5 mi., 300 ft.

Make sure to get on, and stay on, the correct trail to **Lake Margaret**, as granite knobs, many streams, and abundant flora create a maze difficult to navigate off-trail. Water-loving flowers will be tucked away in several choice spots along the way.

About halfway to the lake, you'll cross a fork of Caples Creek. Once at Lake Margaret, make your way around to the left, the southwest shore, and you'll find good lunch spots. A granite island lies a hundred feet or so offshore, in waters that are not as chilling as many Sierran lakes.

LAKE MARGARET

7. KIRKWOOD LAKE

WHAT'S BEST: Enjoy a far-western sunset view while scrambling granite. You'll find solitude on the busiest of summer days.

PARK: Turn on Kirkwood Lake Rd., .75-west on Hwy. 88 from the entrance to Kirkwood Ski Resort. Look for a turnout and unofficial trailhead within .25-mile on left, before reaching the lake. At 7,700 ft. **Map:** Silver Lake

HIKE: Caples Creek Buttes, 6 mi. (3 mi. off-trail), 600 ft.

Before attempting **Caples Creek Buttes**, you may wish to take a gander from the Carson Spur, that precarious section of Highway 88 west of Kirkwood; from a turnout at the top is a full view of this multifaceted drainage. Study a route. At the trailhead, head downstream (on the south bank) and cross Caples Creek after 1 mile, which can be problematic even in late summer because the flow is controlled by a dam. Make your way north-northwest, continuing to lose elevation—perhaps marking your path with stone piles—until walking out onto one of several granite promontories. From here are long views to the west, capturing fading daylight. Many swimming lakelets and mini-falls are in this area. *Be Aware:* Granite benches and brush make for deceptively difficult navigating. Keep your bearings.

FISH: Shore casting and float tubing are popular at **Kirkwood Lake**. This is a classic little lake to paddle around.

8. AMERICAN RIVER POTHOLES

WHAT'S BEST: Enjoy wildflowers and cool off on a hot summer day in granite pools with falls. The potholes are popular, but you can work your way downriver to find private delights.

PARK: At Silver Lake West Campground, on Hwy. 88, which is across the highway from Kit Carson Lodge at the north shore of Silver Lake. At 7,300 ft. **Map:** Silver Lake

HIKE: Along the Silver Fork to the American River Potholes, 4 to 8 mi., 500 to 1,200 ft.

Find the river at the campground—the **Silver Fork of the American**—and walk down on its north bank; you'll find the trail. The **potholes**, natural pools scooped out of granite bedrock, begin about 1.5 miles from the campground. On hot summer weekends, you may hear boomboxes and coconut oil. But you can find solitude by walking granite benches downriver, finding more pools and falls, named the Roman Baths by locals.

More Stuff: An unpaved road at Martin Meadows leaves from Highway 88, about 1.75 miles up the grade from Silver Lake; you'll see a sign for the meadow and for FS10N16A. The road descends toward the river and becomes a trail after 2 miles. The trail continues down for 1.5 miles and reaches the Silver Fork of the American, well below the potholes. This route crosses lush wildflowers, including a profusion of purple delphiniums. This road is parallel to the river on the north—it bellies up and away from the river midway on the hike. Game trekkers with topo maps can create loop hikes by walking down from Martin Meadows, dropping down southward (to the left) to hit the river, and walking back via the potholes.

FISH: Fly-fishermen will have success on the **Silver Fork of the American** looking for rainbows and browns, especially in the fall when the campground has cleared.

9.   SHEALOR LAKES   HIKE

WHAT'S BEST: A short day hike reaches smooth-granite swimming in lakes and nearby lakelets.

PARK: Look for a trailhead sign on Hwy. 88, about 1.5 mi. west of Kit Carson Resort Rd. and spillway at Silver Lake. It will be on your right coming up the hill, before reaching Plasse Rd., which drops down to the left. At 7,400 ft. **Map:** Tragedy Spring

HIKE: Shealor Lakes, 3 mi., 500 ft.

The trail to **Shealor Lakes** rises through the forest, tops a knobby granite ridge, and drops on a rock-strewn switchback with a view of the largest lake. The lakes—there are maybe a half-dozen if you include the smaller lakelets—drain into Tragedy Creek and the headwaters of the American River. The outlet is on the north end of the biggest lake, to your right as you approach. You can head down the creek to the smaller lake, about a mile away and down to an elevation of nearly 6,000 feet. *Be Aware:* This is a fun area to explore off-trail among the lakelets and glacier-polished granite, but it's easy to get lost in the basin. Keep your bearings.

10.   SILVER LAKE   HIKE, FISH

WHAT'S BEST: A fire-and-ice hike takes you from volcanic to granitic, through wildflowers and old-growth junipers and giant red fir. The waters of Silver Lake are ideal for swimming and kayaking—a summer-fun lake that is among the Sierra's most beautiful.

SILVER LAKE

PARK: At the north end of Silver Lake at Kit Carson Resort Rd. It's just off Hwy. 88, 11 mi. west of Carson Pass. At 7,300 ft. *For Horse Canyon Trail to Scout Carson Lake*, use the Oyster Creek picnic area, which is .75-mi. up Highway 88 (toward Carson Pass) from Kit Carson Rd. at Silver Lake. **Map:** Caples Lake

HIKE: Silver Lake to Granite Lakes and Treasure Island, 4 mi., (.5-mi. off-trail) 200 ft.; Horse Canyon Trail to: Scout Carson Lake, 10 mi., 1,300 ft., or Horse Canyon view, 12 mi., 2,500 ft.

For the leisurely hike to **Granite Lake and the shore of Silver Lake**, walk down Kit Carson Resort Road. Islets and inlets add interest to a lovely shoreline. (You will want to pop in at Kit Carson Lodge, where you can enjoy a meal or beverage after the hike or check out the gift store.) Nearly .5-mile from the lodge, the road becomes a trail. Continue and veer left past the Campfire Girls Camp as the trail ascends a short distance to the lake. Granite Lake is actually 2 small lakes, and several lakelets that spread out to the south. After enjoying the placid waters, leave the trail and drop down toward the lake. Treasure Island, a forested granite rise, lies in the middle of this southern end of the lake—and ideal spot for swimmers and picnickers. *More Stuff:* The trail continues through forest from Granite Lake to tiny Hidden Lake, almost 2 miles away. From there the it loops down to the southern end of Silver Lake at Plasse Resort. Walking back to Kit Carson Lodge on this route is a loop hike of about 8.5 miles.

For **Horse Canyon Trail to Scout Carson Lake**, you'll head southeast from the Oyster Creek picnic area through red fir and junipers—an unusually large forest of which extends up-slope from this area. Thunder Ridge, a wall of volcanic rock nearly 2,000-feet high, rises above, separating Silver Lake from Kirkwood Resort. The shaded trail crosses streams through a rocky maze and eventually breaks out onto wildflower-dotted open slopes—leaving the volcanic world and entering the world of granite. Continue on the open trail, reaching **Scout Carson Lake**.

To **Horse Canyon view**, continue southeast from the Scout Carson Lake and follow the trail as it drops steeply into the canyon, heading toward the deep drainage of Summit City Creek. About 600 feet down from the trail's highest point, you'll reach a trail that contours around the top end of Horse Canyon and takes you back up to the Horse Canyon Trail. *Be Aware*: Motorized dirt bikes are allowed access to the Horse Canyon Trail.

Fish: Large browns and rainbows can be found by trolling deep around **Silver Lake's islets**. Boat rentals are available and canoe fishing is popular. Fly-fishermen may want to float tube, since summertime brings shore-casters to the lake.

11.   THUNDER MOUNTAIN   Hike

What's Best: You'll feel airborne on this wild and wide-open ridge. Keep an eye peeled for eagles.

Parking: A trailhead turnout is on Hwy. 88, 2 mi. west of Kirkwood. Heading west, look to your left just past the Carson Spur vista point; the trailhead is just after a small pond. **Map:** Caples Lake

Hike: Martin Point, 3.25 mi., 1,200 ft.; Thunder Mountain, 7.25 mi., 1,500 ft.

Thunder Mountain is the 9,408-foot southern anchor of a 4-mile-long wall between Kirkwood and Silver Lake. **Martin Point**, at 9,250 feet, forms the north end of the ridge. For both hikes, you begin with a steady uphill through red fir and hemlock, climbing to the snow fences and eagle nest area above the cliffy Carson Spur. *Be Aware:* Road workers blast to control for avalanches in this area, so don't get curious should you happen upon a shell. From the fence area, you continue ascending along the east side of the ridge, and then take a short series of switchbacks to its top—just beyond a route that leads down to Kirkwood. Martin Point is the knob to your right as you break out to the top of the ridge.

The trail continues south, jogging east and west of formations piled on top of the ridge. You dip through an open saddle, which can be fiercely windy, and take a spur trail to your right, or west, to the top of noble **Thunder Mountain**. The west side of the peak is nearly 2,000-foot above Silver Lake. *Be Aware:* Watch out for drop offs, and, as the name suggests, don't be up here during summer thundershowers.

More Stuff: The trail continues beyond the Thunder Mountain spur trail, curling around to the east and then dropping down to join the Horse Canyon Trail—which comes out to Highway 88 near Silver Lake at the Oyster Creek picnic area. See TH10 on page 45 for parking directions. You'll do about 10.5 miles on this car-shuttle hike.

12. KIRKWOOD HIKE, BIKE, SKI

WHAT'S BEST: Explore ski slopes in summer with wildflowers and grassy ridges. In the winter, try some of the Sierra's deepest snow.

PARK: Turn at Kirkwood Ski Resort off Hwy. 88, 6 mi. west of Carson Pass. Drive in 1.5 mi. toward the main ski lodge at southwest section of the valley. You'll see a gated road, where the main road makes a sweeping left. At 7,600 feet. *For the Emigrant Valley car-shuttle* park second car at Caples Lake, TH 13. **Map:** Caples Lake

HIKE: Thimble Peak, 7 mi. (3 mi. off-trail), 1,800 feet; Emigrant Valley car-shuttle, 7.5 mi. (.75 mi. off-trail), 1,000 ft.

Plan on spending time nosing around Kirkwood Resort. Known for the deepest snow in the Alpine Sierra, the valley is becoming more popular for summertime adventures. **Both hikes** start out easy, up the road that curves to the left and crosses Kirkwood Creek. You'll have a point-blank look at the sheer face of Thimble Peak at this point. The road then curves left and climbs around the peak's northeast promontory, and comes to an end. You'll be looking down toward Caples Lake and Emigrant Valley.

To climb **Thimble Peak**—still 1,000 feet above you at this point—make your way to the top of the promontory and walk the ridgeline southward. It's reasonably sloped for the next .5-mile, but then you have to switchback up the last 600 feet to the top. *Be Aware:* Only experienced hikers who don't mind a challenge should attempt this peak—but they will be rewarded with a fantastic view of Kirkwood Meadows and beyond.

THUNDER RIDGE

For the **Emigrant Lake car-shuttle**, continue southward from the end of the road, for another .5-mile or so, to the head of Emigrant Valley. Drop down to your left, about 150 feet, and you'll hit the trail that contours down to the south shore of Caples Lake. You go left along the shore to the parking at the dam on the west end of the lake. *Note:* You won't see Emigrant Lake on this hike—unless you leave the trail and contour around the steep shoulder at the head of Emigrant Valley.

BIKE: Park at the entrance to **Kirkwood** to explore the grounds of the resort. It's a leisurely ride of many miles, mostly on pavement, in a beautiful mountain valley. A new **mountain biking park** has been established at Kirkwood. Check it out at the south end of the valley, near the trailhead parking. Rentals and advice are available.

SKI: Kirkwood Cross County Ski Center, on the highway before you turn into the ski resort, offers rentals and some 59 kilometers of groomed trails for all levels of experience. The center is managed by Alpine Sierra legend, Debbie Waldear, who is among the top skiers in the world in her class. Telemark skiers can also buy lift tickets at the downhill resort.

13. CAPLES LAKE   HIKE, FISH

WHAT'S BEST: Commune with evergreens and wildflowers on a midsummer day hike to a dramatic lake. Or take a swim and kayak paddle over an expanse of water.

PARK: At Caples Lake dam lot, .5-mi. east of Kirkwood on Hwy. 88, on the west end of lake. At 7,800 ft. *For the Silver Lake car-shuttle,* park a second car at Oyster Creek picnic area, TH10. *For the Carson Pass car-shuttle,* park a second car at Carson Pass South, TH4. **Maps:** Caples Lake, Carson Pass (for Carson pass car-shuttle)

HIKE: Emigrant Lake, 8.5 mi., 850 ft.; Carson Pass car-shuttle, 9.5 mi. (1.5 mi. off-trail), 1,600 ft; Silver Lake car-shuttle, 11 mi., 1,500 ft.

Begin the walk to **Emigrant Lake** along Caples Lake's forested southwest shore—to your right as you face the water at the dam. About a mile from the trailhead, pass a right-hand junction for a trail up Emigrant Valley (this trail bypasses Emigrant Lake, but it shortens by about .5-mile the car-shuttle hike to Silver Lake). At the southern tip of Caples Lake, the trail starts up the creek. After about .75-mile along the creek, you pass another right-forking trail, which also goes to Silver Lake. Just past this second junction, the Emigrant Lake trail fords the stream and climbs steeply over the last mile or so to the lake basin; this last part is between a fork of two streams. Emigrant delivers a scenic punch, surround by a U-shaped escarpment. *Be Aware:* The lake won't be disappointing, unless you forget mosquito repellant in July. In early summer, snow can

CARSON PASS

also be a problem on this north-facing trail in the woods. *More Stuff:* You can shorten this hike by about .5-mile by parking at the boat launch on the east end of Caples Lake; follow the shore to the south end of the lake to pick up the trail.

For the **Silver Lake car-shuttle**, take either of the two right-forking trails that are described in the paragraph above—the first is the shortest and recommended route. The trail traverses steadily upward in the Emigrant Valley. You top out at a saddle on the east side of Thimble Peak, and jog to the east—atop the 1,000-foot wall of rock above Emigrant Lake. The trail turns south, climbing a little more through a notch before dropping to pick up the Horse Canyon Trail above Scout Carson Lake. From there it's a long steady ramp down to Silver Lake, at first through open, granite slopes and ending up in the red-fir, volcanic forests. *Be Aware:* After dropping over the high saddle above Emigrant Lake, keep right at all trail junctions.

For the **car-shuttle to Carson Pass**, follow the hiking directions toward Emigrant Lake. About .25-mile from the lake, you want to go left, or east, around the base of the rocky knob that forms the east wall of the lake. (You'll probably want to see the lake and double back to this point.) Keep *contouring* eastward, crossing the basin and the headwaters of two streams. After about .75-mile of contouring, head to your right, or east again, climbing about 300 feet to a granite saddle—from where you will see Round Top Lake. Head to the lake's north shore and pick up the trail down to Winnemucca Lake and Carson Pass. *Be Aware:* Make sure not to take the trail that drops to Woods Lake when you get to Round Top Lake. This cross-country hike is not difficult to navigate, but you want to have a map along to be safe.

FISH: On the north shore, **Caples Lake Resort** rents boats. Fishing is good all day for brook, rainbow, brown, and mackinaw trout. Anglers also shore cast from **spillway area at the west shore.** The best tip, however, is to take your small craft to the **public boat launch at Woods Creek,** on the east shore of the lake (headed toward Carson Pass). Shore casting is also good from this locale.

14. WOODS LAKE

HIKE, SKI, FISH

WHAT'S BEST: Family picnic at this sylvan lake, well suited for a swim or paddle. Then walk a flower-rich streamside to a high-mountain lake.

PARK: *Two roads* from Hwy. 88 lead into Woods Lake—they join about .5-mi. from the highway. The first is a dirt road, almost 1 mi. west of Carson Pass; the second, paved access is about 2 mi. west of the pass. On either road, you drive in 2 mi. to trailhead parking near the lake. Park on the right before you get to the campground. At 8,200 ft. **Map:** Caples Lake

HIKE: Round Top Lake, 4.5 mi., 1,100 ft.; Fourth of July Lake, 7.5 mi., 2,100 ft.; Winnemucca Lake, 3.5 mi., 750 ft.

Before embarking on the hikes, you'll want to wander over and enjoy the placid view at the shore of Woods Lake, one of the more pleasant picnic spots in the Alpine Sierra. The trail to **Round Top Lake** and **Fourth of July Lake** (signed as 17E4) is to your right as you face the water—off the campground loop. You immediately walk by historic Lost Mine Cabin, a photographer's favorite. Then you ascend along Round Top Lake's outlet stream as it tumbles by, watering nests of wildflowers. The trail to Fourth of July Lake is south from Round Top Lake, climbing at first and going down a 1,200-foot ramp to the lake. Less energetic hikers can get a good look at the remarkably scenic lake without going all the way down.

For the walk to **Winnemucca Lake**, go to the left as you face the water at Woods Lake. The trail (signed as 18E06) crosses Woods Creek on a bridge—shutterbugs, start clicking. You then take an upward traverse on a hillside that can be zany with wildflowers in the early summer. The trail arcs toward the creek before topping out at the west shore of one of Alpine's cover-shot lakes. *More Stuff:* These lakes are also accessible from Carson Pass South, TH4. You can fashion car-shuttle hikes between these two trailheads.

SKI: Park at Highway 88 and take the road in toward **Woods Lake** (noting there are two entrances from highway separated by about a mile). This is winter wonderland-type skiing when snow is lacing the conifers. As an option, you can also ski **Old Highway 88** down to the Woods Lake roads; access is about .25-mile west of Carson Pass, across the street from the Meiss trailhead.

Fish: In **Woods Lake** await rainbow trout. Accessible by car. The Orvis catalogue could be shot here.

15. RED LAKE   Hike, Bike, Ski, Fish

What's Best: Take an autumn hike or bicycle ride on this pioneer route with mountain vistas. You can also ski or drive to the great divide in the center of the Alpine Sierra.

Park: Look for a turnout off Hwy. 88, at the east end of Red Lake, 2 mi. east of Carson Pass. It's at the bottom of the long grade. At 7,900 ft. **Map:** Carson Pass

Hike: Forestdale Divide, 7 mi., 1,100 ft.; Faith Valley, 8 mi., 400 ft.; Devils Ladder, 3 mi., 600 ft.

Note: Forestdale Divide Road, a.k.a. FS146, is a 4WD track that runs a distance of 9 miles from Red Lake in the north to Upper Blue Lake to the south; see TH18, page 56 for directions to the southern terminus. Only one narrow section on the upslope a few miles from Red Lake will cause drivers to grip the wheel. It sees few vehicles, except for busy summer weekends. Autumn weekdays and early summer, when snow still lingers to discourage vehicles, are the best times to walk the road.

To hike to **Forestdale Divide** and **Faith Valley**, you start out down the road that drops immediately to your left as you drive in from the highway. You begin under a canopy of aspen and lodgepole pine, as well as other conifers. About 2 miles in, heading south, you'll reach the bridge at Forestdale Creek. The route to **Faith Valley** is to the left, or east, after crossing the bridge. You follow the waters of Forestdale Creek. Several streams join in from the south, including the headwaters of the West Carson River, about 1.5 miles from the bridge. You'll want to turn around when you break into the open in Faith Valley. Blue Lakes Road will be dead ahead, less than .5-mile away.

To continue to **Forestdale Divide**, keep right at the Forestdale Creek bridge. After climbing gradually southward to the top, you'll reach the divide, where westerly runoff heads for the Pacific Ocean and easterly for the Carson Valley. Take a walk around this wide-open country to get vistas at all points of the compass. *More Stuff:* If you drive in about 4 miles on Forestdale Divide Road you'll reach a trailhead for Summit City Canyon and the "back way" to Fourth of July Lake. You'll need an SUV for this one. The trail drops 1,200 feet down the narrow Summit City Canyon to a junction (on the right, or north) to a trail that climbs back up 500 feet to the lake. Plan on 9 miles, round-trip, for this jaunt.

Devils Ladder is a nickname given to a portion of a horrendous segment of pioneer road east of Carson Pass—known back then as the Amador Carson Valley Wagon Road. It takes off from the parking area up the south shore of Red Lake to Carson Pass. This walk is a good choice for low-energy groups and families. *Local lore:* Although Red Lake, which is dammed, and modern roads have obscured some of the past, keen observers can spot wheel scrapes on granite and scars on trees from cables used to hoist wagons.

BIKE: **Forestdale Divide to Blue Lakes** is an excellent selection for pedal pushers. It shares the same vistas with the Pacific Crest Trail for this segment. (The PCT crosses the road at Forestdale Divide.) Cyclists can also ride toward Faith Valley on **FS093 at Forestdale Creek** bridge. And, just before the bridge, **FS013A** makes a small loop that may also be of interest. A few spur roads in the region are unsigned, making it a good choice for riders who want to explore.

SKI: The bowl north of **Forestdale Divide** is a Nordic skier's dream, although snowmobiles may be encountered on busy weekends.

FISH: **Red Lake** is accessible by car. Tube and boat fish the lake for trophy-sized brook trout known to frequent the inlet at the west end of the lake. Or stream-cast **Red Lake Creek**, flowing from the lake's eastern shore. In **Forestdale Creek**, 2 miles in and reachable by car, you'll find brook trout. Forestdale Creek flows into West Carson River, off Blue Lakes Road in Faith Valley.

16. CHARITY VALLEY   HIKE, BIKE, SKI

WHAT'S BEST: Take a group day hike through a meadow and then down to the region's most popular Alpine valley. Or solo on an easy-walking road to Markleeville Peak's backside where human footprints are seldom seen.

PARK: Take Blue Lakes Rd., which is off Hwy. 88, 3 mi. west of Picketts Jct. Go 6 mi., park on left at a trailhead sign—before dropping slightly and reaching an old log structure and gated road, also on the left. At 8,000 ft. *Note:* The pavement used to end here; it recently has been extended to Blue Lakes. *For Jeff Davis Peak*, park at turnout on left, 1.5 mi. south of old log structure. *For Grover Hot Springs car-shuttle*, park a second car at TH33, as noted on page 80. *Note:* Some areas around Charity Valley are private property; heed signs. **Maps:** Carson Pass, Markleeville

HIKE: **Grover Hot Springs car-shuttle**, 7 mi., minus 1,900 ft.; **Sawmill Creek Meadows**, 5.5 mi., 400 ft., **Markleeville Peak loop**, 10 mi. (3.5 mi. off-trail), 1,700 ft.; **Jeff Davis circumnavigation**, 6 mi. (all off-trail), 300 ft.

RED LAKE RAINBOW

From the trailhead, you can look east across Charity Valley to roundish Markleeville Peak, elevation 9,415 feet. The trail to **Grover Hot Springs car-shuttle** contours the gently sloping hillside, up from and parallel to the dirt road that leads northeast through a section of private land. It dips and turns through granite sand and mule ears, joining Charity Valley Creek at the east end of the valley. The view bluffs here are a majestic destination for non-car-shuttle hikers. Not long after reaching the creek, the trail drops into upper Hot Springs Valley, and then follows Hot Springs Creek through mixed conifer forest and yellow-granite benches before reaching the meadow of the state park. *More Stuff:* Before beginning its serious descent into Hot Springs Valley, the trail joins the Burnside Lake Trail, which connects to TH21, page 60. Go left, or north, here and you can be at Burnside Lake in about 20 minutes.

To get to **Sawmill Creek meadows and the Markleeville Peak loop**, start out on the trail for the Grover Hot Springs car-shuttle. About a mile into the hike, you need to drop down off the trail to your right, or south—past the private home(s). You'll join a road, which is not shown on any map and which crosses Charity Valley Creek over a broken plank bridge. The road turns easterly and then southerly as you ascend through forest. The road curls around to behind Markleeville Peak—breaking out into the open at the high meadows of upper Sawmill Creek. This basin holds a huge stand of willows, though a careful hiker will have no trouble navigating through them.

The road ends higher up the Sawmill Creek. Here, make your way off trail, westerly up the creek drainage. Hook northerly as you near the rounded top of Markleeville Peak. Near the top, start making a clockwise circle—to your left. You want to circle around and pick your way down the southwest face of the mountain, coming down in the southern end of Charity Valley. At the bottom, walk the creek through the meadow back to the car. *Be Aware:* There are many possible routes up Markleeville Peak. Avoid the escarpments on the west-facing wall (toward Charity Valley) and you'll be fine. Experienced hikers will have no problems on this hike; others should avoid it.

Jeff Davis Peak is the volcanic plug due south of Markleeville Peak. To walk clockwise around Jeff Davis, take off due east, headed for the notch in the saddle halfway between Markleeville Peak and Jeff Davis. Stay high, contouring in and out of volcanic outcroppings, and being mindful of steeper cliffs below you on the southeast side of the peak. You'll do a full circle at roughly the same elevation. *Be Aware:* This is not a hike to break in new boots. Only confident backcountry hikers will enjoy it.

BIKE: East from the Charity Valley Trailhead are **Forest Service Roads**, including FS093, that encircle the valley and connect with **Forestdale Divide Road**. No map shows all the roads. This is a great place to get lost on purpose, keeping in mind that Blue Lakes Road runs north-south through the whole region.

SKI: Park at the entrance to **Blue Lakes Road**. The road, plus the open gentle slopes northwest of Markleeville Peak, make for good Nordic skiing. *Be Aware:* Snowmobiles frequent this zone, especially on weekends and holidays.

17. LOWER BLUE LAKE   HIKE, BIKE, SKI, FISH

WHAT'S BEST: The full regalia of car-camping American-style is on display at popular Blue Lakes in the middle of the summer. Early fall and late spring are quieter times. Several nearby hikes invite hikers for a loop.

PARK: Take paved Blue Lakes Rd., 3 mi. west of Picketts Jct. Go 10 mi. to Lower Blue Lake. Park at dam. At 8,000 ft. **Map:** Carson Pass, Pacific Valley

HIKE: Twin Lake, 1.75 mi., no elevation; Meadow Lake, 5.75 mi., 300 ft.; Evergreen Lake loop, 6.5 mi. (2 mi. off-trail), 700 ft.; Hermit Valley via Clover and Deer Valley car-shuttle 7 mi., minus 1,100 ft.

Large **Twin Lake** is an easy walk (or drive) to the southwest of Lower Blue Lake—although snow lingering in the shaded forest can make for soggy footing. The trail to **Meadow Lake**, through pine and fir, extends westward from Twin Lake—via a rough road that most SUVs can drive almost all the way. The cowboy dam at the west end of Meadow Lake offers a pleasing sunset view.

To find hidden **Evergreen Lake**, follow the drainage that spills into Meadow Lake at its northeast shore (to your right as you reach the lake). You'll climb about 500 feet and come upon little Rice Lake. From here you want to veer right, or northeast, still following the meandering stream. Keeping this course for about .5-mile on a gradual uphill, you'll reach Evergreen Lake, tucked away in the forest. After making peace with the lake, walk due north through rumpled terrain, gaining about 200 feet, until you hit the Granite Lake Trail. This trail is less than .5-mile from Evergreen Lake, so have faith. Go right, or east, on this trail, which comes out between Upper and Lower Blue Lakes. From there go right on the paved road through the campground and back to your car.

The trail (Jeep road, FS9N83) to **Clover Valley, Deer Valley and Hermit Valley** on Highway 4, takes off due south from the trailhead parking at Lower Blue Lakes. Since the driving distance between Blue Lakes and Hwy. 4 is so great, hikers might also opt for an in-and-out to Deer Valley instead of a car-shuttle. In spite of the motorized travelers who use this road, you can find some wild country by wandering up Deer Creek, which is almost 3 miles south of the trailhead. *Be Aware:* Don't wander too far, as it's easy to get lost in these parts.

BIKE: Cyclists might share the **road from Blue Lakes to Hermit Valley** with an occasional Jeepster. Terrain and rocks make this a challenging ride through a slice of beautiful country. A very long loop is possible by taking Highway 4 down to Markleeville and Highway 88 back up to Blue Lake. In the spring, **Blue Lakes Road**, beginning at the turnoff on the highway, is often snow-free and car-free, due to snow higher up at Blue Lakes; scenic pavement pedaling possible. Catch it at the right time and this ride is a keeper.

SKI: Although **Blue Lakes Road** into Faith and Charity valleys is a good beginners' ski track, snowmobiles may make this a poor choice, particularly on weekends. Blue Lakes is a better Nordic choice during storms, on weekdays, and for moonlight skates.

FISH: **Lower Blue Lake** and **Twin Lake** have small boat access for trolling. The lakes are heavily stocked, providing a good chance of landing a trout. Float-tube casting is popular in Meadow Lake. Look for rainbow and cutthroat.

18. UPPER BLUE LAKE

WHAT'S BEST: Hike to a prime backpack lake or trek through old-growth red fir to a box canyon dappled with wildflowers. Blue Lakes can be a zoo in the summer, but short walks lead to the wild country of Mokelumne Wilderness.

PARK: Take Blue Lakes Rd., 3 mi. west of Picketts Jct. Go 10 mi., pass Lower Blue Lake on east shore, and drive through the campground to trailhead parking at south end of Upper Blue Lake. At 8,100 ft. **Maps:** Carson Pass, Caples Lake

HIKE: Granite Lake, 4 mi., 600 ft.; Grouse Lake, 10 mi., 1,900 ft.; Devils Corral loop, 8 mi. (4.5 mi. off-trail), 1,600 ft.

The **Granite Lake** trail immediately crosses a stream between the two Blue Lakes, then climbs easily through pleasing forest. Pretty Granite Lake is set among yellow-granite formations, which make for good side-scrambles to big time views. The **Grouse Lake** trail leaves westerly from Granite's south shore, hooking south and then west again. It weaves through a rocky jumble. At the end, you then descend to Grouse Lake, tucked away among aspen and mixed conifers. *Be Aware:* It's easy to go astray upon leaving Granite Lake, so make sure to follow the trail. Rock cairns will aid navigation in spots. *Local lore:* Grouse Lake and its environs, with lakelets and maze-like topography, provide hidden backpack getaways, even on busy weekends. Just south of here is where Alpine's legendary recluse Monty Wolf stayed lost for years.

The **Devils Corral loop** is one of the best wildflower hikes in the Alpine Sierra. Begin north and up from the east shore of Upper Blue Lake. You'll ascend through a forest of huge red firs. The trail then hooks west (to your left) and drops down Summit City Canyon, following the creek. Keep your eyes peeled: After a little more than a mile of descent, the trail will begin to veer away from the creek, which will be down the hillside to your left. A narrow box canyon, which is Devils Corral, will be south, or to your left. Leave the trail, crossing the creek and heading up into the canyon. You'll want to contour around the slope on the far side of the creek. Head up the creek and you'll break out into the open in Devils Corral, where tall mountain walls encircle a falling creek. Willows and wildflowers abound, shaded by some magnificent western white pines. Ascend along the banks of Devils Corral Creek, which can be difficult at times due to our friends the willows. This stairway to heaven continues for about 1.5 miles, hooking to your left (or eastward) as you climb. Leave the creek at the top, and head due east through a forested saddle with granite buttresses—about 200 feet above the highest meadowlands of the creek. From the saddle you'll see Upper Blue Lake. Switchback down and cut across the flat lands on the north shore of the lake.

BIKE: Expect people on summer weekends, but mountain bikers can ride from **Lower Blue Lakes to Lost Lakes**, northeast of Upper Blue, or up the Forestdale Divide, which is north of Upper Blue. Also see TH17 and TH16 mountain bike notes.

FISH: Boat trolling and shore casting for trout is popular in **Upper Blue Lake**. The beaver ponds at **Lost Lakes**, a short distance from Upper Blue, support large numbers of good-sized brook trout. Walk into **Granite Lake** to fly-cast for cutthroat.

19.   WET MEADOWS   HIKE, BIKE, FISH

WHAT'S BEST: Hike to a high cirque that is the crown jewel among Alpine Sierra lakes. Sit beside its waters, or hike up to one of the craggy peaks that rise above.

PARK: Take Blue Lakes Rd., 3 mi. west of Picketts Jct. At 9 mi. in, take left fork toward Sunset Lakes and Wet Meadows on an unpaved road (FS097). After 2 mi., take right fork to Indian Valley. *For Indian Valley and Reynolds Peak*, go right, or south, after about .5 mi.; continue for another .5-mi. and park in the open area before the road crosses the creek. *For Raymond and Pleasant Valley*, continue east for another 1.5 mi., avoiding left-turn options to Lower Sunset or Summit lakes. The road will curve around the east side of all the lakes and end at the north shore of Wet Meadows Reservoir. At 7,900 feet. **Maps:** Markleeville, Ebbetts Pass

HIKE: Raymond Lake, 11 mi., 1,200 ft.; Raymond Peak, 13.5 mi. (2 mi. off-trail), 2,200 ft.; Indian Valley, 6 mi., 500 ft.; Reynolds Peak, 11 mi. (5 mi. off-trail), 1,700 ft.

A short distance from the Wet Meadows parking spot, the trail to **Raymond Lake** joins the PCT. Go southbound, or to your right. You begin at the backside, or west, of the saw-toothed, volcanic ridge of Raymond Peak. The trail wiggles a contour all the way around to approach from the east. About 5 miles into the walk, a spur trail leaves the PCT and climbs to the lip of the lake. Raymond Lake is in a cirque below the peak. You have dramatic views north to Carson Valley and the Tahoe Sierra.

To reach **Raymond Peak** (elevation 10,014 feet) from the lake, go around to the left, or east, as you face the water. Tighten your laces and proceed off-trail, up that shoulder. Except for possible snow, it's easy but steep going until you get to the peculiar rocks at the top. Loop to your right toward the peak. You'll have to use hands as you make your way the last bit up Ray's spires, but it's not a hard climb. *Be Aware:* Approaching Raymond Lake or Peak from the west seems like a tempting shortcut, but it's not a good idea. It becomes steep and craggy, leading to precipitous cliffs. Also, stay on trails in the Wet Meadows basin; it holds 6 or 7 small lakes, and creeks that run parallel in opposite directions with no great vantage points—all this spells l-o-s-t.

More Stuff: About 2 miles from the trailhead—just as the Raymond Lake turns east around steep cliffs, and breaks into the open—a trail branches to the left into Pleasant

Valley, TH31. This for years has been a popular car-shuttle hike, and also a route used by PCT trekkers who wished to rest in Markleeville. Recently a private landowner in Pleasant Valley has put a locked gate at the trailhead. A dispute between public interest and the landowner has yet to be resolved. Use your own judgment.

Underrated **Indian Valley** boasts pockets of wildflowers and a panorama of the back-side of Raymond and Reynolds peaks. Walk the road south from the parking area. It becomes just a trail after 1.5 miles, climbing gradually to an open ridge that overlooks the Ebbetts Pass area. The vantage point is among large junipers and other conifers, amid dwarf brush and a host of flowers. To do **Reynolds Peak**, go off-trail at this Ebbetts overlook, bearing west along the flat, open ridge for 2 miles, and then dipping through a saddle. After the saddle, you make a 1,200-foot scramble up Reynolds' south-east shoulder. From the peak, you can loop left back into Indian Valley. *Be Aware:* The very top is a spire, difficult to climb.

BIKE: You can park at the **left-fork toward Wet Meadows** from Blue Lakes Road. Then ride into Wet Meadows on a forested, 7-mile circuit among 5 lakes, named in fishing notes below. Not many cyclists visit this great ride-around area. The roads are all fairly flat, which will attract intermediate and beginning level riders.

FISH: Tamarack, Upper and Lower Sunset, Summit, and Wet Meadows lakes, all accessible by road, have brook and cutthroat trout. Try early season fly-fishing and boat fishing later on. The lakes are grouped together, beginning at the turnoff from Blue Lakes Road. Hike into **Raymond Lake** for golden trout—which you may wish to catch-and-release since this is a rare species and popular spot.

20. HOPE VALLEY   HIKE, SKI, FISH

WHAT'S BEST: Alpine's serene yet dramatic valley draws people seeking per-fect picnics, fall color, photograhs, fish, a plunge in the river, moonlight skis, and family walks. This is the place to ... be.

PARKING: Three choices for strolls, all in the same vicinity: *Pony Express turn-out*, on Hwy. 88/89, immediately east of Picketts Jct.; *Hope Valley Wildlife Area turnout*, off Hwy. 88 on the right, .25-mi. heading west of Picketts; and *Rogers Rock turnout*, where the West Carson River crosses under Hwy. 88, 1 mi. head-ing west of the junction, on the left. At 7,000 ft. **Maps:** Freel Peak, Carson Pass

HIKE: Three short walks, up to 4 mi., no elevation.

Hope Valley, with its pastoral majesty, cannot be described without hyperbole. The **Pony Express** turnout is where the first horseman, Warren Epson, got a fresh ride and forded the river on his westward journey in 1860. Cross the fence and walk to your right .25-mile across the often-wet meadow. You'll reach the confluence of the West Carson River and Willow Creek, a place to let the dog swim or to enjoy a book or a bottle of wine. From the new parking area for the **Hope Valley Wildlife Area** an old wagon road meanders through the heart of the valley, 1.5 miles north toward Luther Pass. This section is also known as Snowshoe Thompson Trail. You'll get out in the open of the valley by scaling the low rise to the right of the trail.

From the **Rogers Rock** turnout, walk an abandoned road upriver passing many spots for picnics, reflection, or wading. About .5-mile in, look for a large granite tabletop named for artist and Sierran trekker Roger Duchein. On hot days this is the perfect place to take a plunge. You can also continue on a fishermen's trail for a mile or so upriver, before the route curves toward the highway.

SKI: Moonlight skiing in Hope Valley is superb on the **Snowshoe Thompson Trail** from the **Hope Valley Wildlife Area**. Often, the surface freezes to a crust at night and Nordic skiers will be skating over a vast, sparkling snowfield. This is also a relatively safe spot to venture out during storm conditions.

FISH: The **West Carson River** runs from upper Hope Valley to Woodfords, mostly accessible by car. River habitat ranges from free-flowing water and pools in Hope Valley to white water in Woodfords Canyon. You'll find four species of trout:

, HOPE VALLEY, WEST CARSON RIVER

cutthroat, rainbow, brown, and brook. Fishing platforms at the **Hope Valley Wildlife Area** make it easy for family fishermen to access the water.

21. BURNSIDE LAKE

HIKE, BIKE, SKI, FISH

WHAT'S BEST: Visit a historic peak that is easy to scale, or rest at a small cascade and wildflower meadow. This road offers many options for muscle-powered sports.

PARK: Take Burnside Lake Road (FS019, unpaved), due south at Picketts Jct., where Hwy. 88 meets Hwy. 89. Drive in 6 mi. to Burnside Lake. Keep left as you reach the lake and park at road's end. *Note:* Four-wheel drive recommended, but passenger cars normally can make it. At 8,100 ft. *For Hawkins Peak,* turn left at Cal Pine Mine Rd. which is to your left at an open flat area, about .5-mi. before Burnside Lake. Drive in about .5-mi. and park where a gated road goes uphill to the right. At 8,200 ft. *For the Grover car-shuttle,* park a second car at Grover State Park, TH33. **Maps:** Markleeville, Carson Pass

HIKE: Hot Springs Valley overlook, 2.5 mi., no elevation; Grover car-shuttle, 4.5 mi., minus 2,100 ft.; Burnside Buttes loop, (3.5 mi. off-trail), 900 ft.; Hawkins Peak, 6 mi., (3 mi. off-trail), 2,000 ft.

For both the **Hot Springs Valley overlook** and the **Grover car-shuttle**, take the trail southeast from Burnside Lake. Stay on the east, or left, side of the willow-fringed meadow as you walk from the lake. Beyond the far end of the meadowland, the trail crosses the creek. You'll come to an overlook where benches of yellow granite afford views of the valley—just before the trail begins its descent. Also, the sculpted granite upward from the east side of the trail is an interesting side jaunt for non-car-shuttle hikers. This is the ridge most visible from the hot pool at the park. To **Grover Hot Springs car-shuttle**, take the switchbacks on down from the overlook area, through cedar and pine forests. The last mile or so of the walk is on the flat through the forest.

The **Burnside Buttes loop** is an off-trail saunter up that gives up big views of Hope and Charity valleys. From the south end of the lake, head up and to your right, crossing the lake's outflow. You begin following some loggers' skid roads. When the skid roads end, keep to your left, ascending southeasterly up a draw. Near the top of the ridgeline, you'll want to veer left as you reach the crest—comprised of several granite knobs. Then keep veering left along the ridge. You'll be on the edge where the forest gives way to the mule ears and dwarf scrub of upper Charity Valley. As you near the end of the ridge, make sure to keep left, or north, rather than dropping down toward Hot Springs Valley. You'll pick up the trail that leads from the overlook described in the first hike above. *Be Aware:* Only hikers with orienteering experience should attempt this hike—on the other hand, this a good one for beginners who want to gain some off-trail skills. The old Catch 22.

To reach **Hawkins Peak**, march up the gated road to your right. You'll swerve skyward until you get a big view of the peak. The road eventually curves left in front of the base of the mountain. Don't go that way. Head off trail to the right, following the shoulder to the right, on the south side of the peak. You'll be on the open slopes of Hawkins, which sports dwarf sage and mule ears. Wind up steeply through dwarf trees, and then circle around behind the peak. The last few hundred feet is up talus and rock. It is not difficult, but be careful on this stuff, particularly coming down. The very top of Hawkins is a man-made rock tabletop. *Local lore*: Near the top—maybe 75 feet south of the tabletop—look for a rock inscripted by Harry Hawkins, one of Alpine's pioneers whose ranch house still stands on the east side of Highway 89, one mile south of Woodfords— on private property. *Be Aware*: If lightening is anywhere in the area, do not attempt Hawkins Peak. Also note that the Hawkins today is host to an array of telecommunications equipment, which is a good thing if you want to make a cell phone call.

BIKE: Park at south side of Picketts Junction and ride 6 mi. into Burnside Lake. **Burnside Lake Road**, a.k.a. **FS019**, also presents a number of options. On the return run (or heading up) about 2 miles from Picketts Junction, **FS053** branches off to the east. This road climbs toward **Pickett Peak** and then snakes down **to Sorensen's Resort**. Gung-ho pedal pushers can also do **Cal Pine Road**, as per the **Hawkins Peak** hike; you cross on the west side of the mountain to some intriguing highlands. From Burnside Lake Road you can also go west **toward Hope Valley** on FS205 and 205A; these spur roads are to the right about 5 miles from Picketts Junction. All in all, Burnside should get high marks from intermediate-level cyclists.

SKI: Park at Picketts Junction. Forested **Burnside Lake Road** has reliable snow, with some good downhill runs on the road itself, and off-trail options toward Hawkins Peak and into Hope Valley.

FISH: Drive to **Burnside Lake** to tube or shore cast for rainbows and brookies. This spot is a favorite among car campers.

22.   SORENSEN'S CLIFFS   HIKE, BIKE, SKI

WHAT'S BEST: Fall colors border the route to a commanding vista of Hope Valley. Less energetic hikers can sit beside a river cascade.

PARK: At turnouts .75-mi. east of Picketts Jct., on Hwy. 88/89. Look for spaces on either side of highway, just west of Sorensen's Resort. Resort patrons can use their lot. At 7,000 ft. *For West Carson Cascade*, park at Hope Valley Resort, .5-mi. east of Sorensen's. **Map:** Freel Peak

HORSETHIEF CANYON

HIKE: Sorensen's Cliffs, 3.5 mi., 1,000 ft.; Pickett Peak, 8 mi. (3 mi. off-trail), 2,100 ft.; West Carson Cascade, .5 mi., 200 ft.

All hikers will want to check out the scene at venerable Sorensen's Resort. Its gift shop-slash-bookstore is the best in the eastern Sierra, and the café is normally a hot ticket. This is the place to enjoy a hot or cold beverage on the resort's aspen-shaded deck and commune with fellow lovers of the Alpine Sierra. The rustic cabins draw visitors from around the globe.

To **Sorensen's Cliffs**, take the gated road up from the highway, FS053, as it switchbacks through mixed conifers, aspen, and willow groves. You'll reach an open area and see the flat cliff tops fingering out to the right. Head down and pick a spot—but don't get too close to the edges. The volcanic cliffs view Hope Valley and Woodfords Canyon, as seen by red-tailed hawks. *Local Lore:* One summer, John Brissenden of Sorensen's climbed ten peaks that surround Hope Valley, all the while wearing the same tattered pair of khaki pants. Upon completing the feat, the pants disappeared from their hanging peg at the resort, and thereafter have been sighted walking by their lonesome on full-moon nights. Don't be alarmed should you see these pants. They will not harm you.

To reach **Pickett Peak**, Hawkins' neighbor, continue on the road until the point at which it starts to lose elevation—due north of the peak. At that point go off-trail through a tree buffer and then up the peak's northwest shoulder. Brush and boulders require some creative trailblazing near the top. *Be Aware:* The talus and boulders that comprise Pickett Peak will be a problem to dogs and people not comfortable with bouldering. *Note:* You can also hike Pickett Peak with less elevation gain by driving Burnside Lake Road, TH 21, and then turning left, east, on FS053.

The **West Carson Cascade** is visible from Highway 88 and accessible by taking the short walk through the Hope Valley Resort campground and down to the river; boulder up a few feet from the bridge. *Be Aware:* The water here can be powerful, so make sure to watch your step.

BIKE: The uphill pump on **FS053** connects up with the Burnside Lake system of roads. You can begin here and loop back to Hope Valley via **Burnside Lake Road**.

SKI: Marked trails from near the resort connect with Burnside Lake Road and Hope Valley. Check with **Hope Valley Outdoor Center** and **Sorensen's** for info and rentals.

23. HORSETHIEF CANYON   HIKE, FISH

WHAT'S BEST: Get a high-country experience early in the season, entering pockets of tall wildflowers beside falling water. The quick vertical of this trail is popular among locals getting in shape for the hiking season.

PARK: At the signed trailhead, 4 mi. west of Woodfords on Hwy. 88/89, which is across from Snowshoe Springs Campground. At 6,600 ft. *For the Fay Canyon car-shuttle*, park a second car at Fay Canyon, TH28, as described on page 75. **Maps:** Freel Peak, Woodfords

HIKE: Horsethief Canyon, 4 mi., 1,300 ft.; Cary Peak, 8 mi. (1.5 mi. off-trail), 2,200 ft. Horsethief to Fay Canyon car-shuttle, 10 mi. (3.5 mi. off-trail), 1,800 ft.

Horsethief Canyon trail begins steeply, making switchbacks through granite sand and then skirting a white-water stream below volcanic buttresses. Water thunders by. At the top are large junipers that lead the way to sloping meadows. Continue straight across a Forest Service road, following a trail that features lush wildflowers in midsummer, especially at the upper end of the meadows. Pick your own turnaround spot. A few trails meander the margins of the creek. Your main hazard is getting swallowed by willows. *Local Lore:* In the 1850s, horse thieves preying on California emigrants would bring stolen stock up this canyon and loop eastward back into the Carson Valley, where they would sell the fattened animals back to other emigrants.

To **Cary Peak** (sometimes spelled "Carey") turn eastward on the logging road at the top of the canyon. Continue as the road makes S-turns and climbs. You will hook eastward, around the tops of Hidden and Acorn canyons, which are between Horsethief and the shoulder of Cary Peak. Leaving the road too early will send you into a rumpled maze. The final approach is from due south of the peak, off-trail across a forested ridge that drops off steeply to the east. The last bit of the walk is the most difficult, across brush and boulders. But, darn it, keep going and you will be rewarded with a place on a granite ledge that overlooks Woodfords and is near the source of the sacred Washoe falls (as the hawk flies). *Be Aware:* Water is scarce after you leave the Horsethief trail.

Locals and experienced hikers with topo maps will want to try the **Horsethief to Fay Canyon car-shuttle**, which drops from alpine heights into the arid Carson Valley. Go left when you reach the logging road (FS025) at the top of Horsethief Canyon. Continue on an upward grade as the road parallels the east side of the valley, heading toward the willow-choked saddle at the far north end. When the road hooks east (and continues to Willow Creek, TH24), leave it and switchback through the willows. The slopes of the Carson Range will rise high to your left, and the lower crags of Wade Peak and Annie and Beth peaks will be on your right, to the east. Go north, making sure to pass the eastern peaks—heading east too soon will take you down Fredricksburg Canyon. After descending *steeply* for several hundred feet, you'll pick up the beginnings of Luther Creek, your guiding light that runs down Fay Canyon to the trailhead. A well-built trail will help cushion the knees for the last two-thirds of the hike. *Be Aware:* Manzanita and other brush dominate the head of steep Fay Canyon. Do not attempt to go down all the way off-trail or you will curse the day you picked up this book. If in doubt, retreat, even though it may mean climbing back up some.

FISH: Walk in 1.5 miles to **Horsethief Creek** at top of canyon to fly-cast for brookies. Relatively few fishermen make the effort.

24. WILLOW CREEK HIKE, BIKE, SKI, FISH

WHAT'S BEST: Groups and families can spread out on this trail and enjoy views of Hope Valley and the Sierran Crest. Autumn leaf-peepers, cyclists, and skiers will also want to take note.

PARK: At gate for FS025, on the right .5-mi. driving north from Picketts Jct. on Hwy. 89. At 7,000 ft. *For Horsethief car-shuttle*, park second car at TH23. **Map:** Freel Peak

HIKE: Hope Valley view, about 5 mi., 1,000 ft.; Horsethief Canyon car-shuttle, 6.5 mi., 1,500 ft.

Both hikes begin on Willow Creek Road—FS025, gated—with a mellow saunter across the creek and through primarily lodgepole pine and aspen. Then begins a series of long, gradual switchbacks, topping out at a forested ridge with spot-on **views of Hope Valley**. Wildflower pockets also will be found at several ephemeral drainages up higher. Hope Valley lays out before you on the downward leg. *More Stuff:* Willow Creek is well suited for a fall-color meander. Instead of taking the switchbacks up the Forest Service road, go left at fork not far after the bridge. You can make a 3-mile, counter-clockwise loop through the conifer and aspen forest. Follow Willow Creek through meadowlands on the homestretch. Some of this hike will be off-trail.

For the **Horsethief car-shuttle**, continue on the road across an intervening level zone before descending into upper Horsethief Canyon meadows via switchbacks. Early in the summer, at the saddle on the road itself, notice the pine cone seeds sprouting young Jeffreys and lodgepole. You follow the road south in Horsethief Canyon. Make sure to branch off on the trail to your right at the extreme south end— if you start back up on the road, you've gone too far.

WILLOW CREEK

BIKE: To do the **Horsethief Canyon loop**, you will have to walk your bike the last fraction of a mile down the Horsethief Canyon trail, and then ride Hwy 89 back to the Willow Creek parking area. It's a good riding surface, other than that. From the higher reaches of Willow Creek Road, you can branch off to explore other roads toward Horse Meadow, TH25.

SKI: Moonlight skiing is choice at the forested, lower part of the **Willow Creek Road**. Downhill runs are good for beginning and intermediate skiers as you return on the road. You can also go across the highway into the open area of **Hope Valley**—another good starting point for a moonlight run and for novice skiers.

FISH: Use this trailhead to fish **Willow Creek** and the **West Carson River** before it falls into Woodfords Canyon. Most fishermen group together near Picketts Junction, where the river is visible from the road.

25.   HORSE MEADOW   HIKE, BIKE, SKI

WHAT'S BEST: Scale the three peaks with Tahoe and high-desert views and return on a downhill run through granite sand. Cyclist and skiers can take a trip through an old-growth juniper forest.

PARK: Drive about 1.5 mi. toward Tahoe from Picketts Jct. on Hwy. 89, to about .25-mi. past the old barn on big bend. Turn uphill on a dirt road, FS051. Go about 4.5 mi., passing a right fork option after almost 2 mi. (Although 4WD is recommended, passenger cars should be able to drive this road.) *For Fountain Place and Star Lake*, turn left at the bridge and drive .75-mi. to parking at Armstrong Pass. *For Freel, Jobs, and Jobs Sister*, continue straight at the bridge for about a mile. Go left off the road as it curls to the right in Horse Meadow. *For Jobs Peak*, shortly after this left, take a right fork, which then ends after about .25-mi. For Freel Peak and Jobs Sister, take the left fork and park where the road ends after about .25-mi. At 8,400 ft. **Maps:** Freel Peak, Woodfords

HIKE: Fountain Place, 6 mi., 900 ft., Star Lake, 9.5 mi., 1,800 ft.; Jobs Peak, 6 mi., 2,200 ft.; Jobs Sister and Freel Peak loop, 7 mi., 2,900 ft. *Be Aware:* You'll find sketchy trails leading up to the peaks, and good trail segments at the top, but the peak routes require mostly off-trail orienteering.

A short connector trail leads up a steep switchback from the parking area to Armstrong Pass. For **Fountain Place**, you follow the creek, straight over the pass—not the Tahoe Rim Trail that takes off to the right. Fountain Place is the confluence of two creeks below Freel Peak that form Trout Creek, a major tributary of Lake Tahoe. This trail continues to Meyers as Fountain Place Road, FS1201. To reach **Star Lake**—a topaz jewel set in the forest below the peaks—go right, or north, on the Tahoe Rim Trail.

From Armstrong Pass the route does some serious climbing on the steep west face of Freel Peak. You then cross the stream in the crease between the two peaks and descend to the lake, which sits at 9,100 feet.

The three peaks are the giants of the Carson Range, lording over the Carson Valley to the east and Big Blue northwest. To climb **Jobs Peak**, proceed off-trail and steeply from the parking area. Keep the steep drainage on your left, and switchback skyward. The first part of this hike is the most rugged. Make sure not cross into the drainage. After climbing about 500 feet, you will top-out above the larger conifers and contour easterly and to your left. Aim for the saddle between Jobs and Jobs Sister. To Jobs Peak from the saddle—which would be one, yahoo ski run down to the Carson Valley—a trail takes off southeasterly. With the security of this trail, you'll curl around to the east of an unnamed peak, across a saddle, and then up the last segment to the summit, sitting at 10,633 feet. Jobs Peak's east face is a steep and rugged drop of almost 6,000 feet to the Carson Valley. *More Stuff:* Energetic hikers can backtrack to the saddle and scale Jobs Sister on this hike. A steep trail ascends though rock and granite sand.

The **Jobs Sister and Freel Peak loop** hike isn't complicated for hikers accustomed to off-trail travel, and who are in condition. From the parking area, cross the creek and wind your way through the lowlands. At the outset you want to aim for the rise that is between the two peaks—which can be mistaken for Freel Peak. Switchback and climb in a northwesterly direction. As you reach higher elevations, veer right, or easterly. You want to stay right of sandy hogback (false Freel) that is between the two peaks. You'll reach a level area with dwarf whitebark pine. The trail to Jobs Sister will be to your right, climbing up the last distance to the 10,823-foot summit.

You'll backtrack on this trail to pick up Freel Peak on the homeward leg of the hike. A trail traverses the north side of false Freel and then winds up through rock formations that comprise the peak. Freel stands at 10,881 feet, the tallest in the Tahoe Basin. From Freel, drop off due south through hundreds of feet of sandy descent, down to the middle of Horse Meadow. Cross the stream and find the road back up to the car. *More Stuff:* To do Freel Peak without Jobs Sister, park just after the bridge at Fountain Place road, and approach Freel directly from its south side—making switchbacks at will, as your legs and lungs dictate. *Be Aware:* From the top of any of these peaks, get a bearing on where you parked your car. Three streams converge in Horse Meadow, making micro navigating hard after you've descended. Finding the car may prove more difficult than reaching the summits.

BIKE: Park at the gate at Hwy. 89 for a 12-mile ride up **FS051 to Horse Meadow.** Adventurous cyclists can also push the pedals over **Armstrong Pass** to Meyers in the Tahoe Basin. Use the Fountain Place hiking description. The trail joins **FS1201** and curves down Trout Creek, which is off **Pioneer Trail Road in Meyers**. You'll need a second car or face a hellish loop ride on the highways.

SKI: **Horse Meadow road** is great for larger groups of intermediate skiers, with steeper runs optional for those who go off road. A sleeper area.

26. TAHOE RIM TRAIL-LUTHER PASS   HIKE, SKI

WHAT'S BEST: Take an out-of-the-way hike through old-growth conifers and lush wildflowers to a seldom-scaled, but famous peak with Hope Valley views.

PARK: On Hwy. 89, about 4 mi. toward Tahoe from Picketts Jct. The trailhead is on the west end of Grass Lake, 2 mi. west of the Alpine-El Dorado county line. At 7,700 ft. **Map:** Freel Peak

HIKE: Tahoe Rim view, 5.5 mi., 1,100 ft.; Freel Meadows, 6.75 mi., 1,400 ft., Thompson Peak, 8.5 mi. (3 mi. off-trail), 1,800 ft.

Tahoe Rim Trail, only recently completed, circles the lake; this is one of its many trailheads. **For all hikes**, take the first .5-mile of this connector trail that climbs several hundred feet that joins TRT coming up from Big Meadow—2 miles to the left on a less-interesting segment of the trail. Go right at the junction. The trail does a squiggly climb for the next 2.5 miles, ascending to a point above Tucker Flat, from which is a **view of Lake Tahoe** amid the architecture of monolithic granite.

From the view spot, the trail undulates for a mile or more before reaching the wild-flower expanse of **Freel Meadows**. Find a spot to kick back and commune with nature at this tucked-away garden. For the easy climb of **Thompson Peak**, continue on the TRT to the east end of the meadow. The forested shoulder of the peak slopes up to the right. From the trailhead, you will have circled up and behind the mountain. It's an easy off-trail walk to the tree-dotted top, not a giant at 9,340 feet. Named for Snow-shoe Thompson, the peak overlooks the skier's route through Luther Pass and gives you a good look at Hope Valley and the Sierran Crest.

SKI: Popular skiing is across the highway from the trailhead, at **Grass Lake**, which is a Sno-Park (permit required, available at Sorensen's). The best ski, however, may be at the **Luther Pass** turnout. A road, old Highway 89, leads out the south side of the parking area, making an exhilarating run into Hope Valley—on a section called the Snowshoe Thompson Trail.

27. BIG MEADOW   HIKE, BIKE, FISH

WHAT'S BEST: An old-growth, red fir forest shades the way to two, first-class camping lakes. Wildflowers dot a lush meadow on the way.

PARK: Look for an improved trailhead parking lot on Hwy. 89, 3 mi. north of Luther Pass. Heading toward Tahoe, it's on the right on the downhill grade. At 7,200 ft. **Maps:** Fallen Leaf, Freel Peak

HIKE: Big Meadow, 1.5 mi., 300 ft.; Dardanelles Lake, 6.5 mi., 1,100 ft.; Round Lake, 5.75 mi., 1,000 ft.

For all hikes, cross the highway and walk down the road a short distance. The Big Meadow trail begins up a north-facing, steep section for the first mile or so. You may encounter snow in early summer. **Big Meadow** features a host of wildflowers for most of the summer, and its creek, which can be deep but not dangerous to cross, makes a good lunch spot. *More Stuff:* You can walk from here to Scotts Lake, which is above Hope Valley. Keep to your left as you reach the meadow. See TH1, page 33.

Dardanelles Lake is a beauty in the woods, with a complex shoreline and rock ledges hanging over its loden green waters. To get there, head through Big Meadow on the Tahoe Rim Trail. For the next 1.5 miles you'll climb gradually and contour around to a hillside of huge red fir—now in the drainage for the Upper Truckee River. From a trail junction at that point, the trail to Dardanelles Lake drops down to the right and across the drainage. You snake through the forest for another mile before coming to the lake. *Be Aware:* Take heed to stay on the trail, since the lake is easy to miss.

To get to **Round Lake**, you also head south on the TRT from Big Meadow. Then continue south past the trail to Dardanelles Lake. You'll climb and dip through a confusing zone of hidden lakelets before reaching the lake. Towering above Round Lake is an enormous "buffalo head" outcropping, a feature which can be seen from many points in this area. *More Stuff:* This trail continues to Meiss Meadow and Carson Pass, about 5 miles distant. See TH3 on page 34.

BIKE: Mr. Toad's Wild Ride, a tough downhill run of 12 miles to Meyers, begins by heading northeast to Tucker Flat on the Tahoe Rim Trail. You begin at the back end of the parking lot. Follow the northwest, left-forking trail down the Saxon Creek drainage, and keep taking left-fork options on roads as you get closer to Meyers. Bikers can also take an easier, and equally scenic, route down from Big Meadow. An unpaved road, the old highway, leads down to **Christmas Valley** and then follows the **Upper Truckee River** along a road through neighborhoods, popping out at Meyers. The road begins at the back of the Big Meadow parking lot and crosses Highway 89 a mile later.

FISH: Day hike or backpack to **Round Lake**—stock varies. Multi-taskers can daydream while casting into placid waters.

Markleeville

WASHOE RABBIT ROBES

PHOTO COURTESY NEVADA HISTORICAL SOCIETY

Markleeville didn't become the county seat for Alpine's first 11 years, not until Silver Mountain City near Ebbetts Pass went bust in 1875. During those Silver-boom years, the regional population was a transient 25,000—more than five-times that of Los Angeles—with miners and entrepreneurs roaming six mining districts. Today, Alpine's population hovers above 1,200, by far the smallest among California counties. Agriculture was the county's mainstay for most of the twentieth century, and many family holdings operating today date back to pioneer days. But remnants of other, bygone homesteads dot this region; ranchers, farmers, and sawyers who kept the mines supplied and were gone when it was over.

In recent years, Markleeville's mountains and rivers and meadows have become the silver mine, as recreational tourism has become a primary economic force. Scenic resources are complemented by ranching families who to date have withstood pressures to develop private holdings adjacent to public lands. Local groups, such as Friends of Hope Valley and Sierra Nevada Alliance, as well as individuals, work to maintain Alpine's natural resources.

East and north of Markleeville are piñon forests and sage lands with volcanic outcroppings, the historic wintering grounds of the Washoe Indians. The Washoe—whose ancestors 8,000 years ago blazed trails that exist today—were hunters and gatherers. They harvested thousands of plants and animals from the wild gardens of the Sierra. Washoe baskets are known as the finest in the world, and those woven by Dat-So-La-Lee are coveted museum pieces. Other than baskets, obsidian arrowheads and grinding rocks found throughout the region are physical reminders of the ancient Washoe nation. In Woodfords is one of several regional communities of Washoe.

Washoe lands are cleaved by the East Carson River, running

WEBSTER SCHOOL, ALPINE COUNTY HISTORICAL COMPLEX

through a canyon leading to Nevada. The East Carson Canyon was the route taken by Jedediah Smith and other trappers, the first white men in California in the late 1820s. It was also the passage for the Expedition of the Western Territories by Captain John C. Fremont. Led by Kit Carson in the early 1840s, this was the first recorded passage through the Sierra.

The upstream drainage of the East Carson River—Hot Springs Valley, Pleasant Valley, Wolf Creek, Silver King, and Bagley Valley—is ideal for all kinds of alpine recreational pursuits. Wolf Creek is a prime trailhead for the Carson-Iceberg Wilderness. Saw-toothed Raymond Peak and massive Silver Peak, landmarks visible due south from Reno, are just two mountains hanging around town.

Ebbetts Pass, with Scossa Cow Camp and the Silver Mountain City ruins nearby, was once planned as the first railroad route through the Sierra, but its engineer suffered an untimely death by drowning. Now the Pacific Crest Trail is the major route. West of Ebbetts, the Mokelumne River flows to the San Joaquin and the San Francisco Bay. Lands bordering the pass are part of the Mokelumne Wilderness. East of the pass, Silver Creek and many other streams feed the East Carson River, headed for the Carson Sink in the Great Basin.

Monitor Pass was completed in 1954, the last pass engineered in California. On top of Monitor are the broad shoulders of Leviathan Peak, with its sage, pine, and aspen expanses. Basque sheepherders have left many artful carvings on trees in

WOLF CREEK CARSON-ICEBERG

the hinterlands of this region. The westward view is of the Sierra Nevada, an ocean of peaks, and to the east are the sublime Slinkard and Antelope valleys, with the Sweetwater Mountains a short hop south.

During winter months, Highway 89 leading into Markleeville is a dead end—Monitor and Ebbetts passes to the south are closed. Although not much commerce travels Monitor, almost all camel traffic in the Sierra took this route. Camels were coaxed through Monitor in the late 1800s, on the last leg of a long journey from their middle-Eastern homelands and headed to haul salt in the Lahontan area of Nevada. The animals balked at the cliffs, but when the first one was pulled along the rest followed—down "Dump Canyon," which leads from south of Monitor's Company Meadows into to Slinkard Valley.

MONITOR PASS, EAST FORK CARSON RIVER

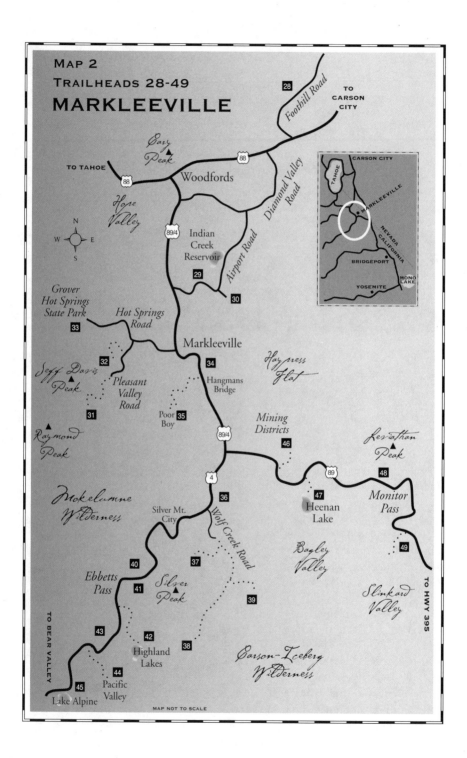

MAP 2
TRAILHEADS 28-49
MARKLEEVILLE

T R A I L H E A D S

		28-49
HIKE :	DAY HIKES AND LONGER TREKS	
BIKE :	MOUNTAIN AND ROAD BIKE TRIPS	
SKI :	CROSS COUNTRY SKIING AND SNOWSHOEING	
FISH :	LAKE, STREAM, AND RIVER FISHING	

TH = TRAILHEAD, FS = FOREST SERVICE ROAD, NUMBERED

All hiking distances in parentheses are ROUND TRIP, unless noted for car shuttles. Elevation gains of 100 feet or more are noted. Maps listed are USGS topographical, 7.5 series. See Resource Links for recommendations for other optional trail maps.

28.   FAY CANYON-LUTHER CREEK   HIKE

WHAT'S BEST: Get ready for the summer hiking season with a jaunt from the sagebrush to the Jeffrey pines in the east-Sierran canyon. You'll be able to get in here when snows cover much of the higher country.

PARK: From Woodfords, take Hwy. 88 north. As you drop into the Carson Valley, at the bottom of the grade, turn left on Fredericksburg Rd. Follow for several miles and turn left on Foothill Rd. Look for signed trailhead parking on the left. **Maps:** Freel Peak, Woodfords

HIKE: Fay Canyon-Luther Creek, up to 6 mi., 1,300 ft.

The **Fay Canyon-Luther Creek trail** starts out as a flat, granite-sand track through sagebrush. Jobs Peak looms to your right, only a few horizontal miles away but more than a mile in the sky. You'll then enter a Jeffrey pine forest and climb nicely graded ramps that are also frequented by equestrians. Shortcut trails provide options near the lower reaches of the trail; keep to your left and keep going up.

After a mile or so, the canyon narrows and you'll become aware of Luther Creek—which will have precious little water near the end of summer. Manzanita makes off-trail walking foolhardy, as the route veers south and gets deeper into the crease of the mountains. Choose a turnaround before the trail peters out. You'll find a few vista points, with looks toward the Carson Valley. *More Stuff:* With some orienteering required, you can walk from Fay Canyon to Horsethief Canyon. This hike is described beginning on the other side, in TH23, page 64.

29. CURTZ LAKE-INDIAN CREEK   HIKE, BIKE, SKI, FISH

WHAT'S BEST: Head here to explore Washoe country—early-season flowers, bald eagle sightings, and mountain bike rides. A short hike leads to a historic spot on the East Carson River.

PARK: Turn on Airport Rd. off Hwy. 89/4, midway between Woodfords and Markleeville. *For Summit Lake and Fremonts Crossing,* park on the left at Curtz Lake, 2.5 mi. in from the highway. At 6,200 ft. *For Markleeville car-shuttle,* park second car in Markleeville. *For Indian Creek car-shuttle and Stevens Lake,* park a second car at Indian Creek Reservoir, 3 mi. from Curtz Lake on Airport Rd. **Maps:** Woodfords, Markleeville

HIKE: Summit Lake, 2.5 mi., 200 ft.; Summit Lake to Indian Creek car-shuttle, 4.5 mi., elevation loss. Fremonts Crossing, 4 mi., 1,000 ft., Fremonts Crossing to Markleeville car-shuttle, 4.5 mi. (2.5 mi. off-trail), 300 ft.; Stevens Lake, .5-mi., no elevation.

To **Summit Lake**, take the trail that begins at the gate on the north side of Curtz Lake. Keep an eye out for eagles and hawks, as well as waterfowl on the way to this small lake. For the **Indian Creek car-shuttle** take the trail out the northeast side of Summit Lake—to the right as you approach the lake. You'll cross an intervening flat over rock cobbles and then turn east. The trail curves down through piñon forest to the campground at the reservoir. For **Stevens Lake**, drive to Indian Creek Reservoir and take the short walk from the far end of the campground. Waterfowl like this little lake.

The trail to **Fremonts Crossing** is on the opposite side of the road from Curtz Lake. It takes you 2 miles down to the East Carson River Canyon, where Fremont's expedition

SUMMIT LAKE

passed through in 1844. Today during the early part of the summer you might see rafters shooting by this stretch of the river. This hike is a locals' favorite in spring and fall. For the **Markleeville car-shuttle**, head upriver from the crossing, off-trail, scrambling and side-hilling outcroppings for the first mile. Then you walk through Jeffrey pine forests that border the pastures leading to the town. *Note:* The pastures are private property, so stay in the trees.

More Stuff: An interpretive trail begins at the south end of Curtz Lake, across the highway. And you can extend this ho-hum nature walk by going off-trail from the southerly loop of the trail. Head up, southerly, to the volcanic nubs with dead-on views of Raymond and other peaks above Markleeville. You'll feel a long way away after only a short walk.

BIKE: **Airport Road**, unpaved, cuts through BLM lands on the east shore of **Indian Creek Reservoir**. You connect with Diamond Valley Road, which can be ridden west toward Woodfords and then back to the car via Highway 89/4, making about a 10-mile loop. This under-used cycling route is a scenic sleeper.

SKI: After or during big storms, **Airport Road to Indian Creek** is a good Nordic choice. **Stevens Lake** is often frozen in midwinter and can be used as a rink for ski-skating; this should only be attempted during the coldest weather, as breaking ice is extremely dangerous.

FISH: Walk in to **Summit Lake** to float tube for brook trout, or drive to **Indian Creek Reservoir** for some of the area's biggest rainbows, brooks and Lahontan cutthroat. A boat ramp available.

30. ALPINE AIRPORT   HIKE, BIKE, FISH

WHAT'S BEST: Get to an eagle's perch above the deep East Carson River canyon—or switchback down and dip your feet to be at one with the fish. This out-of-the way trailhead is keeper, especially in the spring and fall.

PARK: Turn on Airport Rd. off Hwy. 89/4, midway between Woodfords and Markleeville. Continue about 3 mi., passing Curtz Lake, and park on the right amid pine trees—where the road makes a sweeping left on its way down to Indian Creek Campground. The two wide runways will be straight ahead. **Map:** Markleeville

HIKE: East Carson River vista, 1.5 mi., 240 ft.; Carson River, 3.75 mi., 800 ft.

For both hikes, walk across the two broad runways, making sure to avoid running into cows that laze about the tarmac. (If cows had wings they would be the only aircraft you'd likely see; no buildings fringe the runways.) Veer over to the right and look for a rough road perpendicular to the runways, and a couple hundred feet from their southerly end. Amid a pinon forest, start up the road and keep left at a junction. You'll top out the ridge, where the road ends and you pick up a trail that veers right, or south. (The trail also goes left, but no matter.)

For the **East Carson River vista**, take the trail over the saddle and descend about 100 vertical feet. You'll see an outcropping just to the left off the trail. A rocky perch affords a miles-long view on the green river snaking through its volcanic gorge. *More Stuff:* To make a loop of the vista hike, head south along the rim of the gorge and circle to your right back to the airport. Brush makes the first quarter-mile of this loop tricky, but you reach an even better view of the river gorge as well as big views toward Markleeville. To reach the **East Carson River**, descend on the trail for another 500 feet and stop when your feet get wet.

More Stuff: A marked trail leads upstream at the river and winds around a rock outcropping to Fremonts Crossing, making for a possible car-shuttle hike; see TH29 above. Only goats and sure-footed hikers will like one short section of the trail along the river, although it is not dangerous. You can also reach Fremonts Crossing by taking the road down through the Jeffrey pine forest that goes south from the Alpine Airport parking described above. The road meets the Fremonts Crossing trail that comes down from Curtz Lake, about .75-mile from the river. Use this road to make an Alpine Airport loop hike—but you'll have an easier time finding your way by heading up to the vista described above, walking the river to Fremonts Crossing, and returning on this road.

BIKE: Parking at the **Alpine Airport** is an option for cyclists wishing to pedal the route described in TH29 above. Cyclists will be pleasantly surprised.

FISH: Although it takes a bit of walking, you can get a wilderness fishing experience by taking the trail down to the **East Carson River**. This long section of the river has some big pools that see relatively few anglers.

31.   PLEASANT VALLEY   HIKE, BIKE, SKI, FISH

WHAT'S BEST: This aptly named valley is a top pick for fall color and early-season flower hikes. When the big snows fall, it's also a choice for skiers.

PARK: Take Pleasant Valley Rd., 1.5 mi. west of Markleeville on Hot Springs Rd. Keep right, uphill past homes for 3 mi. (2 mi. unpaved) into Pleasant Valley to end of the county road. At 6,000 ft. *Be Aware:* A landowner has recently gated the trailhead and posted no-trespassing signs. This occurred after many decades of public use and maintenance, and in spite of the trail's historic and prehistoric use by early settlers and Washoe. Although a legal opinion supports the notion that the trail remains a public easement to a national wilderness area, the matter has yet to be litigated. Stay tuned. Use your own judgment about this trail access. **Map:** Markleeville

HIKE: Pleasant Valley trail, 2 to 7 mi., 100 to 800 ft. *Note:* The trail continues to Mokelumne Wilderness and Wet Meadows, TH19.

Pleasant Valley rests beneath saw-toothed Raymond Peak and supports cottonwoods, aspen, and mixed conifers, all nourished by a winding stream. It's a great place for both dawdling and serious hiking. Along the creek are sandy beaches for wading and pools for swimming. Energetic hikers can continue on the trail as it gains elevation after about 2 miles, crossing the fanned-out drainage on its way up to Wet Meadows and Raymond Peak.

If you don't cross the drainage, and continue up the northwest sector or the valley, a hidden falls lies just off-trail, about two miles up from the creek crossing. The trail peters out—stay lower to avoid manzanita, walking up granite faces in a few places. Several trail-side perches afford misted looks at white-water shooting through a narrow section of the bedrock. *Local lore:* History buffs might try Raymond Canyon midway on the south side of Pleasant Valley—rural legend tells of miner's goodies stashed away in a cave that were left one winter and not retrieved in the spring.

BIKE: Mountain-road cyclists touring Markleeville will want to take a side-trip up **Pleasant Valley Road**, including the last 2 miles of unpaved surface that leads into the valley.

SKI: Ski in and down the 2 miles at the end of the road and then west into the **Pleasant Valley**. A very good area when snowpack is adequate—with the same caveat regarding the trail closure given in the parking note above.

FISH: **Pleasant Valley Creek** is a renowned catch-and-release fly-fisherman's' haven, that was stocked by the State of California for many years. Recently it has been turned into a private fly-fishing stream. Permit requirements are posted. See *Resource Links* for further information.

32. THORNBURG CANYON   HIKE, BIKE

BEST FOR: Take a short walk to a view of Pleasant Valley or strap on the trekking gear and scale rugged cliffs in the high country.

PARK: Turn on Pleasant Valley Rd., 2 mi. east of Markleeville off Hot Springs Rd. Go about .25-mile and veer right on unpaved Sawmill Rd., FS071. Pass homes on left and continue about 2.5 mi. until the county road ends. At 6,200

ft. *Note:* The road crosses two creeks, pesky in early spring and summer, when 4WD is required. High clearance always recommended. *For Blue Lakes Rd. car-shuttle*, park a second car on Blue Lakes Rd.—2 mi. beyond the Charity Valley Trailhead, or 1 mi. before the road forks to Wet Meadows. (See TH16, page 52.) The volcanic plug of Jeff Davis Peak will be to your left. **Maps:** Markleeville, Carson Pass (car-shuttle)

HIKE: Pleasant Valley overlook, 1.25 mi., 250 ft.; Thornburg Canyon cliffs, 7 mi. (1.5 mi. off-trail), 1,800 ft.; Blue Lakes Road car-shuttle, 6.5 mi., 1,500 ft.

For all hikes, take the Thornburg Canyon trail that rises out of a lush forest of Jeffrey pine and aspen, and into an open area covered with manzanita and granite sand. A few hundred feet to the south, or to the left, of this spot is a **Pleasant Valley overlook**. Then rejoin the trail as it jogs north, or to the right, and climbs steeply in the shade of alder and mixed conifers, alongside Spratt Creek. *Be Aware:* Due to shade, snow may linger to early summer in the middle section of this hike.

The top of Thornburg Canyon, which is a rugged zone between Jeff Davis and Markleeville peaks, offers off-trail scrambling to spires of the **Thornburg Canyon cliffs**. These platforms afford commanding views eastward. *More Stuff:* As the crow flies, Grover Hot Springs is a short distance from here north as you reach the top of the canyon—an opportunity for a car-shuttle hike. But the intervening country is extremely rough and complex.

For the **Blue Lakes Road car-shuttle**, continue on the trail as it heads westerly between Markleeville and Jeff Davis peaks. Spratt Creek will peter out as you ascend gradually and reach the saddle that is the hike's high point. You will cross the waters of Jeff Davis Creek, but don't follow their southerly course. Make sure to keep the crumbly escarpments of Jeff Davis Peak to your left. Due to vegetation and topography you may not see Blue Lakes Road until you stumble upon it.

BIKE: Park at Pleasant Valley Road and ride in **Sawmill Road** for round-trip ride of about 5 miles. Stop at wilderness boundary and walk to overlook described in hike.

33. GROVER HOT SPRINGS   HIKE, SKI, FISH

WHAT'S BEST: A soak in a hot pool awaits after a walk to the falls above this classic Alpine valley. Pockets of wildflowers hide in the margins of the creek. Many fond memories of the Sierra have their origins at this state park.

PARK: At Grover State Park, 4 mi. west of Markleeville on Hot Springs Rd. A day use fee may be charged for trailhead parking. Additional free parking at pool. At 5,900 ft. **Map:** Markleeville

GROVER HOT SPRINGS

HIKE: Grover Falls, 4 mi., 800 ft.

The main **Grover Falls trail** is on the north side of the meadow, through Jeffrey pine and the region's best cedar grove. (Most cedars were taken for buildings.) It's a flat stroll along the creek for a mile, and then up through granite benches to the falls—which are more a cataract. The hot ticket is the top of the rock formation above the falls. Another trail leads back to the park on the south side of the creek, ending up at the hot pool. Pockets of some of Alpine's best wildflowers are tucked away in the little streams that feed the meadow. *Local Lore:* The verdant valley and its lush forests were spared a horrific wild fire in 2002, when Ranger Paula Pennington sniffed the smoke and single-handedly ran hoses to snuff the blaze—a feat of Bunyon-esque proportions.

More Stuff: Two trails lead out of Hot Springs Valley, one to Burnside Lake, TH21, and another to Charity Valley, TH16. See those trailhead descriptions. Both are ideal starting points for day hikes down to the park. Additionally, the Charity Valley East trailhead is about a mile before the entrance to the park—on the right before the road crosses the creek and takes an uphill left turn. This trail continues to the park, connecting with the above-described hikes. The intervening mile-long section will appeal to strolling campers. On hot days, try a refreshing walk up the creek without a paddle.

SKI: Hot Springs Valley offers leisurely forest skiing, with some uphill excursions possible on the slopes opposite the pool. Fallen trees and a number of brooks make for hassles when snowpack is insufficient. Pick a full-moon evening for a sparkling adventure on the meadow.

FISH: Markleeville Creek, which runs along Hot Springs Road, has a number of fishing holes for fly-casters looking mostly for rainbows. **Six or seven creeks**—with headwaters in Hot Springs Valley, Thornburg Canyon, and Pleasant Valley—all come together by the time they reach Markleeville Creek just west of town. This creek, formerly called the Middle Fork of the Carson River, joins the East Carson a mile downstream from Markleeville. All of which is to say, fly-fishermen have plenty to explore.

34. HANGMANS BRIDGE   HIKE, BIKE, SKI, FISH

WHAT'S BEST: Early- and late-season hikes are available in the piñon forests of Washoe country along the East Carson River. Full sun keeps the ridge open and sprinkled with early-season wildflowers. Walk up for panoramic views westward toward the Sierra.

PARK: At Hangmans Bridge, 1.5 mi. south of Markleeville on Hwy. 89/4. The parking area is immediately south of bridge. At 5,500 ft. **Maps:** Markleeville, Heenan Lake

HIKE: Carson Confluence, 3 mi., 200 ft.; Barney Riley Jeep Trail-East Carson Canyon loop 6 to 10 mi. (2 or 3 mi. off-trail), 900 ft.

To reach the **Carson Confluence**, where the East Carson River meets Markleeville Creek, take the road leading from the gate. After a mile or so through sage country dotted with piñon pines, look left for a short spur road down to the river. From the main trail, you'll be able to see a point of land across the river that is the point of confluence—but it's also easy to miss. A nice beach and pool lies below volcanic cliffs when you get down to the water. *More Stuff:* You can extend this walk by continuing on the overgrown road downriver through the canyon another couple miles. *Note:* Portions along the river are private property; heed signs.

The **Barney Riley Jeep Trail** takes off to the right, uphill, about .25-mile from the gate at the parking area. It leads to an open, often-sunny ridge with vistas of a wave of Sierran peaks to the west. BRJT continues over hill and dale into Nevada. To make the loop, you'll want to pick a spot at the top, near where the trail contours eastward from the river canyon for the last time—and go down off-trail to the river. At the bottom, find the old road and head upriver to the trailhead. *Be Aware:* The off-trail portion of this hike is rough. Avoid a precipitous escarpments by staying mainly in the creases of the slope rather than coming down its shoulders.

BIKE: The **BRJT** also connects with roads leading to **Haypress Flat** and the **Leviathan Mine**, which are accessed from Highway 89 below Monitor Pass—see TH46 and TH48. Near the Hangmans Bridge trailhead, clay soil can make for sticky going in the spring.

SKI: The **Barney Riley Jeep Trail** is a good choice after or during a winter storm that dumps in Markleeville. Due to southern exposure and arid locale, snow is unreliable.

FISH: You can walk down the **East Carson River**, fly-casting for browns and rainbows. This downriver section is a California Department of Fish and Game Wild Trout Area, with special restrictions. To fish upriver, drive Highway 89/4, looking for turnouts and spur roads along a stretch that extends beyond the turnoff to Wolf Creek Road, on Highway 4.

More Stuff: Hangmans Bridge is a renowned put-in for rafters. The East Carson Canyon has hot springs, cliffs and mixed conifer forests. Takeout for this overnight or day trip is before the dam off Highway 395 south of Gardnerville. Kayakers and adventurous rafters put in at several spots upriver from Hangmans, making for more exhilarating runs and less hassle with the car-shuttle. Several white-water chutes can be spotted from the highway along the upper section—tailor made for kayakers by the flood of 1998.

EAST FORK CARSON RIVER

35. POOR BOY CANYON

WHAT'S BEST: Explore an out-of-the-way canyon with vistas and varied evergreen forests. Keep an eye out for Mr. Bear and other wildlife.

PARK: Take unpaved Indian Creek Rd., FS040, a right turn 1 mi. south of Markleeville on Hwy. 89/4. At 5,700 ft. The top of the road is at 7,500 ft. Passenger vehicles are often okay, but 4WD is recommended. **Map:** Markleeville

HIKE: Silver Mountain City overlook, 11 mi., 1,900 ft. Shorter and longer hikes, depending on how far you drive.

Hikers to the **Silver Mountain City overlook**—those in four-wheel drive vehicles—will want to drive in (and up!) about 6 miles on Indian Creek Road to a gate that marks a private property inholding. After about .5-mile from the highway you pass a spur road to the right for a heliport—from which you can take a postcard shot of Markleeville. Farther up, you will pass two left-forking spur roads, the first being Poor Boy Creek Road some 4 miles from the highway.

About a mile beyond the closed gate you come to the high point of the road. Continue down the other side for views of Silver Mountain City, which is on Highway 4 on the way to Ebbetts Pass. The green oasis of English Meadow is to your right after you get into the flats on the other side. Before topping out on the road, you will pass a large juniper on the right, a viewing spot for the Carson Range and Tahoe Sierra to the north. Poor Boy Canyon is a likely place to see wildlife, including bear, since it is less frequently used than other trailheads. *Be Aware:* Some of Poor Boy is private property; heed signs. The area has been logged and most old-growth conifers are gone.

More Stuff: Off-trail exploring can lead to old mines and artifacts, as this area borders several historic mining districts. Watch your step. Remains of a historic trail can be found walking up the drainage of Poor Boy Creek, from near the bottom at the little pond. For the best off-trail journey in the area, head to your right, or west, from the top of the road, just before it drops down the other side. You can contour around some steep forested slopes to reach open vistas of Raymond Peak and Pennsylvania Creek.

BIKE: Although clay soil can be nasty at times, **Indian Creek Road, FS040,** is a very large and interesting area for mountain bikers. A more leisurely contour is **Poor Boy Creek Road**, a left-forking spur about 4 miles from the highway. A second, similar spur forks left about 1.5 miles above the first. Both roads are almost 2 miles. You can park the wheels and walk out for views of the East Carson River Canyon.

SKI: Snow is unreliable, but during or after heavy storms Indian Creek Road up **Poor Boy Canyon** has plenty of elevation and open tracts for Nordic trips. This is a very good midwinter choice, if snow is on the ground in Markleeville.

36. SILVER HILL

WHAT'S BEST: Hike or bike off the beaten path through an old mining district. Big views await on top of Silver Hill.

PARK: At Silver Hill Road, FS198, on Hwy. 4, 1 mi. south of jct. with Hwy. 89. The road goes uphill to the left. *Note:* Barring snow, 4WD vehicles can easily drive in 2 miles. Subtract driving distances from the length of the hike. At 5,700 ft. *For the Bagley Valley car-shuttle,* park second car at Heenan Lake, TH45. **Map:** Heenan Lake

HIKE: Silver Hill, 7 mi. (2.5 mi. off-trail), 1,800 ft.; Bagley Valley car-shuttle, 8.5 mi. (3.5 mi. off-trail), 2,000 ft.

To **Silver Hill**, a landmark for one of Alpine's historic mining districts, take the road as it climbs and twists. After about 2 miles, look for where the road makes a big sweeping left over an ephemeral stream drainage. *Note:* This is where drivers should park. You'll know you've gone too far if you pass rustic cabins as the road climbs again. Leaving the road, head up the crease of the stream drainage, climbing about 400 feet in a half-mile. You'll reach a big open saddle. Silver Hill is to the right, or south, in this saddle—up another gradual 200 feet. At 7,500 feet, the hill is not the highest point around; an unnamed peak of 8,031 feet lies a mile to its northeast.

To drop into **Bagley Valley for the car-shuttle**, head east off-trail, from the north side of Silver Hill. Aim for the saddle between the tall unnamed peak to the northeast, its 7,956-foot high neighbor. From that saddle, make the steep descent, due east, until you reach the road along the west shore of Heenan Lake. The lake is your beacon. *Be Aware:* This rugged route is not a challenge for experienced hikers and other masochists.

BIKE: Silver Hill, via FS198, is a leg-burner for cyclists. The road continues past the hike's parking area for another mile, and spur roads will take adventuresome pedal pushers toward Silver Hill to the south. This is an area to call your own for the day.

37. SILVER PEAK
HIKE

WHAT'S BEST: A monster hike through wild country leads to top of a major Sierran peak. Trim your toenails and tighten the bootlaces for this baby.

PARK: Take Wolf Creek Rd., off Hwy 4, 3 mi. south of jct. of Hwys. 89/4. Go several miles as the road (recently paved) climbs. At the top, before the road drops into Wolf Creek—and just past the rock quarry—take the road that veers off to the right, which should be signed FS032C. It's 4WD only. Go about 1.5 mi. until road forks and park. At 7,200 ft. If you don't want to drive in this last road, plan on another 3 mi. and 800 ft. of elevation. **Maps:** Ebbetts Pass, Wolf Creek

HIKE: Silver Peak, 11 mi. (all off-trail), 3,500 ft.

Silver Peak, standing at 10,774 feet, is a tough hike and should be attempted only by fit, experienced hikers who can read a topographical map. On the other hand, it is doable and delivers an out-there, big-time Alpine Sierra experience. The first part of the hike is the most challenging. From the parking area, walk a north-heading branch of a road into an old logging landing. Then turn west, to your left, and climb like a big dog through the trees. You need to make about 1,300 feet from the get go.

If in doubt of your mirco-route, take the southerly or left-heading options, since the summit is almost 2 miles south of here. You'll pop out into an open area, with scree slopes, brush, and series of knobs. Keep climbing with a general bearing of southwest, up a shoulder between scree and brush. Be wary of going up false peaks, as you are still several miles from Silver Peak at this stage.

After this initial scramble, you'll break out to the top of this lower shoulder and have easy going for a while. To the south and west, you'll recognize the shoulder you can observe from the Carson Valley, heading away from you and toward the summit. Follow the shoulder south. You'll reach a ledge at a high meadow, where the Dixon Creek drainage will be visible far below to the south.

The meadow, with an ephemeral stream, is a good resting spot before making your way up and around an intervening craggy ridge that stands between you and the final 800-foot climb to Silver Peak. It's still a good mile away from the most-easterly peak on this ridge, which rises to 10,174 feet. Go to the right, or north of the ridge. Then, at last, you'll see the ramp up to double-peaked Silver. Purists may wish to climb the more difficult left side of the double knob, which is the actual peak. The rest of us will take the right knob, which is closer and easier to climb—and damn near the same height. *Be Aware:* Leave at the crack of early for this hike and carry lots of liquid. In certain years, or late in the season, you'll find little water. Plan for weather extremes.

38. WOLF CREEK MEADOW   HIKE, FISH

WHAT'S BEST: A forested creek canyon opens into the Carson-Iceberg Wilderness, the best of mid-elevation Alpine Sierra hiking. Many day-hike and backpack options are possible among the high peaks that encircle the head of the canyon.

PARK: Take Wolf Creek Rd., 3 mi. south of the jct. of Hwys. 89/4. The road is unpaved after 2.5 mi., but two-wheelable. Continue south in Wolf Creek Meadow for 2.5 mi. and park at trailhead parking. At 6,200 ft. *For car-shuttles,* park second car at Wolf Creek North, TH39. **Maps:** Wolf Creek, Disaster Peak (for car-shuttle and loop hikes)

Hike: Wolf Creek, 3 mi. to 20 mi., 400 to 1,800 ft.; Car-shuttle or loop hike via Murray Canyon and High Trail, 22.5 mi. 3,700 ft., or via Carson River Trail, 21.5 mi., 3,100 ft.

Wolf Creek runs north-south, leading to a number of trails into the Carson-Iceberg Wilderness. You can pick your hike, ranging from a family picnic walk to a full-on day trek or multi-day backpack. A little more than a mile into the walk, the trail joins the creek as it collides with a rocky bluff—a worthy destination for short trippers. It then continues through cottonwood meadows, under siege from beavers, and climbs gradually through mixed conifers. After 2.5 miles you must cross Dixon Creek, difficult in early summer.

At 4.5 miles, just after a spectacular rocky gorge with junipers as its guardians, you'll come to the Bull Canyon Trail; Nobel Lake lies 3.5 miles to the west of this junction, up and over a saddle. At 6 miles in from the trailhead, to the left off the Wolf Creek Trail, is a good lunch stop—with views of Bull Peak and a cataract cut through a metamorphic gorge. *Note:* Heed private property in this area—a ranch cabin inholding in the wilderness area.

WOLF CREEK

Continuing south of the ranch inholding for less than a mile you'll reach the lush upper reaches of Wolf Creek, where the Elder Creek Trail takes off and up to the west, to your right. A half-mile later, for the monster **loop hike or car-shuttle via Murray Canyon**, take the Murray trail east, or to your left. You climb up and out of Wolf Creek into Falls Meadow—this will get you aerobic. From there, proceed east to the Soda Springs Ranger Station in Dumonts Meadow. From Dumonts, walk north 2 miles to where the High Trail forks to the left, and the East Carson River Trail forks right—both trails lead back to Wolf Creek North trailhead.

More Stuff: For non-loop hikers, stay on the Wolf Creek Trail past the Murray Canyon Trail junction. This trail leads to the Pacific Crest Trail. From the PCT, you can turn north toward Highland Lakes or Nobel Lake, or south toward Golden Canyon into lovely Falls Meadow. The PCT continues south to Sonora Pass. These options are more for backpackers.

FISH: Fly-fishing is fairly good in **Wolf Creek**. Walk upriver from parking into Carson-Iceberg Wilderness, fishing for mostly rainbows. From the trailhead you can also fish downstream in **Wolf Creek Meadow.** Brook trout dominate. Some anglers park at the north end of the meadow, at the bridge, and fish the rugged canyon downstream.

39. WOLF CREEK NORTH   HIKE, BIKE, FISH

WHAT'S BEST: Go high or low on a less-trod forested ridge, and then make your way into the canyon to watch the river flow. Available in early summer, these Carson-Iceberg Wilderness spots invite hikers and horsemen.

PARK: Take Wolf Creek Rd., 3 mi. south of jct. Hwys. 89/4. The road is unpaved after 2.5 mi. After dropping into Wolf Creek Meadows, take the first left. Beyond the corral, don't turn toward Dixon Mine after the uphill section, but keep right until reaching an improved trailhead parking area. At 6,200 ft. **Map:** Wolf Creek

HIKE: East Carson River Trail to: Wolf Creek Lake, 1.5 mi., 600 ft.; Grays Crossing, 4 mi., 1,300 ft.; Silver King Valley, 11 mi., 1,400 ft.; High Trail to Dumonts Meadow loop, 12 mi., 2,200 ft.

For all hikes, take the trail that is up and to the left behind the horse trailer parking spot and rest rooms. To reach **Wolf Creek Lake**, pass the High Trail junction and head over the saddle from the trailhead. Just down the other side is the little lake that is transforming into a meadow. To **Grays Crossing**, continue 1.5 miles beyond the lake, then take a trail branching to left, downward, toward the East Carson River. (The right-fork at this junction is East Carson River Trail south to Dumonts Meadow.)

Grays Crossing was an early settlers' north-south route from Markleeville to Bridgeport. You'll find some good camp and picnic spots less than a mile upriver from Grays Crossing, but the canyon walls soon encroach on the water—which is why the southbound trails are higher up. *More Stuff:* Across the river is Bagley Valley and a trail out to Highway 89 at TH47. Conifers give way to sage country of the Great Basin at the crossing.

To lovely **Silver King Valley**, take the right fork described above, the East Carson River trail—which does not drop to the river at this point. Continue for another 2 miles along the sidehill of the river canyon. The trail reaches the green valley, with Silver King Creek snaking through it. This place is a slice of pastoral heaven. You'll have to drop down and cross the river to get into it. The valley holds the confluence of the East Carson River and Silver King Creek.

To take the **High Trail to Dumonts Meadow**, look for the trail just a couple hundred feet from the parking area, as it takes off up to the right, south. The High Trail climbs for several miles before dropping down at the north end of Dumonts Meadow. Here the High Trail joins the East Carson River Trail. Turn left, or north, to walk the seven miles back via Silver King. Mountaineers can shorten this hike by leaving the trail sooner and dropping (steeply) cross country to hit the East Carson River Trail.

More Stuff: Wolf Creek North is a family backpacking area, flat and sandy (decomposed granite) along the river. It's also an early-season choice for extended treks, with many options. Some possible routes are south to Carson Falls and White Canyon to Sonora Pass. You can also cross more easterly to reach Highway 395 at Little Antelope via Poison Flat. Or stay in the region and walk to Wolf Creek Meadow via Murray Canyon. *Be Aware:* Creek crossings can be a problem during high-water years.

BIKE: In the spring, **Wolf Creek Road** is gated at Centerville Flat campground due to snow, making this a route for mountain bikers who don't mind walking bikes over a packed snow for short stretches. You can ride into Wolf Creek Meadow and Dixon Mine. Wilderness trails are closed to bikes.

FISH: The hike along **East Carson River** leads to some big pools holding cutthroat, rainbows and browns—beginning at **Grays Crossing** and continuing to Silver King Valley, Dumonts Meadow, and Falls Meadow. It's a winner for backpacking or horseriding fishermen. Ditto for **Silver King Creek**. *Note:* The river above Carson Falls is protected and closed to fishing.

40.   EBBETTS PASS NORTH   HIKE, BIKE, SKI, FISH

> **WHAT'S BEST:** Volcanic formations rise above fields of wildflowers in this prime Sierran panorama. Pick an easy stroll or keep on trekkin' to a high mountain lake.

WEST FROM DOROTHY LAKE

PARK: At Ebbetts Pass turnout on Hwy 4. At 8,700 ft. *Note:* The Pacific Crest Trail crosses Hwy. 4 about .25-mile east of the Ebbetts Pass turnout. When taking the trail north, you need to backtrack downhill a short distance. Even so, the turnout parking is shorter than the signed PCT trailhead parking, which is about .5-mile east of Ebbetts and is not convenient for northbound hikes. *For Dorothy Lake:* Take the short, unpaved spur road that is to you right, or north, just west of the Ebbetts Pass sign. **Map:** Ebbetts Pass

HIKE: Pacific Crest Trail to: Upper Kinney Lake, 3.25 mi., 400 ft.; Raymond Meadows, 7 mi., 750 ft.; Pennsylvania Creek, 12 mi., 1,200 ft.; Raymond Lake, 20 mi., 1,800 ft.; Dorothy Lake, .75-mi., 450 ft.

For all PCT hikes, head downhill on the north side of the road and pick up the trail. The crumbly knob of Ebbetts Peak will be to your left as you pass it. You'll undulate through forest, passing ponds before reaching **Upper Kinney Lake**. Backpackers love this place. It features some nice granite monoliths that serve as viewing platforms, which are to the right as you approach the lake. Farther down the trail, **Raymond Meadows** sports several brooks that join to make a creek, nourishing willows and wildflowers beneath the volcanic buttresses of Reynolds Peak. You can't see Raymond Peak from here—a ridge intervenes.

For **Pennsylvania Creek**, continue along the level and circuitous trail, around a skyline of craggy spires. Dwarf brush and flower fields give way to pockets of mixed conifers. The formation of Raymond Peak is the wall due north of Pennsylvania Creek.

The trail to **Raymond Lake**, doable as a day hike for the fittest of hikers, loops around this volcanic ridge and reaches the east side of Raymond Peak. From there you climb an 800-foot ramp to the lake, a beautiful cirque beneath a saw-toothed ridge. *Be Aware:* It's tempting to cut across the high ridge at Pennsylvania Creek, climbing through a notch, you think, ha ha, and dropping down to Raymond Lake. This route is folly at best, due to unstable escarpments.

The short hike to cute **Dorothy Lake** serves up a Sierran panorama seen by relatively few hikers. The trail climbs a rock-scrabble face on the west side of Ebbetts Peak, the sentinel of the pass. The route flattens out in an open swale. Walk off-trail a short distance for a 360-degree view. You then drop into the snow-fed lake, an ideal kids' backpack destination. *More Stuff:* Heading northwest from Dorothy Lake is easy-walking, open country that makes for a pleasant off-trail escapade. After nearly 2 miles, veer right, or east and you will reach the Pacific Crest Trail at Raymond Meadows. Or head east earlier above Dorothy and you'll hit the PCT near Upper Kinney Lake.

BIKE: In spring, **Ebbetts Pass Road**, Highway 4, is gated, either down below at the Monitor Pass turnoff, or higher up at Silver Creek. Park at either gate and ride in along the river on pavement, avoiding the season's rock-falls and perhaps pushing the bike over the occasional snow patch. This car-free highway next to running white water makes for an A+ outing. Be prepared to climb.

SKI: After heavy winter snows, drive to the junction of **Highways 4 and 89**, where both roads are gated, and ski up **toward Ebbetts Pass**.

KINNEY LAKES BASIN

Fish: Kinney Reservoir, which is on Highway 4 about 1 mile east of Ebbetts Pass, draws float tubers and casters looking for rainbows. Rainbows are also the most prevalent trout at **Upper Kinney Lake**, which can be reached via the above hiking description. To try the rainbows at **Lower Kinney Lake** take a trail beginning at Kinney Reservoir dam. The lower lake is about a mile away.

41. EBBETTS PASS SOUTH   Hike, Fish

What's Best: Trails curve southward on the Pacific Crest, presenting high-altitude hikers with varying degrees of difficulty. Find a spot to commune with nature or go for the gusto.

Park: At the Pacific Crest Trail parking lot, about .5-mi. west of Ebbetts Pass on Hwy. 4. At 8,700 ft. *For the Nobel Canyon car-shuttle*, park a second car at "Cadillac Curve," 1.5 west (up) from Silver Creek Campground. (Trail also leads to the PCT and Nobel Lake.) *For the Wolf Creek car-shuttle*, park second car at Wolf Creek Meadow, TH38. **Maps:** Ebbetts Pass, Wolf Creek (for car-shuttle)

Hike: Nobel Lake, 9 mi., 1,800 ft.; Nobel Canyon car-shuttle, 9 mi., 400 ft.; Tryon Peak, 12.5 mi. (4 mi. off-trail), 2,800 ft.; Bull Lake, 15.5 mi., 2,000 ft.; Highland Peak, 17 mi. (5 mi. off-trail), 3,900 ft.; Wolf Creek car-shuttle, 16.5 mi., 1,500 ft.

The **Nobel Lake** hike has commanding vistas of the canyon and of giant Silver and Highland peaks. The walk in, which follows the rim of the canyon, will please tree and flower fans. After about 3.5 miles, as you near the head of the canyon, the Noble Lake Trail joins from the left. For the **Nobel Canyon car-shuttle**, hang a left on this trail; you'll descend in forests below the craggy ridgeline, reaching the highway at Cadillac Curve. The PCT continues to Nobel Lake, crossing to the other side of the canyon and making switchbacks up its barren west face. The lake itself may be somewhat disappointing, as algae has taken its toll and marauding cattle have trashed the shoreline.

To reach **Tryon Peak**, with its fascinating geology and 360-degree view, take the PCT southerly from Nobel Lake. From the saddle at the south, leave the trail—which continues into Elder Creek and Paradise Valley—and make your way west and up, climbing steeply toward Tryon's shoulder. You'll top out onto a sandy flat area with dwarf hemlocks and whitebark. Then proceed up the last few hundred feet of scree, heading due north now, to the moonscape top of Tryon Peak. The route seems hairy from a distance, but it gives up ample passage.

To reach cozy **Bull Lake,** take the Bull Canyon Trail east from Nobel Lake, around to the backside of the stand-alone ridge above the lake's east shore. The trail will be to the south, on your right, after climbing through a notch and descending into lush Bull

BULL RUN LAKE

Canyon. The walk to remote **Highland Peak** is a murderous slog that takes all day in the middle of summer. Take the Bull Canyon Trail east from Noble Lake, but do not descend into the canyon. Instead, branch off north, to your left. (You will want a quad map for this one.) Begin the long ascent off-trail, over jagged footing, up Highland's southwest shoulder. Continue until you run out of up, will power, or daylight.

For the **Wolf Creek car-shuttle**, take the Bull Canyon Trail from Nobel Lake, up and through the narrow, forested saddle. Don't be surprised to see a bear or other residents of the lush forests during your descent. Once down to Wolf Creek, you'll meet the trail at a point about .5-mile from trailhead parking at TH38. Go to your left at the trail junction. This car-shuttle hike, one of Alpine's best, takes you through varied terrain and is not particularly difficult, in spite of the distances.

More Stuff: One of the best hikes in this area is the sketchy trail on the east side of Tryon Ridge—the Pacific-facing side. Park at the turnout right at Ebbetts Pass. To begin—facing south—head around the ridge to your right, making sure to stay fairly low at first. (High routes lead to craggy buttresses, and you end up having to drop down to continue south.) Lots of wildflowers and bouquets of evergreens accent a wide-open view of the Tryon Meadows and headwaters of the Mokelumne River. The trail follows a lower contour, and then leads up a draw to the saddle above the treeline from which you can see Nobel Lake. Follow the deer. This saddle is 2-plus miles from the pass. From the saddle, you can take a mountaineer's route southward to Tryon Peak. Or, climb through a gunsight saddle and drop down to Nobel Lake to make a loop hike. The first part of the descent is steep; choose your switchbacking course with care. The return route for the loop is the PCT, beginning at Nobel Lake.

Fish: **Bull Lake** is a 2-mile side trip south off the trail, not far from the saddle above Nobel Lake. The lake is a perfect one-night stand for backpackers with poles. Cut-throat trout is your most likely catch.

42. HIGHLAND LAKES   Hike, Bike, Fish

WHAT'S BEST: A variety of trees and flowers highlight the high country hikes into the Carson-Iceberg Wilderness. For mountain bikers, getting there will be more than half the fun.

PARK: Take Highland Lakes Rd. off Hwy. 4, 2 mi. west of Ebbetts Pass. Go 5 mi., through Bloomfield Camp to Highland Lakes. Park at east end of the larger of the two lakes, to the left as you drive in. The road is normally okay for passenger cars. At 8,700 ft. **Maps:** Ebbetts Pass, Dardanelles Cone, Disaster Peak

HIKE: Upper Gardner Meadow, 2.5 mi., 250 ft.; Asa Lake, 5 mi., 400 ft.; Paradise Valley, 13 mi., 1,200 ft.; Carson-Iceberg Meadow, 16.5 mi., 2,200 ft.

CARSON-ICEBURG WILDERNESS

For all hikes, head away from the lake through Bear Tree Meadow. The trail to **Asa Lake** takes off to the northeast, to your left, at a trail junction about a mile from the trailhead. After about a mile, you reach the Pacific Crest Trail. Go left here for less than .5-mile and you'll find the lake tucked away in the woods. PCT trekkers like to layover at little Asa Lake. *More Stuff:* After crossing the PCT, the trail continues east through Wolf Creek Pass and follows Elder Creek down to the upper end of Wolf Creek. Seven miles to the south is the parking for TH38, Wolf Creek Meadow.

To reach **Upper Gardner Meadow**, the next drainage over from the trailhead, turn south, to your right, when you reach the junction about a mile from the trailhead. Walk south about .5-mile to another junction, where a left-fork follows Disaster Creek and a right-fork follows the banks of Arnot Creek—this is your turnaround spot. On the home leg, you may choose to veer to the northwest from the trail to pass several lakelets including Half Moon Lake, which is nearly .5-mile east of the trail.

To reach **Paradise Valley**, continue south through Upper Garner Meadows. At the trail junction, veer left, or east, on the trail that follows Disaster Creek. Rugged Paradise Valley lies at the foot of Disaster Peak. To reach **Carson-Iceberg Meadow**, continue south on the trail, losing elevation, following Disaster Creek. You may wish to stop up high, a mile or two from the meadow and view the Iceberg from on top. *Note:* Iceberg Meadow can be reached more easily on foot by taking a long drive to Clark Fork/Cottonwood Campground Road, 20 miles west of Sonora Pass off Highway 108. The trailhead is 9 miles in from Highway 108.

More Stuff: Hiram Peak rises to a pointed 9,795 feet at the south shores of Highland Lakes. A hike to its summit is about 3 miles, round trip, with a gain of 1,500 feet. From between the two lakes, ascend in a direction just east of the peak. On the way up, you'll pass some pretty lakelets set 600 feet below the north side of the peak. These pools are the headwaters of Arnot Creek.

BIKE: Park at the Highway 4 junction or at Bloomfield Camp 2 miles down the **Highland Lakes Road**. This is an excellent run along the Mokeumne River and through Tryon Meadows. You'll find side roads to explore, as well as the road that runs along the north shore of the lakes. This is a five-star mountain biking area, and well-suited for intermediate and beginning cyclists.

FISH: **Highland Lakes** are fished for brook trout. The road is usually open by mid-June. By stopping at **Bloomfield Camp**, 2 miles in from the highway, you can fish a fairly flat section of the **Mokelumne River** for rainbows and browns.

43. HERMIT VALLEY   HIKE, BIKE, FISH

> **WHAT'S BEST:** Get away but be careful not to get lost on these streamside hikes.

> **PARK:** At Hermit Valley Campground, on Hwy. 4, about 4 mi. west of Ebbetts Pass. At 7,200 ft. **Maps:** Pacific Valley, Ebbetts Pass

HIKE: Grouse Creek, 6 mi., 600 ft.; Deer Valley, 7 mi., 600 ft.; Stevenot Camp, 12 mi. (4.5 mi. off-trail), 800 ft.

The **Grouse Creek** trail takes off southeast from Hermit Valley, on the south side of the highway. You climb about 350 feet in the first half-mile, and enter lush streamside habitat of Beayer Meadow. At the head of this narrow meadow, the trail veers left, along with the main fork of Grouse Creek. Here you climb another 250 feet and reach Willow Meadow, where the trail peters out. Water-loving wildflowers will be pocketed along the margins of Grouse Creek throughout the summer.

For **Deer Valley** and **Stevenot Camp**, take the trail heading northwest, on the north side of the highway. After about a mile of varied terrain, the route turns northward and joins the Jeep road, FS9N83, which comes south from Lower Blue Lakes. After 3 miles of rugged uphill the road crosses Deer Creek at a point south of its confluence with Blue Creek. Now you're in Deer Valley. *Be Aware:* On busy summer weekends you may encounter motorized humans on the road, a corridor through the wilderness. The Mokelumne River provides a number of spots to get far away without going very far off trail. But be careful: Snowshoe Thompson said Hermit Valley was the only place he ever got lost.

At the road's creek crossing, you need to depart the trail to get to **Stevenot Camp**— contour southwest out of the drainage. After 1.5 miles on this contour you will reach the lakelet and pleasant overlooks of the camp, set between two 8,000-foot knobs. On your return trip, make sure to contour back before dropping down to the road. You don't want to follow Deer Creek down to Highway 4. *Local Lore:* Members of the Murietta Gang are said to have whiled away hours resting up in the Deer Valley and Stevenot Camp area.

BIKE: **Hermit Valley trailhead north to Deer Valley** is the southern terminus of a crude road, FS9N83, from Lower Blue Lake. This is a rugged bike ride, steeply uphill from this end. Another option is a hike 'n' bike: Walkiing off the main trail quickly puts you into some of the Alpine's most remote country.

FISH: **North Fork of the Mokelumne River** passes under highway at Hermit Valley, a parking spot for two river fishing walks. One stretch to catch rainbow trout is downriver for about 1.5 miles from the road; lots of pools and white water—and rugged footing. A second spot is upriver from Highway 4, where the fishing is good for rainbows and brown trout, and the terrain is easier to walk.

44. PACIFIC VALLEY   HIKE, FISH

WHAT'S BEST: Take a family picnic walk in search of flowers and in view of peaks.

PARK: Take Pacific Valley Campground Rd., south off Hwy. 4, 7 mi. west of Ebbetts Pass. The road, FS8N12, veers south just as the highway begins to climb

Pacific Grade Summit. Drive in 1 mi. on the unpaved road. At 7,600 ft. **Maps:** Pacific Valley, Spicer Meadow Reservoir

HIKE: **Pacific Creek Meadow, 3.5 mi., 400 ft.**

Pacific Creek Meadow is the water-sluiced clearing below Bull Run, Henry, and Lookout peaks. Two streams meet, and both fall color and wildflowers are profuse in their season. This is a destination that invites more energetic hikers to explore the environs while others catch up on some creekside R&R.

More Stuff: The trail forks in Pacific Creek Meadow, providing day-trekkers and backpackers with intriguing options. The right fork follows Pacific Creek up to the saddle between Bull Run mountain and Henry Peak—a worthy destination. (Bull Run is the farther west, or to the right.) The trail continues southward, dropping through fanciful geology to Dardanelles Cone. The left-forking trail in Pacific Creek Meadow climbs Marshall Canyon. From the top of this canyon you can go east, or left, for 6 miles on a bumpy trail that connects with the Highland Lakes Road, in Tryon Meadow.

FISH: From the Pacific Valley Campground, walk **Pacific Creek**, casting for brook trout and some browns, along a 2-mile stretch. **Mosquito Lake**, a jewel right on Highway 4, about 1.5 miles west of Pacific Valley, is home mainly to brook trout.

45. LAKE ALPINE   HIKE, BIKE, SKI, FISH

WHAT'S BEST: Summer in the Sierra doesn't get any better—for hikers, swimmers, and cyclists. Bring the family for a lakeside picnic and then take a stroll of the shops and eateries of nearby Bear Valley.

PARK: On Hwy. 4 at Lake Alpine, 16 mi. west of Ebbetts Pass, 7 mi. east of Bear Valley Resort. At 7,300 ft. *For Bull Run Lake,* drive in 1 mile on Stanislaus Meadow Rd., FS8N13, south off Hwy. 4. The road is about 3.5 mi. east of Lake Alpine. At 7,800 ft. **Maps:** Tamarack, Spicer Meadows Reservoir, Dardanelles Cone, Markleeville

HIKE: **Lake Alpine and Duck Lake, 2.5 mi., 350 ft.; Bull Run Lake, 6.5 mi., 900 ft.**

Serene **Lake Alpine** has an undulating shoreline, with shaded pine pockets, beaches, and low granite cliffs—enticing strollers to find places to hang out. To **Duck Lake**, walk past cabins on Lake Alpine's east shore, continuing east and a little south. The trail begins near the Silver Valley Campground. This hike, on a gradual downhill at the beginning, is a favorite among lake dwellers. *More Stuff:* Hikers might also check out the trails from Lake Alpine's southwest shore, leading along a granite-banked stream— pools and troughs await dipping. You can hike FS7N17 along pretty Silver Creek.

For **Bull Run Lake** follow the trail out of Stanislaus Meadow as it turns east up the beginnings of the Stanislaus River. Your path then climbs and twists to the south, through a different drainage, and finally ascends to the forested lake. Islets just off-shore will beckon swimmers, and backpackers will be happy to pitch a tent. *Be Aware:* Stay on the trail in this bumpy and overgrown country. *More Stuff:* Bull Run Peak— about a mile east of the lake—is a challenging non-technical climb.

More Stuff: About 2 miles east of Lake Alpine, at Woodchuck Basin, is a trail to isolated Wheeler Lake. Look on the north side of the road at a bend where you cross a creek. It's a 10-mile, round-trip trek that ascends 800 feet to a saddle. You then drop down the same distance and curl through Avalanche Meadow on the way to the lake. Several trails fan northward into the Mokelumne Wilderness from Wheeler Lake. The best is to the right, or west, which crosses four creeks over a 5-mile course. This trail reaches Highway 4 at Sandy Meadow, which is a mile west of Mosquito Lakes. This makes for a superb car-shuttle hike, beginning at the Wheeler trailhead.

BIKE: From **Lake Alpine** are a number of mountain bike paths, including one around the lake and one to **Uttica Reservoir**. Some of the riding is on Forest Service roads, some on bike paths. Another option is the **Poison Canyon Road, FS7N93**, which veers to the right, just as you start up the main road to Mount Reba Ski Resort. Bike rentals and expert advice is available in Bear Valley at the Bear Valley Adventure Center. This is an underrated zone for mountain bikers.

SKI: **Bear Valley Cross County and Adventure Center** is located west of Lake Alpine in Bear Valley (accessible only from the west during winter). The center has rentals and some 65 kilometers of groomed track.

FISH: **Lake Alpine** is big enough to get out in the middle and have plenty of space to fish, for rainbows and brookies.

46.   LOOPE CANYON   HIKE, BIKE

> **WHAT'S BEST:** Explore Markleeville's historic mining district and Basque sheepherder's pastures—on foot or by mountain bike. Get ready for splashes of color in the fall.
>
> **PARK:** Take Hwy. 89 from its junction with Hwy. 4. Continue 2 mi. and turn left, or north, on Loope Canyon Rd., FS190. Drive in 1.5 mi. (avoiding your first left turn at the top) and park Forest City Flat. At 6,900 ft. **Map:** Heenan Lake

HIKE: Markleeville Lookout, 3 mi., 1,000 feet; Haypress Flat, 6 mi., 1,100 ft. (without doing lookout); Little Cottonwood Canyon, 12 mi., 2,100 feet.

To reach **Markleeville Lookout**, stay left, heading westward from the parking area in Forest City Flat. (The right forking-road is FS322; all roads up here interconnect in a fishnet pattern.) Jogging around a spur, you will then cross the ephemeral Mogul Canyon drainage after .5-mile. Keep to your left, or west again, now on FS190B. Switchback up and take a short spur road on the left to the top of the knob, which is the lookout.

To **Haypress Flat**, backtrack from the lookout, and continue north on FS190B for about a mile, reaching a wide-open area with a spring and aspen. On the way, you'll pass a left-forking road, which is FS306. On the north end of Haypress are views of the Carson Valley. *Local Lore:* Haypress Flat's aspen groves are known for artful Basque carvings from the late 1800s and early 1900s.

For the hump to **Little Cottonwood Canyon**, take a road—FS310—to the west out of the southern end of Haypress. (Other roads curve right and loop southward). On the Cottonwood trail, you'll descend for 1.5 miles—passing a north-heading trail 1 mile from Haypress, and also passing two other roads that will be on your left, heading south. The Little Cottonwood trail curves north, or to your right, through the lush crease, and ends after 1.5 miles. On the homeward leg, you can walk to your right, or south, on FS306 and shave almost a mile from the hike. *Be Aware:* This entire region is a former mining district. Exploring old mines can be dangerous; heed signs.

BIKE: Park at Highway 89 at **Loope Canyon Road**—and enter an excellent mountain biking tract. A system of old roads runs through historic Mogul Mining District, including to **Haypress Flat**, as described above. By veering right at Forest City Flat, on FS322, you'll go by **Morningstar Mine**. From there take a right-turn options, to the east and south, following FS190. You can connect with the **Leviathan Mine Road**, FS052, which comes back out to Highway 89 at Heenan Lake. From there you ride back down the highway to Loope Canyon Road.

Note: Many paths lead through this underused mountain cyclists' heaven, which covers about 30 square miles of the old mining district. A map is worth a thousand words: Check out the Heenan Lake USGS quadrangle, or the Toiyabe National Forest-Carson Ranger District map. On the other hand, riders with a sense of direction and a pocket full of Power Bars can pedal their way around without maps. Just avoid FS052, Leviathan Mine Road down the canyon to the north; you'll wind up in Nevada.

47. HEENAN LAKE HIKE, BIKE, FISH

WHAT'S BEST: Bagley is an open valley, where the Jeffrey pine belt gives way to the Great Basin. Wildflowers will brighten late springtime hikes.

PARK: Take Hwy. 89 about 4 mi. east from its junction with Hwy. 4. Veer right on an unpaved road that is .5-mi. before (west of) the turnout for Heenan Lake.

ALONG HEENAN LAKE TRAIL

Drive in .25-mi. and park at a locked gate. *For Heenan Lake*, continue on the highway and park at the turnout for the lake. At 7,100 feet. **Map:** Heenan Lake

HIKE: Bagley Valley, 5 mi., 300 ft.; Grays Crossing, 9 mi., 900 ft; Silver King Valley and Vaquero camp, 12 mi., 850 ft. Heenan Lake fish ponds, 1.5 mi., 100 ft.

Bagley Valley is an open sweep of East Sierran sagebrush, flanked by copses of Jeffery pine and accented by wildflowers early in the season. Take the road from the gate along the west shore of Heenan Lake. You'll top a rise and drop into the upper valley, where decrepit ranch buildings provide a valley view—and a place to get out of the sun.

To reach **Grays Crossing**, continue south, swerving down through Bagley Valley. You'll descend gradually before turning west through an obvious opening in the landform—at a right-forking road. (Notice that the ridge to your right has sloped down to trail level, providing an easy way through.) Grays Crossing was the old route across the East Carson River. If the river is too deep to cross here, don't plan on crossing it anywhere. *More Stuff:* Provided you can get across the river, it is a shorter walk from here to Wolf Creek North, TH39, than back up the valley: A-plus car-shuttle potential.

To **Silver King Valley**, bear left, or south, at the road fork at the southern end of Bagley Valley. The additional 2-mile walk takes you into an emerald meadow, where the Silver King Creek makes lazy bends and meets the East Carson. **Vaquero Camp** is in the valley, about 1.5 miles from the fork in the road. *Local Lore:* The camp, a bunkhouse for cowboys of yesteryear, is part of a ranching history that predates the mining districts of the 1860s. It makes for a scenic rest stop. *Be Aware:* Both of these hikes are in the open sun, so bring plenty of water. The walk can be deceptively difficult.

Heenan Lake is a state fishery. To see the **fishponds**, follow the road from the lakeside parking area along the north shore of the lake. You'll see the breeding ponds at the east shore, where Heenan Creek enters the lake. *More Stuff:* To hike up to Company Meadow, continue on the road as it ascends up the courseway of the creek. Don't quit when the road does. Continue up the creekbed, keeping left at a fork of the waters. The going is fairly steep, until you top out in a grassy swale that is dotted with conifers, mostly Jeffrey pine. This hike is about 6 miles, with 850 feet of elevation and 2.5 miles off-trail. *Note:* The meadows are more easily reached from Monitor Pass.

BIKE: This is attractive biking terrain, although clay soil and coconut rocks can make for tough going in places. **Bagley Valley** is first class cycling venue. Try it, you'll like it.

FISH: Heenan Lake is the only Lahontan cutthroat stock lake in California. To protect this rare breed, special restrictions apply. To determine current restrictions, you need to check when buying your fishing license.

MONITOR PASS

48. MONITOR PASS

HIKE, BIKE, SKI, FISH

WHAT'S BEST: Fall color and a quick hike to a big peak with Sierran crest views will attract hikers and cyclists. Many travelers rate wide-open Monitor as the most scenic pass in the Sierra.

PARK: *For Leviathan Peak,* drive in .5-mi. on peak road, 1 mi. east of Monitor Pass on Hwy. 89. *For other hikes,* park where unpaved FS083 meets Hwy. 89, .75 mi. west of Monitor Pass. *For car-shuttle,* park second car at Indian Springs Road 085, 2 mi. east of Monitor Pass. At 8,300 ft. **Maps:** Heenan Lake, Topaz Lake

HIKE: Leviathan Peak, 2 mi., 1,200 ft; Leviathan circumnavigation car-shuttle, 5 mi. (7 mi. without car shuttle), 300 feet; Company Meadow, 2.5 mi., 400 ft.

The easy walk up to **Leviathan Peak** is on a trail along open sage slopes, often replete with dwarf wildflowers and Alpine's signature flower, mule ears. The lookout station at the top (at 8,963 feet) provides a view in all directions, taking a wide-angle on the Sierran Crest, bucolic Antelope Valley, and Topaz Lake. Humpbacked Leviathan is the highest point around for miles.

For the **clockwise trip around Leviathan**, begin northward on the road from the parking spot. This is a flat walk through open country, with only a small climb over the saddle of High Peak to the northwest of Leviathan. As you continue around, look for Big Spring, a sleeper lunch spot. Then follow the road to circle around the mountain to the highway. You can walk back along the road if a car-shuttle isn't convenient, adding 2 miles to the hike.

Company Meadows is south of Highway 395 from the trailhead at FS083. The road ends after a mile, where the meadows extend to the east. *More Stuff:* On the south side of Monitor Pass, a series of spur roads and trails squirm through piñon and aspens, as well as other pine and fir. One destination is a knob due south, from which you can view Slinkard Valley below treacherous cliffs to the east. In this direction is Dump Canyon, down which camels were cajoled in the old days in a failed effort to replace mules.

BIKE: **Monitor Pass** has numerous mountain biking roads to explore, including those mentioned in hiking description. **Indian Springs Road**, FS085, continues for a number of miles north, and can actually be ridden down to Highway 395. From the south side **Company Meadows**, you can ride down toward Grays Crossing and Heenan Lake. In the spring, when the road is gated at the junction of Highways 4 and 89, you can ride the pavement up to Monitor. If you've ever wanted to yodel, this is the place to do it. *Note:* The USGS quadrangle maps, or the Toiyabe National Forest-Carson Ranger District map will be helpful—though not absolutely necessary.

SKI: **Highway 89** is closed for winter at the junction of Highway 4. When snowfall cooperates, beginning skiers can use it as a track. When the road is first opened in the late spring, skiing on top of **Monitor Pass** is excellent, if the winter's snowpack is above normal.

FISH: **Mountaineer Creek** will be a pleasant surprise for fly-fishermen. Take Indian Springs Road, FS085, and park at Big Spring, just after a left-fork. Fish the creek down and north from the spring.

49. SLINKARD VALLEY   HIKE, BIKE, FISH

WHAT'S BEST: Get a feel for sage country in this dramatic pocket in the Eastern Sierra. An old-timey Western could be filmed here.

PARK: Take a dirt road (FS203) to the south off Hwy. 89, 3.5 mi. west of the jct. with Hwy. 395, or 6 mi. east of Monitor Pass. Park at a gate that less than .5-mi. in from the highway. At 6,000 ft. **Map:** Topaz Lake, Coleville

HIKE: Slinkard Valley, from 5 to 15 mi., 200 to 1,000 ft.

Slinkard Valley State Wildlife Refuge is the sublime hanging valley best viewed from Highway 89 east of Monitor Pass as you drop down the Sierra. Hiking on Slinkard's gated road southward allows you to choose the length of your hike. You can also explore a number of side trails and roads into the valley's several ravines. Try this hike when clouds gather to tweak the cinematic effect to the max; you'll be in the middle of a sphere of scenic beauty. *Local Lore:* The remains of an ingenious catchment and irrigation system, as well as a number of outbuildings and mine structures, are to be found along the breadth and depth of Slinkard Valley.

More Stuff: Slinkard can be used to access Upper Fish Valley and Llewellyn Falls, via Rodriquez Flat. But a more direct access to those areas is from Little Antelope, TH50. Slinkard is more commonly a trip-ending trailhead for backpackers.

BIKE: Though the surface is rocky and rutted in places, mountain biking may be the best way to see all that's worth seeing in a day in **Slinkard Valley**. This wildlife area is a great place to get away and mountain bike-hike.

FISH: Fly fishermen are apt to find a treasure of hungry brookies hanging out among the watercress in the small pools of **Slinkard Valley Creek**. The creek is a favorite of fly-fishing guru Richard "Doc" Harvey, a lifelong Sierran angler.

PACIFIC VALLEY

Sonora

BODIE STATE HISTORICAL PARK

Like Markleeville, Bridgeport is a California town that wound up on the east side of the Sierra. In 1875, most people debated, but few really cared, where California ended and Nevada began. Then rich ore was discovered and better surveys decided the issue in favor of the Golden State. Even so, Bridgeport faced stiff competition for the honor of county seat from bustling Bodie and several tent-cities pitched on top of mining claims.

Unlike Markleeville, this region has never seen much traffic, aside from local miners in the late 1800s. Sonora Pass is closed in the winter and the nearest trans-Sierra route is 80 miles north, after making it through rugged Walker River Canyon. The Great Basin sprawls hundreds of miles to the east and the Sierra juts to the west. To the south, Yosemite's Tioga pass was not even an engineer's dream, and local Paiutes took a foot path over Mono Pass, just to the south of today's highway.

But the same geographic conditions that have historically created economic isolation now provide the region with a wealth of recreational tourism. As you take Highway 395 down the east Sierra, every 15 or 25 miles a road leads into a hanging valley of the Sierra Nevada. Sonora Pass, Walker River, Little Walker River, Twin Lakes, Buckeye Creek, and Green Lakes are all entrances to mountainous watersheds and river valleys. All drain into the Great Basin via northern flowing Walker River, which is the world's longest landlocked riparian environment.

OFF HIGHWAY 395

Thousands of years ago, ancient peoples roamed the Sonora region, then a central part of the Lahontan Lakeland Empire—a plentiful region of woodlands and huge, interconnected lakes that stretched from Pyramid Lake north of Reno to the Colorado River. Although these lakelands have dried out to form high desert, many primary lakes remain, shrunken, but still large. Walker, Topaz, Bridgeport, and Mono lakes are four. These catchments for Sierran snowmelt provide a safe haven for millions of migrating waterfowl, as well as open water for humans to enjoy.

The ancestry of these ancient people can be traced through the language they spoke—Hokan—to the Paiute Indians who were in the region when the first European people came through in 1833, as part of an expedition led by Captain Joseph Walker. No Mother Lode or Comstock was discovered in this region to create a massive boom, although Bodie, ten miles south of Bridgeport, was a thriving mining town for a decades, beginning in the mid-1800s. Bodie has been preserved almost intact as a State Historic Park.

Part of Mono County's high country was annexed into Alpine County by the California Legislature in 1864. People have long memories. Twenty years later, when Alpine was down in the dumps due to the Silver bust, Mono hatched a political scheme to get its portion back, and then some.

UPPER FISH VALLEY

When a murderer was on trial in Markleeville, his Mono county attorney applied successfully for a change of venue, arguing no fair trial could be had in Markleeville, which was true due to a number of eye witnesses to the mishap. Transporting the prisoner and paying for a lengthy trial would've bankrupted Alpine County at the time, thus facilitating Mono's takeover. Fearing this, a group of Alpiners cut through the red tape. They caught up with the Mono-bound prisoner a mile south of Markleeville and did frugal justice at soon-to-be-named Hangmans Bridge.

This Mono-Alpine sibling rivalry was ameliorated in 1954 when Monitor Pass was completed, ending the isolation between the two, and making it at last possible to drive to and fro without going into Nevada.

TOWARD UPPER PAIUTE MEADOW, STAMP MILL NEAR GREEN LAKE

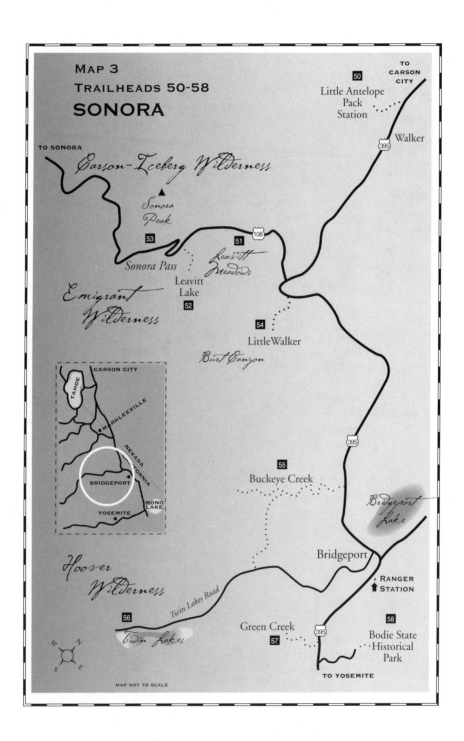

MAP 3
TRAILHEADS 50-58
SONORA

TO CARSON CITY

50 Little Antelope Pack Station

395 Walker

TO SONORA

Carson-Iceberg Wilderness

▲ Sonora Peak

53 Sonora Pass

108

51 Leavitt Meadows

Leavitt Lake

52

Emigrant Wilderness

54 LittleWalker

Burt Canyon

CARSON CITY

TAHOE

MARKLEEVILLE

NEVADA CALIFORNIA

BRIDGEPORT

MONO LAKE

YOSEMITE

395

55 Buckeye Creek

Bridgeport Lake

Bridgeport

RANGER STATION

Hoover Wilderness

Twin Lakes Road

56 Twin Lakes

Green Creek

395

57

58 Bodie State Historical Park

W N S E

TO YOSEMITE

MAP NOT TO SCALE

TRAILHEADS

HIKE :   DAY HIKES AND LONGER TREKS
BIKE :   MOUNTAIN AND ROAD BIKE TRIPS
SKI :   CROSS COUNTRY SKIING AND SNOWSHOEING
FISH :   LAKE, STREAM, AND RIVER FISHING

50-58

TH = TRAILHEAD, FS = FOREST SERVICE ROAD, NUMBERED

All hiking distances in parentheses are ROUND TRIP, unless noted for car shuttles. Elevation gains of 100 feet or more are noted. Maps listed are USGS topographical, 7.5 series. See Resource Links for recommendations for other optional trail maps.

50.   LITTLE ANTELOPE PACK STATION   HIKE, BIKE, FISH

WHAT'S BEST: Backpackers and day-trekkers can launch from this high-altitude trailhead on an early-season foray into the Carson-Iceberg Wilderness. Start with a panorama and then drop down for the details in a classic alpine river valley.

PARK: Take Little Antelope Pack Station-Mill Canyon Rd., an unpaved road off Hwy. 395 a few miles north of Walker. Veer right just after leaving the highway. Drive in (and up!) 6 miles to Rodriquez Flat and go left a short distance to park at the spaces near—but not at—the pack station. 4WD recommended but not always required. At 8,200 feet. **Maps:** Coleville, Lost Cannon Peak

HIKE: Slinkard Valley overlook, 3.5 mi., 800 ft.; Llewellyn Falls loop, 14 mi., 2,200 ft.

The drive up to the pack station will get you deep into the mountains at this backpackers' jumping-off spot. Boots, start walking on the Corral Valley-Driveway Trail that begins behind the pack station. The **Slinkard Valley overlook** is a steep walk up from the pack station through mixed-conifer forest. After the initial climb, you enter the Carson-Iceberg Wilderness and come to an exposed area that features a display of sun-loving wildflowers. The trail contours southwesterly on this exposed shoulder.

The **Llewellyn Falls loop** takes you over hill-and-dale through a number of ecosystems, including pine-fringed meadows set under steep peaks. Beyond the overlook, you'll reach a junction where the Driveway Trail is to the right and the Corral Valley

Trail is to the left. Head left toward Corral Valley. You drop into the smallish valley, with volcanic rocks and a confluence of streams. The trail then climbs out the valley's narrow saddle, continuing south into Coyote Valley, which features huge junipers—among the Sierra's oldest trees. In Coyote Valley, go left, southeast, at a trail junction, taking you down into Upper Fish Valley at Connells Cow Camp, .5-mile above Llewellyn Falls. *Note:* You could take a right-bearing trail in Coyote Valley, northwesterly, which drops into Long Valley and shortens the hike by about 4 miles.

From the cow camp, take the trail downstream along Silver King Creek, the home of the protected Paiute Trout. You'll pass the cataract that is Llewellyn Falls and descend into Lower Fish Valley. Continue over a rise and then into Long Valley, another meadow cleaved by the creek. About .75-mile from the southern end of Long Valley—at a creek crossing that is the junction of a trail to Poison Flat—keep your eyes peeled for the Driveway Trail heading up and to the northeast, or to your right. The Driveway Trail climbs back to the junction of the Corral Valley trail.

More Stuff: The Fish Valleys and upper Silver King Creek are comfortable, scenic backpacking areas, best early in the season, say late June. The area is popular with horse campers later in the summer. Llewellyn Falls is a good base camp to explore upper Silver King Creek or dramatic Whitecliff Lake. This trailhead also is a starting point for 1-to 3-night car-shuttle trips heading easterly via Snodgrass Creek or Poison Flat to Dumonts Meadow. From there go northerly to come out at Wolf Creek North, TH39.

BIKE: **Rodriquez Flat** is a starting point for an excellent East Sierra car-shuttle ride into **Slinkard Valley**. Park a second car at Slinkard Valley, TH49. From 1 mile east of Rodriquez Flat-Little Antelope Pack Station, take an old road, FS203. It's on the right, where the road makes a hairpin left. You start out on a steep decline before reaching the more gradual descent through the long valley. The ride covers 13 miles and drops 2,000 feet. *Be Aware:* Make sure you start out on the right road: There are spur roads to mines, which are east of the road you want.

FISH: Horsemen and backpackers with poles like **Silver King Creek** in Lower Fish Valley and Long Valley. **Poison Lake**—2 miles west and up from Long Valley—is known for good camping and catching the limit. *Be Aware:* Certain areas are closed to fishermen to protect Paiute Trout habitat. Included are Corral Valley, Coyote Valley, and Silver King Creek above Llewellyn Falls, including Upper Fish Valley. Inquire locally for current restrictions.

51. LEAVITT MEADOWS   HIKE, FISH

WHAT'S BEST: Take long hikes with minimal elevation gain into river meadows with wildflowers and forested lakes. You have many options at this backpacker's entry trailhead.

PARK: At Leavitt Meadows Pack Station and trailhead parking, on Hwy. 108, 6 mi. west of Hwy. 395. At 7,100 ft. **Maps:** Pickel Meadow, Tower Peak (for longer hikes)

HIKE: Poore Lake loop, 6 mi., 300 ft.; Roosevelt and Lane lakes, 5 mi., 400 ft.; Fremont Lake, 12 mi., 1,100 ft.; Upper Paiute Meadows, 20 mi., 1,200 ft.

SLINKARD VALLEY

All hikes begin on the trail from Leavitt Meadows that follows the Walker River upstream for about 12 miles to its headwaters beneath craggy Tower Peak. After crossing through sage lands bordering Leavitt Meadow, the trail ascends gradually. For the **Poore Lake loop**, take a left-forking trail about 2 miles from the trailhead—it's after the trail begins its switchbacks. Make your way through statuelike rock formations for about .75-mile and you'll reach the west end of the long lake. To return, backtrack for about .5-mile and take a trail to the right that parallels the trail back to the trailhead, only higher up from the river. Secret Lake, a small one, lies to your right off this trail, less than a half-mile from the trail junction. *Be Aware*: Vehicles can get to Poore Lake, via a Forest Service Road.

To reach forested and popular **Roosevelt and Lane lakes**, which are separated by a long stone's throw, take the right-forking trail, the main trail, as you ascend from Leavitt Meadows. You won't see the lakes until you come upon them. To **Fremont Lake**, take a climbing, west-bearing trail that is 2-plus miles south of these lakes. Fremont is a beauty. For **Paiute Meadow**, continue along the river trail, south. The river snakes through the lush valley, beneath dramatic views southward of the craggy peaks of northern Yosemite.

More Stuff: Fremont Lake is ideal for a first-night lake layover for packers headed west toward Emigrant Wilderness or Helen and Mary lakes of northern Yosemite. Upper Paiute Meadows fills the bill for fishermen and as a base camp for hikes to Kirkwood Creek and Tower Lake. Point-to-point packers can continue on a several-day trip and come out at either Buckeye or Twin Lakes.

Fish: The **Walker River** will yield trout for fly-fishermen, beginning in Leavitt Meadow just south of the trailhead. **Roosevelt and Lane lakes** also have fish, but see a number of fishermen. Backpackers who like to fish should bring a pole to **Upper Paiute Meadows**, where the Walker River makes big sweeps.

52. LEAVITT LAKE   Hike, Bike, Fish

What's Best: Yaaa-hoooooo! This peak hike takes you flying and provides quick, if arduous, entry into the High Sierra.

Park: Turn south, or left, on Leavitt Lake Rd., FS077, off Hwy. 108, 10 mi. west of the junction with Hwy. 395. The road is about 2 miles west of Leavitt Meadows Pack Station, where Hwy. 108 makes a hairpin right. Drive in 3.5 mi. to Leavitt Lake and keep left to trailhead parking. The road in is not advisable for 2-wheel drive. At 9,500 ft. **Maps:** Pickel Meadow, Emigrant Lake, Tower Peak

Hike: Leavitt Lake Pass, 2 mi., 1,000 ft.; Big Sam, 11 mi., 3,200 ft.

Geologist will marvel at the convergence of forces on this sky-high hike at the border of the Emigrant and Hoover Wilderness Areas. The short trail to **Leavitt Lake Pass** is a butt-kicker right out of the car, climbing up and south from the parking area on the east shore of Leavitt Lake. You are rewarded with a commanding view of Sierran peaks to the south, as if gigantic storm-tossed waves were frozen in time.

To **Big Sam**, you drop down from Leavitt Lake Pass to the upper reaches of Kennedy Meadow Creek. Here the Pacific Crest Trail crosses your path. Stay on your trail—an old mining road that is a monument to cowboy engineering—as it contours around to your right and then makes some steep switchbacks. The road goes smack dab over the top of Big Sam, a barren dome standing at 10,824 feet. From the peak are the most diverse vistas possible: the granite sheets of the Emigrant Wilderness, the severe red slopes of the Hoover, the alpine meadows and granite crags of northern Yosemite. *Be Aware:* Mineralized Big Sam seems to draw lightning; early afternoon is prime time for summer storms. Don't attempt the hike if clouds are gathering during thundershower seasons. Always bring rain gear and warm clothing.

More Stuff: Backcountry destinations include the Emigrant Wilderness high country and Helen Lake area of northern Yosemite. The upper reaches of Kennedy Creek—sometimes called Hollywood Basin—which is down the backside of Leavitt Lake Pass, provides a sheltered, first-night camp spot with reliable water.

BIKE: Park at the highway and ride **Leavitt Lake Road**, FS077, a bumpy round-trip ride of 7 miles through aspens and mixed conifers. Spur roads allow for riding around the lake basin, but you'll have to stash the wheels and walk to take in the view from Leavitt Lake Pass. *Be Aware:* Heed wilderness signs, and don't ride in those areas.

FISH: Pulling a trailer into **Leavitt Lake** is a risky proposition, but many fishermen have good luck from craft on this lake.

53. SONORA PASS   HIKE

> **WHAT'S BEST:** A notable peak hike takes in a variety of wildflowers and links with longer north-south pack trips.

> **PARK:** At Sonora Pass, Hwy. 108, 14 mi. west of jct. Hwy. 395. At 9,600 ft.
> **Maps:** Sonora Pass, Pickel Meadow

HIKE: Sonora Peak, 6.5 mi. (1.5 mi. off-trail), 1,800 feet; Wolf Creek Lake, 7 mi., 1,200 ft.

High-altitude parking gives you a jump-start on the peak hike. **For both hikes**, start out north on the Pacific Crest Trail, ascending immediately as you switchback westerly, then easterly, and finally north, through lichen-splotched rock formations of the massive mountain. To climb **Sonora Peak**, head off-trail about .5-mile after the trail turns north, before the trail begins a descending traverse. You should find a sketchy trail, up and due west of the PCT. Sonora Peak has a comfortable rock shelter on top and 360-degree views. *Note:* At 11,462 feet, Sonora Peak is the highest peak in Alpine County—the Alpine and Mono county boundary line runs through the top of the peak, as does the boundary between Toiyabe and Stanislaus national forests.

For **Wolf Creek Lake**, stay on the PCT north as you walk up and over the east shoulder of Sonora Peak. You'll see the lake below as the trail drops down to it. Wolf Creek Lake is a good first-night camp for late-starting trips. *More Stuff:* Sonora Pass gives you a high-elevation start for 3- to 5-night car-shuttle trips to either Wolf Creek via White Canyon/East Carson Trail, TH38; Ebbetts Pass via the PCT, TH41; or Little Antelope via White Canyon and Poison Flat, TH50.

54. LITTLE WALKER RIVER · HIKE, BIKE, FISH

WHAT'S BEST: This out-of-the-way Hoover Wilderness hike delivers scenic wonders and is one of the most underrated in the Alpine Sierra. An arid canyon leads to forested, hidden lakes and a meadow encased by peaks.

PARK: Turn south on Obsidian Campground Rd., FS066, 1 mi. south on Hwy. 395 from the jct. of Hwys. 395 and 108. (The road is 16 mi. north of Bridgeport on Hwy. 395.) Drive 3 mi. to Obsidian Campground. *For Emma Lake and Mount Emma,* keep right on FS066, cross a bridge and continue for about 2.5 mi. to road's end at Stockade Flat. At 8,600 ft. *For Burt Canyon and Anna Lake,* stay left, not crossing bridge, and follow signs to Hoover Wilderness trailhead parking. At 7,650 ft. *For Molybdenite Creek,* park at the back end of Obsidian Creek Campground. At 7,750 ft. **Maps:** Fales Hot Springs, Tower Peak, Buckeye Ridge

HIKE: Emma Lake, 4 mi., 625 ft.; Mount Emma, 5.75 mi. (1.75 mi. off-trail), 1,950 ft.; Burt Canyon, 9.5 mi., 1,800 ft.; Anna Lake, 12.5 mi., 2,900 ft.; Paiute Pass, 13 mi. (sketchy trail), 2,900 ft.; Molybdenite Creek to McMillan Lake, 8.5 mi., 1,500 ft.

Emma Lake begins as a walk in the woods. From the trailhead, you climb fairly steeply, on a road for a while, through mixed conifers and not catching a glimpse of the lake until you are upon it. Steep talus forms three of its shores. By scrambling up the steep ridge to Emma's southwest you can get some views of the West Walker drainage. **Mount Emma,** at 10,525 feet, is .5-mile southwest of the lake. To climb the mountain because it's there, go up the steep draw due south of Emma Lake, reaching a saddle. From the saddle, walk up the peak's southwest shoulder. Standing alone, Emma gives you a circular view, taking in both the silvery Great Basin and the deep greens of Upper Paiute Meadows.

To **Burt Canyon**, starting at a different parking area, you walk past private cabins and some huge junipers, and into the Hoover Wilderness. Great Basin flora gives way to aspen and conifers as you climb moderately but steadily. You'll pass a large beaver pond and cross the drainage—the Little Walker can be a problem to ford early in the year. Burt Canyon is a high meadow, fringed by varieties of fir and pine, with 11,500-foot Flatiron Butte and Hanna Mountain looking down from their southernmost reaches. We're talking in-your-face Sierra scenery, dappled with wildflowers. *Be Aware:* All hikers should bring along plenty of water and wear sun protection on the Burt Canyon hikes.

To reach **Anna Lake**, take a trail to the west, where a creek drops into Burt Canyon. It's on your right, about 1.5 miles into the meadowlands. The trail is a strenuous hump up to Anna, which often will be frozen well into June. To reach **Paiute Pass**, look for a drainage to the west at the northern end of Burt Canyon—just as you get into an open area with views. Proceeding up the steep drainage, you climb a sketchy trail to 10,300-foot Paiute Pass. From a windswept ridge are spectacular views west. *Be Aware:* Only hardy hikers with quad maps should try Paiute Pass.

The trail up **Molybdenite Creek to McMillan Lake** doesn't see many humans. The ascent is gradual for the first few miles. Then the drainage narrows, in a brushy zone, and you make the last 500 feet on a steep climb to the tiny lake.

BIKE: Park at Hwy. 395. The **Obsidian Campground Road**, FS066, mentioned in the parking directions, is a flat pedal for bikers. Also, explore a whole other network of roads on the north side of Hwy. 395—toward **Burcham Flat** on FS031. *Be Aware:* This is big country, so remember where the car is. The Toiyabe National Forest-Bridgeport District map will paint an enticing picture for mountain bikers.

FISH: For fly-fishermen willing to walk, **Little Walker River** in Burt Canyon is a sleeper for big brookies. Also try the beaver ponds, a couple miles from the trailhead. Catch-and-release recommended.

55. BUCKEYE CREEK   HIKE, BIKE, FISH

WHAT'S BEST: Fall colors or early season wildflowers will please hikers in this less traveled East Sierran canyon. Finish the day in a creekside hot spring.

PARK: Two routes into Buckeye Campground: *From Bridgeport*, take Twin Lakes Rd. for 7 mi. paved and turn right at Doc & Al's Resort toward Buckeye Campground on FS017. Continue for about 3 mi. to the campground. *From 4 mi.*

north of Bridgeport, turn off Hwy. 395 on Buckeye Road, also FS017. The 4WD road is across from an old ranger station. Continue through piñon forest 3.5 mi. to the campground. At 7,250 ft. *Note:* Buckeye Hot Springs is on the river, .5-mi. east of the campground. **Map:** Buckeye Ridge, Twin Lakes

HIKE: Buckeye Trail to: Big Meadow, 10 mi., 1500 ft., or Buckeye Forks, 18.5 mi., 400 ft.; Eagle Creek, 11 mi., 2,900 ft.

For **Big Meadow**, follow Buckeye Creek through a sage-belt valley, with pockets of cottonwoods and aspen. You climb slightly, bearing southwest. You don't see much of the creek from the trail, but golden trees highlight its banks in autumn. More conifers join the landscape and a creek drops in from the north at Big Meadow. About 3 miles up the trail, you reach **Buckeye Forks**, where creeks join together. *More Stuff:* The Roughs begin west of the Buckeye forks, as the trail elevates through a craggy passageway in the Hoover Wilderness. A trail continues to Kerrick Meadows.

Eagle Creek is a rugged, no-exit drainage that collects the water from three big peaks, Eagle (11,847 feet), Victoria (11,732 feet), and Robinson (10,806 feet). The trail begins at the west end of the campground and starts climbing. You follow Eagle Creek up the side of Eagle Peak—the bulwark of the Buckeye Ridge. The trail ends at the upper reaches of the creek. *More Stuff:* Eagle Peak is another 2 miles from trail's end, plus about 1,700 additional feet of altitude. Fit and experienced hikers might as well go for it. Go to the right, or northward above the top of the creek drainage. You want to walk up the south face of the peak.

BIKE: Ride into **Buckeye** and up the creek. This is big sky country.

FISH: **Buckeye Creek** is an under-used fly-fishermen's waterway. Bring the car-camping gear. Have a nice weekend.

56.   TWIN LAKES   HIKE, FISH

WHAT'S BEST: Snowcapped ramparts are a backdrop to serene alpine lakes. These Hoover Wilderness treks will inspire wanderlust among lovers of the high country.

PARK: *Robinson Creek and Horse Creek hikes,* drive 12 mi. from Bridgeport on Twin Lakes Rd., off Hwy. 395. Park at the Mono Village trailhead lot, which is to your left by the boat launch at the farthest (most easterly) end of Twin Lakes. *For Tamarack Lake,* turn left on Lower Twin Lakes Rd. as you get to the first lake. Continue over a bridge past the Lower Twin Campground to trailhead parking. At 7,100 ft. **Maps:** Buckeye Ridge, Twin Lakes (primary maps), Matterhorn Peak, Dunderberg Peak

HIKE: Twin Lakes to Upper Horse Creek, 5 mi. or more, 1,500 ft., Robinson Creek to: Barney Lake, 8 mi., 1,100 ft; or Peeler Lake, 16.5 mi., 2,200 ft.; or Crown Lake, 16.5 mi., 2300 ft.; Twin Lakes to Tamarack Lake, 8.5 mi., 2,500 ft.

The scent of coffee and grilling flapjacks often float in the morning air at Mono Village, a fishermen-and-family camping resort. The **Twin Lakes to Upper Horse Creek** hike is an all-time goody, given its sections of falling white water and views of the aptly named Sawtooth Ridge. The allure for mountaineers is the trail's passageway to big-daddy Matterhorn Peak—the route on which Jack Kerouac beat tracks and memorialized in his writing. The popular trail heads due south from the west end of Twin Lakes—don't walk through the campground to Robinson Creek. At the outset you climb steeply through rugged country toward the north side of Sawtooth Ridge—the signature ridge visible from Highway 395 at Bridgeport. Horse Creek is the confluence of three short streams that are fed by a half-dozen mini-glaciers held by the Sawtooth Ridge. Falls sound a greeting after the hike's first series of switchbacks. Then the trail marches upward, revealing a cover-shot view of the Sawtooth Ridge and Matterhorn's glaciers. In Upper Horse Creek (sometimes called Horse Canyon) the trail levels out.

More Stuff: The good campsites of Upper Horse Creek serve as a base camp for hikers headed for 12,279-foot **Matterhorn Peak**. (Only extreme sport enthusiasts will want to day hike the 16-plus miles, 5,200 feet to the summit.) The easiest ascent of Matterhorn is the south face, that is, up from Burro Pass—which is also accessible from above Crown Lake on the backside of the Sawtooths, a hike described below. From Horse

MATTERHORN CANYON

Creek, head south and climb through dwarf vegetation, talus, and scree. As you reach a bouldered saddle, you need to cut right, or east. Rock cairns and a sketchy trail worn by previous mountaineers will lend a hand. A vast field of scree will be fatiguing and disheartening. Eventually, your right-heading traverse curls northward up Matterhorn's south face. *Be Aware*: This hike requires a lot of sure-footed bouldering. Bring a topo map and watch your step. Also, pack for snow-cold weather 365-days a year.

The **Barney Lake** stomp is popular among the more energetic of campground dwellers. Following the drainage of Robinson Creek, you enter the Hoover Wilderness beginning a gradual climb, at first through sage country and then into aspen and conifers. Steep cliffs on either side plunge into Barney's deep blue waters. The granite bluffs at the far end of the lake are worth the effort. Almost everyone stops at the foot-stamped eastern shore.

To **Peeler Lake and Crown Lakes**, take the trail cut into the steep slope of Barney's west shore. Though pushing the envelope, either of these lakes is doable in a day, and you'll feel like you've been somewhere. Continue along Robinson Creek through an intervening valley, where you cross the creek. You'll begin some serious climbing before reaching a trail junction—where you go right to Peeler Lake or left to Crown. The right-forking trail to **Peeler Lake** continues upward through forested granite outcroppings until reaching cobalt-blue Peeler, perched smack on the edge of Yosemite. *Note:* Peeler is one of the only lakes whose waters drain to both sides of the crest. From the junction, take the left fork to **Crown Lake**, also up a fair distance. You wind past some small lakes—warm for swimming—and then up a last ramp to the lake.

More Stuff: Twin Lakes' Robinson Creek trailhead gets you deep into the Sierra, to bona fide beautiful country with many point-to-point options. On 4- to 6-day car-

GREEN CREEK

shuttle treks, you can curl north from Peeler to Buckeye, TH55, or Leavitt Meadows, TH51. Crown Lake is the jumping off spot for the awesome north-canyon country of Yosemite. You can head south toward Virginia Lakes, TH59, or Lower Tuolumne, TH66—via Burro Pass to Matterhorn Canyon.

The hike from **Twin Lakes to Tamarack** will make you earn your dinner. Set at 9,650 feet, the good-size lake is up there—but the vertical wall of Monument Ridge rises another 1,600 feet from its eastern shore. Put this lake on the list if you're familiar with the area and are looking for something new and challenging.

FISH: **Twin Lakes** has boat launch facilities for deeper-water fishermen. The popularity of the campground is due in large part to lake fishing. Boaters and shore casters disperse around the shores of Twin Lakes. **Barney Lake** is a destination for fly-casters.

57.   GREEN CREEK   HIKE, BIKE, FISH

WHAT'S BEST: Weary car-campers can relax along forested creek banks—and then explore trails into the heart of the Hoover Wilderness. Mountain bikers and fishermen will find many reasons to get their legs tired.

PARK: Take unpaved flat Green Lakes Rd.,FS142, 4 mi. south of Bridgeport on Hwy. 395. Park about 11 mi. in at Green Creek Campground. At 8,050 ft. *Note:* On the way, avoid right-forking FS144 to Upper Summers Meadows and left-forking FS020 to Virginia Lakes. **Map:** Dunderberg Peak

HIKE: Green Lake, 4 mi., 900 ft.; West Lake, 7 mi., 1,850 ft.; East Lake, 7.25 mi., 1,425 ft.; Gilman Lake, 9.5 mi., 1,550 ft.

For all hikes, head southwesterly on the trail from Green Creek Campground and get ready to see the best the Hoover Wilderness has to offer. **Green Lake**, not a difficult walk, offers terrain typical of this wilderness on Yosemite's northeast boundary—pointed, mineral peaks with grand, steep shoulders dropping into lakes. *More Stuff:* On the far side of Green Lake, its eastern shore, is a trail to Virginia Pass via steep Glines Canyon. This breathtaking trail connects with the trail from Virginia Lakes, TH59, on the way to Virginia Return Canyon in northern Yosemite.

To **West Lake**, take the right, westerly, fork of the trail as you approach Green Lake. You'll switchback steeply over 1.5-miles to this body of blue. *More Stuff:* Three small lakes—Berona Lake and Par Value Lakes, rest just west of West Lake. Climb off-trail, up the stream feeding the lake's west shore to reach Berona Lake. This is a short but demanding side-trip. Par Value Lakes are a short distance and a somewhat easier hike. Climb the 500-foot-high wall above West Lake's southwest shore and you'll find a pocket that holds the little lakes.

Hikers to **East Lake** and **Gilman Lake** need to take the southerly, or left, fork at Green Lake. You'll march up 600 feet through forest before reaching East Lake. Gilman is an easy walk from East Lake—continuing south on the trail. You'll pass tiny Nutter Lake and some lakelets along the way. Dunderberg Peak juts to 12,374 feet from Gilman's west shore, the king among the surrounding mountains.

More Stuff: Just as you get to East Lake—at its north shore—a trail forks to the right. This rugged trail climbs to a high saddle between Gabbro Peak and Page Peaks, and to a hidden lakelet held in a small basin. Repeat visitors with a sense of adventure may want to explore this wild nook. For backpackers, a 2-night, car-shuttle trip, with a second car at Virginia Lakes, TH59, is a natural. The trail continues south from Gilman.

BIKE: Park near the highway and ride **Green Creek Road**, FS142. Cottonwoods mingle with conifers, making this a beautiful autumn ride. You can ride to sheep country near **Upper Summers Meadow** by veering right on FS144 about a mile from Highway 395. *Note:* Heed private property signs in this area. A third option is to veer left about 3 miles from Highway 395 on FS020. This road climbs to **Sinnamon Meadow** and continues up (up!) to **Virginia Lakes Pack Station**. All in all, cyclists will find more than 30 miles of East Sierran country to pedal at this little-known trailhead.

FISH: Along **Green Creek** are a number of spots to car camp and walk the creek, fly-casting mainly for rainbow and cutthroat trout. **West Lake** is probably the best to shore-cast, although fishermen try their luck at all the lakes mentioned above.

58.   BODIE STATE HISTORIC PARK   HIKE

WHAT'S BEST: You won't find a better preserved mining town anywhere in the American West. Pick a blustery weekday and you may hear echoes of the past.

PARK: Drive 7 mi. south of Bridgeport on Hwy. 395. Turn east on Hwy. 270 and continue 13 mi. to the state park. *Notes:* The last 3 mi. are unpaved and can be rough, though normally passable by passengers cars. Bodie is open all year, but storms may cause road closures. Summer hours are normally 8 a.m. to 7 p.m.; off-season hours are usually 9 a.m. to 4 p.m. Hours are strictly enforced. A small entrance fee is charged. Changes to operating hours should be posted at gated entrances to the park. Please do not remove or alter any artifact at this historic site. **Map:** Bodie

HIKE: Bodie stroll, up to 2.5 mi., 150 ft.

"Good bye God, I'm going to **Bodie**," was a cry heard throughout the West, as an 1859 gold discovery matured into a massive mining venture for the rest of the 1800s and well into the 1900s. By 1879, some 10,000 gold-lusting miners toiled by day and frequented the town's 65 saloons at night. This was one tough place. The Sierra sun baked the sagebrush in summer and its 8,375-foot elevation invited harsh weather in the winter. Fires, explosions, an occasional avalanche, and frequent street killings could greet the dawn of any new day in Bodie. The town's mining activity petered down in the 1900s and came to a close in 1932 when another fire took much of the town. In 1961 it was declared a National Historic Landmark, and three years later a State Historic Park. In a state of "arrested decay," you get the feeling that miners walked away yesterday. Bodie's remaining 170 buildings are spread out over 1,000 acres.

Though about 200,000 people visit each year, the place is not a tourist trap. There are no food concessions or cutesy gift shops—although a museum, informative brochures, and guided interpretive walks will help you get a handle on the place. You can pick your own route, but you may wish to begin by walking down to the right from the parking area and heading up the old town's main drag, Green Street. You'll find the park office on the left. The museum and visitors center is a block past the office, on the right. Most of the buildings are in the two square blocks behind the park office, although you'll want to wander to the outskirts to capture the forlorn undercurrent of the ghost town. The town cemetery is down the road to the right, or southwest, from the parking lot; you drive by it on the way in. *Be Aware:* The northeast section of Bodie, by the stamp mill, is a hazardous area closed to the public.

More Stuff: You can depart Bodie via Cottonwood Canyon Road, which is a sharp right-turn by the kiosk as you enter the park (or to the left as you leave). This unpaved road winds down a scenic 10 miles to the north shore of Mono Lake. From there you turn right on Highway 167 and continue about 6 miles out to Highway 395. Ask the rangers about current conditions.

BODIE

MT. CONNESS, TWENTY LAKES BASIN

After geologic upheavals and glacial carvings, and centuries of habitation by American Indians, Yosemite Valley was "discovered" by the Western world in 1851. The majesty of the valley inspired the National Parks system, as well as a whole school of American painters and photographers. Now each year millions of admirers are drawn to the high country of Yosemite, Tuolumne Meadows, which rests above Half Dome and other fabled monoliths of the valley.

Yosemite National Park is the largest gathering of people in a hundred-plus-mile radius, and surely the most cosmopolitan, attracting visitors from around the globe. Day trippers from Markleeville can drive to valley viewpoints in about two-and-a-half hours, making it possible to enjoy the park without having to endure what can be overcrowding in the valley below. Mount Watkins from Olmstead Point, North Dome, Clouds Rest, and Yosemite Falls are hikes that pay off with valley panoramas. Accessing the park from the east side of the Sierra also gives visitors the opportunity to see the less-heralded majesty of Virginia Lakes, Lundy Canyon, and Mono Lake.

LOWER TUOLUMNE RIVER

Water from the Yosemite high country forms into the Merced River in Yosemite Valley—via numerous falls that are among the world's highest. The Tuolumne River also flows from the meadows into Hetch Hetchy Reservoir which is parallel to and north of Yosemite Valley. The hike to and below Glen Aulin High Sierra Camp is along both river pools and several roostertailing waterfalls.

In Tuolumne Meadows, with a base elevation of just under 9,000 feet, peaks were taller than the glaciers, so that their shoulders and saddles were scoured smooth as the ice moved by over the centuries, but their tops remained fancifully twisted and pointed. Polished granite bedrock of the high country also makes for streams with both clear pools and runs of white water. A hike to Lyell Canyon is a river lover's favorite, and the Cathedral Lakes Trail is entree to the sculpted peaks.

Thanks to John Muir, Joseph LeConte, Clarence King, and other naturalists, Yosemite became the second National Park. It is a testament not only to America's love of its natural treasures, but also, today, of how these treasures are worth more in economic terms when preserved. Muir and others failed in an attempt to prevent a dam in Hetch Hetchy Valley which was said to be as magnificent.

To the east of Yosemite, at Mono Lake, naturalists similarly failed initially in attempts to prevent water exportation from harming the east Sierran ecosystem. But in recent years, the Mono Lake Committee was able to persuade federal courts that the lake's waters must be substantially restored, a decision that must have sent smiles from on high from Muir. The decision also has given millions of tourists a place to behold and explore. Migrating birds presumably are also much happier.

Hikes north and south out of Tuolumne Meadows give you high-country access without having to make that first 3,000-foot hump up that is typical of east Sierra trailheads as you go farther south. On the north side of Tioga Road, Young Lakes, Ten Lakes Basin, and Mount Hoffman are three prime destinations. Tioga Pass is the most southerly through-route in the Sierra. The historic pass, Mono, can be accessed today via trail that leads to the Ansel Adams Wilderness.

MONO LAKE TUFAS

HALF DOME, YOSEMITE VALLEY; ELLERY LAKE, TUOLUMNE MEADOWS

Yosemite is bordered by two other Wilderness Areas: Emigrant on the north, and Hoover to the east. Several trails, including the Pacific Crest and John Muir, run through the Yosemite high country, all interconnected, making it a hiker's park with unlimited options.

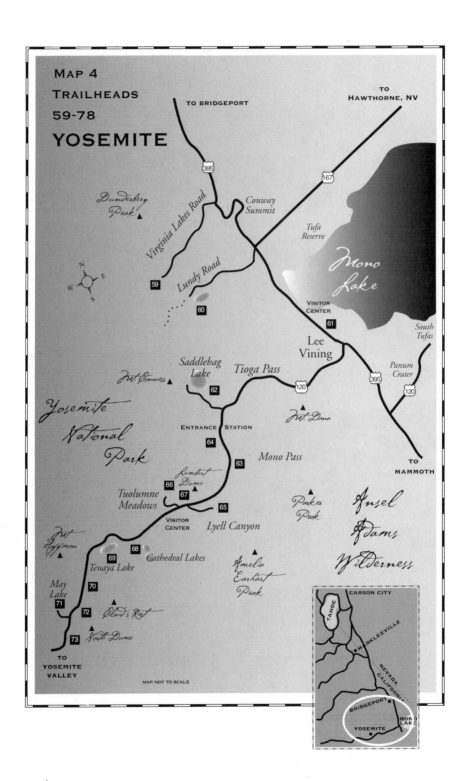

MAP 4
TRAILHEADS
59-78

YOSEMITE

TO BRIDGEPORT

TO HAWTHORNE, NV

[395]

[167]

Dunderberg Peak ▲

Virginia Lakes Road

Conway Summit

Tufa Reserve

Mono Lake

Lundy Road

[59]

[60]

VISITOR CENTER

[61]

Lee Vining

South Tufas

Mt. Conness ▲

Saddlebag Lake

Tioga Pass

[62]

Panum Crater

Yosemite National Park

ENTRANCE STATION

[64]

[120]

[395]

[120]

Mt. Dana ▲

Mono Pass

[63]

TO MAMMOTH

Lembert Dome

[66]

[67]

Tuolumne Meadows

[65]

Parker Peak ▲

Ansel Adams Wilderness

VISITOR CENTER

Lyell Canyon

Mt. Hoffman ▲

[68]

Cathedral Lakes

Amelia Earhart Peak ▲

[69]

Tenaya Lake

May Lake

[70]

[71]

[72]

Cloud's Rest ▲

[73]

North Dome ▲

TO YOSEMITE VALLEY

MAP NOT TO SCALE

W N E S

CARSON CITY

TAHOE

MARKLEEVILLE

NEVADA
CALIFORNIA

BRIDGEPORT

YOSEMITE

MONO LAKE

T R A I L H E A D S

HIKE : DAY HIKES AND LONGER TREKS
BIKE : MOUNTAIN AND ROAD BIKE TRIPS
SKI : CROSS COUNTRY SKIING AND SNOWSHOEING
FISH : LAKE, STREAM, AND RIVER FISHING

59-73

TH = TRAILHEAD, FS = FOREST SERVICE ROAD, NUMBERED

All hiking distances in parentheses are ROUND TRIP, unless noted for car shuttles. Elevation gains of 100 feet or more are noted. Maps listed are USGS topographical, 7.5 series. See Resource Links for recommendations for other optional trail maps. *Notes:* An entrance fee is charged to enter Yosemite. An adequate trail map is provided. Watch for traffic when sightseeing along the highway, and be careful to stay on trails in this popular hiking region. Don't leave food or a visible cooler in your car. Bears *will* break in.

59. VIRGINIA LAKES   HIKE, BIKE, FISH

WHAT'S BEST: This trailhead launches you to vistas of Hoover Wilderness and the gateway to northern Yosemite. Shutterbugs, flex your fingers.

PARK: Take Virginia Lakes Rd., FS021, off Hwy. 395 at Conway Summit, about halfway between Bridgeport and Lee Vining. Drive in 6 mi. to trailhead parking at Virginia Lakes. At 9,800 ft. **Map:** Dunderberg Peak

HIKE: Frog Lakes, 4 mi., 600 ft.; Summit Lake Saddle, 6.5 mi., 1,400 ft.; Summit Lake, 11 mi., 2,200 ft.; Hoover Lakes, 10.5 mi., 2,100 ft.

For all hikes, proceed westward from the trailhead at Virginia Lakes, which caters to car-campers, fishermen, and equestrians. **Frog Lakes**, along with Cooney and Blue lakes, are a series of pools set in dwarf vegetation beneath the towering wall of Virginia Crest. You will pass these lakes, beginning with Blue Lake as you begin the steady climb from the trailhead. Big Dunderberg Peak and Black Mountain rise north and south, 2,000 feet above the lake basin. The Summit Lake Saddle trail veers out the southwest quadrant of the lake basin.

To reach the **saddle and Summit Lake**, you take switchbacks on the face of the breathtaking (in more ways than one) pass, and then more switchbacks down the west side. Snow can be a problem near the top of the pass in early summer in long-water years. Below the west side of the pass is a basin perennially gushing snowmelt from various fissures—a symphony of falling water and flowers. At a trail juncture in this basin, take the west-leading trail up some more to **Summit Lake.** At the lake's western shore is a view the down Return Canyon of northern Yosemite.

To reach **Hoover Lakes**, darlings of the Hoover Wilderness, take the northerly trail when you reach the basin over the saddle. You'll descend a good mile between very steep scree slopes. From Hoover Lakes, you are a mile up the canyon from Gilman Lake. *More Stuff:* Virginia Lakes is a prime backpackers' trailhead. Summit Lake is one possible direction for a 3- to 5-night car-shuttle trip ending up at Tuolumne Meadows, TH67. Hoover Lakes is a direction for a shorter trip, with the second car at Green Creek, TH57.

BIKE: Just before you get to Virginia Lakes Resort—on the right near the pack station— is **FS020**. You can ride this unpaved track down to Highway 395 at **Green Creek Road**, passing Sinnamon Meadow on the way. The descent is more than 3,000 feet over about 16 miles. Have fun. Green Creek Road is 4 miles south of Bridgeport.

FISH: Virginia Lakes lend themselves to small craft fishing. Lake fly-fishermen, in search or rainbow and cutthroat, may want to walk to **Cooney Lake** and **Frog Lakes**. These are good ones take the kids on a fishing outing.

60.   LUNDY CANYON   HIKE, FISH

WHAT'S BEST: With all the marquee attractions in the area, many visitors miss these great hearty hikes up a dramatic hanging valley.

PARK: Take Lundy Lake Rd., which is 5 mi. north of Lee Vining on Hwy. 395— and opposite Highway 167 to Hawthorne. Drive in 4 mi. to the lake. *For Oneida Lake,* veer left when you reach the lake and use trailhead parking. At 7,900 ft. *For Lundy Canyon,* keep right at the lake and continue another 2 mi. on an unpaved road to trailhead parking. At 8,000 ft. *Note:* Lundy Canyon is also the terminus for one of the best car-shuttle hikes in the known universe. See Saddlebag Lake, TH62. **Maps**: Lundy, Dunderberg Peak, Tioga Pass

HIKE: Oneida Lake, 9 mi., 1,850 ft.; Lundy Canyon, 3 mi., 400 ft.—or more!

Oneida Lake is the largest of several lakes in a box canyon that is surrounded on three sides by 12,000-foot-high ridges. Abandoned mine equipment and workings in the area tell its history as a claim—you'll wonder how they got stuff up there in the old days. The trail begins on a steep traverse above the south shore of Lundy Lake. You then hook south on a more gradual ascent up Lake Canyon, following a gushing creek. Little Blue and Crystal lakes are on the left before you make the final rise. A smaller lake lies above Oneida about a half-mile away; head up the canyon the only direction possible. *Be Aware:* Mine workings hold booby traps. Watch your step.

The trail up **Lundy Canyon** is along fast-falling Mill Creek, which is fed by a half-dozen streams over the first 1.5-miles. Incredibly steep escarpments pinch the canyon from three sides, a towering 3,000 feet of seemingly unstable rock. As the trail starts to get steep two or three cataracts gush in from cliffs—called Upper and Lower Lundy Falls. You can keep on humping up the canyon, but the next section of the trail is best walked with gravity as your friend. Start at Saddlebag Lake.

FISH: Anglers hook brooks, browns, and rainbows in the deep lake. **Lundy Lake Resort** has gear and advice.

61. MONO LAKE   HIKE, BIKE

WHAT'S BEST: Attention geologists, photographers, bird watchers, mountain bikers, and hikers on a driving tour: If you stop at Mono Lake plan on spending extra hours. This national scenic area has an inescapable allure.

PARK: The most popular attractions cover a 10-mile section along the lake's western and southern shores. The entire lake is within the Mono Basin National Forest Scenic Reserve: *For Mono Lake County Park-State Tufa Reserve*, drive about 4 mi. north of Lee Vining, turn right on Cemetery Rd. Then turn right immediately into the park. *For the Mono Basin Scenic Area Visitors Center*, drive about 1.5 mi. north of Lee Vining. The center is .25-mi. from the highway. *For Panum Crater and the South Tufa State Reserve*, take Hwy. 395 to 5 mi. south of Lee Vining, turn east on Hwy. 120, and follow signs to south tufas and Panum Crater. *For Mono Craters*, continue east on Hwy. 120. Parking for the craters is about 4 mi. past South Tufa Reserve, near Mono Mills. **Maps:** Mono Craters, Lundy, Negit Island

LUNDY CANYON

HIKE: Mono Basin Scenic Area Visitors Center, up to 1 mi.; Mono Lake County Park-State Tufa Reserve, .75-mi.; Panum Crater and South Tufas, 1 to 3 mi., 300 ft.; Mono Craters, 2 mi., 1,000 ft.

The architecturally stunning **Mono Basin Area Visitors Center** offers excellent interpretive displays, a theater, and an outstanding view of the lake from the back patio. The lake is roughly 9 miles in diameter, with Paoha Island in the center and smaller Negit and Gaines islands to its north. The islands are a sanctuary for migrating birds. The birds, as well as the lake's ecosystem, were threatened when streams were siphoned off to supply water to Los Angeles. Thanks to the Mono Lake Committee and other conservationists, waters have been restored. (The committee's office is in Lee Vining, a must-stop for anyone interested in the lake's natural history.) A nature trail circles behind the center and continues to a tufa view area at the old marina. *Be Aware:* Mono Lake has sensitive habitats that can be harmed by human and vehicular contact. There are also hazards to us humans. The staff at the center will give you tips on safe ways to visit.

Relatively few people visit the **Mono Lake County Park-State Tufa Reserve**. From the parking area, walk down the trail to the boardwalk to view the array of statuesque tufas (pronounce *toofahs*) along the shoreline. Tufas, the creamy-white knobby spires that rise from the water and shoreline, are Mono Lake's trademark attraction. They form when calcium-bearing freshwater springs intrude into the lake water, which is alkaline and rich in carbonates. Calcium and carbonates combine, precipitating out as limestone. Over many years, a tower forms around the mouth of the spring. The tufas above water are only there because the lake level has dropped. Okay, now you can take a picture and be at one with these artful creations. *More Stuff:* Black Point, what's left of a formerly underwater, 13,000-year-old volcano is just east on Cemetery Road from the county park. (Veer right on an unpaved road about 2 miles from the park, and drive out another almost 2 miles to the parking area.) The walk to Black Point, on a cinder trail, is nearly 2 miles, round-trip, with 400 feet of elevation. Fissures at the top are up to 50 feet deep, a foot or two wide, and more than 100 yards in length.

From the parking at the south end of the lake, a .5-mile walk gets you to large, obsidian- and pumice-strewn **Panum Crater**. Its rim affords a panorama of Mono Lake. The obsidian in this crater was the primary trading commodity for the local Paiute Indians. Many of the arrowheads and chips found throughout the Alpine Sierra likely came from this locale. *Be Aware:* Heed posted signs prohibiting removal of rocks. Travelling off-trail across Panum Crater is not recommended. A short drive from Panum Crater to the lakeshore leads to the eerily beautiful **South Tufas**. You can roam around the spires and along the shoreline. West of the tufas is where wide Rush Creek refreshes Mono Lake with snowmelt.

Looking north from a pine forest at the **Mono Craters** turnout is perhaps the best panorama of Mono Lake—seldom photographed, relatively speaking. These volcanic mountains are the youngest in North America, only 650 years old. A trail leads from the roadside to the crater rims.

BIKE: Mono Lake is encircled by a number of dirt and sand roads, which see few cars. On the north and east shores, roads are too soft, and even mountain bikers may have to escort their wheels here and there. *Be Aware:* High brush and dunes can get you lost. Stay on more established roads.

62. SADDLEBAG LAKE   HIKE, FISH

WHAT'S BEST: Take a boat ride and a loop hike of some 20 lakes set in an austere basin above 10,000 feet. Or, start at this lake basin and embark on one of the most dramatic alpine hikes you'll find anywhere, down a 2,500-foot escarpment laced with waterfalls.

PARK: From just south of Lee Vining, go west toward Yosemite on Hwy. 120. At the top before the park entrance, turn right on unpaved Saddlebag Lake Rd. and continue almost 4 mi. to trailhead parking near the resort. **Maps:** Tioga Pass, Dunderberg Peak

HIKE: Twenty Lakes Basin loop, 5 mi., 350 ft; Lundy Canyon car-shuttle, 6 mi., up 350 ft. and then down 2,500 ft. *Note:* During the summer, a water taxi leaves from Saddlebag Lake Resort shore every 30 minutes and takes you to the boat dock at the north end of the lake. A small fee is charged. If you choose to walk rather than ride, add 3 mi. to round-trip hiking distances; take the shorter trail along the west shore of the lake.

SADDLEBAG BOAT TAXI

Resting at 10,087 feet, Saddlebag Lake is by far the largest among the two-dozen lakes in a barren basin. To the west, glacial Mount Conness rises 2,500 vertical feet marking the Yosemite boundary; the east side of the basin is formed by the crumbly, reddled Tioga Crest, which juts up 2,000 feet or more. **For both hikes**, from the boat landing, begin uphill as the trail gradually ascends, passing small Hummingbird Lake. Farther, amid windblown dwarf whitebark pine, you'll pass larger Odell Lake and come upon Lake Helen, which is to the left of the trail.

For the **Twenty Lakes Basin loop**, go to your left, or west, along the north shore of Lake Helen. The trail veers southwest along the north shore of two other lakes, Shamrock and Excelsior, before turning south on the homeward leg. One of the basin's larger bodies, Steelhead Lake, will be to your right at this juncture, and a series of lakelets will be in the basin to your left. (Don't try to count 'em, since the "20" is an approximation.) As you near Saddlebag, you pass large and pretty Greenstone Lake. *More Stuff:* Saddlebag is at the boundary of the Hall Natural Area. A dozen or more small lakes are nestled below Mount Conness and White Mountain.

For the **Lundy Canyon car-shuttle**, hang a right at a trail on the north end of Lake Helen. Take some air-sick pills if heights make you dizzy, because after a tame quarter-mile the trail drops like a rock. During your descent along Mill Creek you pass several cataracts, including Upper and Lower Lundy Falls. After staircasing down more than 2,000 feet over the course of a mile or so, the trail takes a more gradual approach into Lundy Canyon. The thrill ride is over, but you can always do it again.

FISH: Fishermen try **Tioga Lake** and **Ellery Lake**, which greet visitors on Highway 120, on the east side of the park entrance. They are jewels. Fishermen also flock to **Saddlebag Lake** to catch rainbows and browns. They'll fix you up at friendly Saddlebag Lake Resort.

63. MONO PASS   HIKE, SKI, FISH

WHAT'S BEST: Tibetanlike grandeur invites hikers into the Ansel Adams Wilderness, with wildflowers and large conifers along the way.

PARK: On Hwy. 120, drive almost 2 mi. west of the Tioga Pass entrance to Yosemite National Park. Look for parking area on left (south) side of road. At 9,700 ft. **Maps:** Tioga Pass, Mount Dana, Koip Peak

HIKE: Mono Pass, 7.75 mi., 980 ft.; Parker Pass, 10.5 mi., 1,350 ft.; Parker Pass loop, 13 mi., 1,700 ft.; Spillway Lake, 7.5 mi., 750 ft.

For all hikes begin on the trail south, roughly following the historic route of the native peoples through the mountains. The trail crosses the Dana Fork of the Tuolumne River less than a mile from the trailhead. You'll spot a wide variety of wildflowers and some

ABOVE SPILLWAY LAKE

good-sized conifers, many of them lodgepole pine. The trail continues a gradual south-ward ascent, reaching a junction at Parker Pass Creek, about 2 miles from the trailhead. For **Spillway Lake**, veer right here. With the creek rushing by, the trail climbs gradually another 2 miles to the lake—which is set in an open area below the crags and lakes of the Kuna Crest to the west.

For **Mono and Parker passes**, keep left at the junction. In another .75-mile of fairly steep climbing you reach another junction. **Mono Pass** is to the left, or east. After another .75-mile, you can enjoy the view from the 10,604-foot pass—the same one seen by native peoples when this was a primary route. *More Stuff:* To see both passes, double back and continue up; the two-pass hike is about 15 miles.

To **Parker Pass**, continue south at the junction with Mono Pass trail. The trail winds for another 1.5 miles on a moderate climb. You'll see Spillway Lake below to the right. Be-yond the pass and down a couple hundred feet is the outer edge of the Ansel Adams Wilderness, with its steep, stark formations. To the south are Koip and Parker peaks, each pushing 13,000 feet. Mount Lewis lies just east, standing at 12,296 feet. A wild cascade that is just over the pass makes a good resting spot to take in the majesty.

SKI: In the winter when **Tioga Pass** is closed, Nordic skiers drive up the road to the locked gate and ski in toward **Tuolumne Meadows**. Tioga Pass Resort, just before you enter the park, stays open in the winter to accommodate skiers. See *Resource Links* to book a reservation.

FISH: Lake fishermen try **Tioga Lake**, on the road just at the top of Tioga Pass. Down below Tioga Pass (along the several-mile, fairly flat section of Highway 120) are several roads into campgrounds, where fisherman can try their luck along **Lee Vining Creek**.

64. GAYLOR LAKES   HIKE

WHAT'S BEST: Frozen lakes, clear brooks, lawnlike flower gardens, mine ruins: take a picnic lunch and enjoy the afternoon.

PARK: Enter Yosemite via Tioga Pass on Hwy. 120. *For upper Gaylor Lakes and Great Sierra Mine*, park to the right just after passing through the entrance station. At 9,945 ft. *For Lower Gaylor Lake*, continue 4.5 mi. west of the entrance station. Look to the right as the road passes over a creek. At 9,200 ft. **Map:** Tioga Pass

HIKE: Middle Gaylor Lake, 2 mi., 500 ft., Upper Gaylor Lake and Great Sierra Mine, 4.25 mi., 950 ft.; Lower Gaylor Lake, 4.75 mi., 850 ft.

From the entrance station trailhead to the **upper Gaylor Lakes and Great Sierra Mine**, you begin by climbing a ridge that—behind you—affords great views of Mount Dana and the lush lands of Dana Meadows. You drop down about 200 feet from the ridge to Middle Gaylor Lake. To Great Sierra Mine ruins, a stone cabin, proceed north on a trail. You'll pass Upper Gaylor Lake on the way. Pick a spot among the wildflowers and enjoy the alpine vistas. *More Stuff:* Icy Granite Lakes lie about .5-mile west of the mine. The outflow from these lakes feed Lower Gaylor Lake.

From the car, finding the trailhead to **Lower Gaylor Lake** can be difficult. Be mindful of traffic. For the first mile of the hike, the trail climbs through lodgepole forest on the west side of the creek that drains the upper Gaylor Lakes. Then, after about 1.5 miles, it veers left away from that creek and enters the green, high-altitude slopes that lead to the lake. *Be Aware:* Due to the fragile, gardenlike terrain, off-trail walking should not be attempted.

65. LYELL CANYON   HIKE

WHAT'S BEST: Take a miles-long hike with little elevation gain, alongside a glacier-water river in a classic Yosemite canyon. Or go for the gusto to a spectacular High Sierra Camp.

PARK: Enter Yosemite via the Tioga Pass entrance. Go 8 mi. and turn left toward Tuolumne Meadows High Sierra Camp and ranger station. There is a parking lot at the wilderness permit kiosk, and another lot a short distance farther. At 8,800 ft. *Be Aware:* Don't leave any food in your car. Mr. Bear considers that an invitation. **Maps:** Tioga Pass, Vogelsang Peak

HIKE: Tuolumne River Bridges, 1.5 mi., 100 ft.; Vogelsang High Sierra Camp via Rafferty Creek, 15 mi., 1,375 ft.; Lyell Canyon, 8 to 16 mi., 300 ft.

For all hikes, take the trail to your left as it heads along the river toward the tent cabins of the camp. (Put the camp's restaurant on your list for a hearty snack after the hike.) The trail hooks south over a forested rise before reaching the awe-inspiring **bridges over the Tuolumne River**. Deep-flowing waters rush under the bridge's timbers, inviting all to sit a spell. About .75-mile from the bridges, you'll reach a trail junction.

To **Vogelsang High Sierra Camp**, take the trail that forks right. You'll go up gradually through a lodgepole forest, skirting Rafferty Creek. The creek has several cascades and pools. The forest thins as the route staircases to seemingly landscaped meadowlands on the approach to Tuolumne Pass. Keep left at a trail junction, and a mile later you'll reach Vogelsang. The creek sheets over bedrock below the camp and Fletcher Peak rises above. If the kitchen's open you can bag a lemonade to enjoy at the cascade—but make sure marmots don't get your lunch.

Lyell Canyon was once home to one of the the longest glaciers in the Sierra. Stay left at the junction after the river bridges—on the main trail, which is both the Pacific Crest Trail and John Muir Trail at this point. It's is a flat walk along granitoid Tuolumne River, with Kuna Ridge on east side and several large peaks to the west. After about 3 miles on the trail you'll see the first of many spots along the river where the glacial waters have sculpted pools and chutes. The trail junction to Vogelsang via Evelyn Lake is about 6 miles in, just below anvil-shaped Potter Point. Just south of Potter Point, massive Amelia Earhart Peak rises to 11,974 feet. About 2.5 miles past the Potter Point trail junction, the river narrows at a series of bends. Here, Kuna Creek enters from the east. Although Donahue Pass beckons seductively ahead, time management may dictate that you begin the 8-plus miles back to civilization.

More Stuff: Donahue Pass makes a good 3-day excursion, with a base camp 8 miles in, on the north side of Donahue. The pass, with an active glacier nearby, is a magnet for hikers from all over the world. Another backpacking option is to continue south over Donahue into the Thousand Island Lakes basin, coming out eventually at Reds Meadow in Mammoth Lakes. Permits are normally a hot ticket. Check with park rangers. *Be Aware:* Overnight visitors are required to use a bear canister to protect food. They're available for sale or rent at Tuolumne Meadows Store.

VOGELSANG HIGH SIERRA CAMP

66. LOWER TUOLUMNE RIVER

WHAT'S BEST: View one of the world's grandest stretches of falling white water. Take a short stroll or make it an all-day spectacle.

PARK: From the Tioga Pass entrance, go west about 8.5 mi. to the Lembert Dome parking area on right. This area is about .25-mi. before the campground and store. Drive in toward the stables and park at gate or continue and park at the stables. At 8,800 ft. **Maps:** Falls Ridge, Tioga Pass

HIKE: Soda Springs-Parsons Lodge, 1.5 mi.; Tuolumne River views, 4 mi., 150 ft.; Glen Aulin High Sierra Camp, 11.5 mi., 600 ft.; California Falls, 14 mi., 1,100 ft.; Waterwheel Falls, 19 mi., 2,100 ft.

For all hikes, head down the level road. (From the stables, take a connector trail down the hillside.) **Soda Springs**, in a wooden enclosure in the middle of the meadow, is where carbonated water perks from the earth. Some people say to drink it is healthful, but health officials advise against it. **Parsons Lodge** is a historic stone structure on the rise above the springs. When open, you'll find exhibits inside, along with informative park docents. *More Stuff:* A trail leads from near the lodge across a bridge and the meadow to the Tuolumne Visitors Center. You can do a mini-car-shuttle hike if someone is willing to move the car from Lembert Dome.

From the lodge, the trail winds through a forested section before reaching a lovely **view area on the Tuolumne River**. Water sheets over granite as the fanciful peaks of Tuolumne Meadows rise as a backdrop to the south. **Glen Aulin High Sierra Camp** is down the Tuolumne River, on a trail winding its way through the serene meadows with more views to the south—peaks tufted like meringue since they stuck above scouring glaciers. Just above Glen Aulin is Tuolumne Falls, beginning a 6-mile run of cascades and pools as the river drops toward the Grand Canyon of the Tuolumne River. Glen Aulin has a large pool and cascade falling through a reddish rock amphitheater.

Keep going. The trail drops down the face of the amphitheater and winds along the river before reaching the twisting stretch of white water that is **California Falls**. Le Conte Falls is almost a mile below California. A half-mile later you reach the gem of the hike, **Waterwheel Falls**, named for its shooting roostertails of water. In the early summer, the breadth, complexity, and volume of white water is mind-numbing. *Be Aware:* These hikes are downhill from the trailhead; though it is a high-speed trail, you could wind up on a longer hike that you realize.

More Stuff: The popular backpacker camp at Glen Aulin offers many day-hike options. This trailhead is also a good southern terminus for 3- to 5-night pack trips that begin at Twin Lakes, TH56, or Virginia Lakes, TH59. *Note:* Although a backpackers' campground at Glen Aulin has bear boxes, bear canisters are required when camping in the region.

SKI: Adventurers snow camp in **Tuolumne Meadows**, after getting rides to the locked gate on Tioga Road. A primitive group cabin is normally available. Check with park rangers. Tioga Pass Resort, east of the park, caters to Nordic skiers. See *Resource Links*.

67. LEMBERT DOME   HIKE

WHAT'S BEST: See what Tuolumne Meadows looks like from atop a granite monolith—unlike some its cousins in the hinterlands of the park, this dome is easy to get to. Or pick a tougher trek to spectacular, rock-bound lakes.

PARK: From the Tioga Pass entrance, go west 8.5 mi. to the Lembert Dome parking area on the right. At 8,800 ft. *Note:* A second trailhead is on the east side of the dome, at the Dog Lake parking area, near shuttle bus stop number 2 before the Tuolumne Lodge. **Map:** Tioga Pass

HIKE: Lembert Dome, 4 mi., 600 ft.; Dog Lake, 3.25 mi., 375 ft.; Young Lakes, 15mi., 1,200 ft.

For **both Lembert Dome and Dog Lake**, follow the trail up and along the west side of the big rock. You begin northward and then, at a trail junction, turn east around the back. After about .75-mile you'll be on the east side of the dome. For **Lembert Dome** peel off the trail and pick one of the easy routes up the rounded rock. From the top, Tuolumne Meadows lies before you, seen now as a scale model. *Be Aware:*

THE TUOLUMNE, LEMBERT DOME

Those granite ramps can turn too steep imperceptibly as you walk down them. Don't be lulled. Also, don't venture out under thunder clouds, as lightening is a real hazard on domes.

To **Dog Lake**, which is certainly not one, continue on the trail beyond Lembert Dome. Make sure to pass the right-forking trail that leads to the other Dog Lake trailhead at the highway. Less than a half-mile beyond that junction is the west shore of Dog Lake. You might consider doing Lembert Dome for the view and taking in the lake for a lunch.

To **Young Lakes**, start out on the Lembert trail and continue as though you're going to Dog Lake. About 1.25 miles into the hike, go left, or west, at the trail junction that is near Dog Lake. Over the next 3.75 miles of gradual, constant upping you'll cross the upper reaches of Delaney and Dingley creeks. Then comes a trail junction. Go right for the last 2.25 miles around Ragged Peak to Lower Young Lake. There are three lakes, west to east; the highest lake (recommended if you have the energy) is a half-mile away, and another 350 feet up. Young Lakes sit below a skyscraper ridge and afford big views toward Roosevelt Lake and Cold Mountain. *More Stuff:* You can make this a semi-loop hike coming back, adding another mile to the walk. To do the loop, keep right, or, westerly, at the trail junction that is 2.25 miles from Young Lakes. Follow that trail south 3.9 miles, crossing Dingley Creek again, farther downstream. Go left, or east, at the next trail junction and march the remaining 1.75 miles back to the trailhead.

68.   CATHEDRAL LAKES   HIKE

WHAT'S BEST: Tuolumne's sculpted peaks encircle lakes that are popular for good reason. Pay your respects on a day hike to the Cathedrals.

PARK: From the Tioga Pass entrance, go west 10 mi. The roadside trailhead parking is about .5-mi. past the Tuolumne Meadows Visitors Center. *Note:* Consider taking the free shuttle bus to the popular trail during the summer; stop number 7. At 8,600 ft. **Maps:** Falls Ridge, Tenaya Lake

HIKE: Upper Cathedral Lake, 7.5 mi., 1,000 ft.; Lower Cathedral Lake, 7.5 mi., 700 ft. *Note:* Both lakes, 8.75 mi., 1,100 ft.

The **Cathedral Lakes** hike begins on a steady uphill traverse through the forest below Cathedral Peak. About 1.5 miles into the hike, the trail crosses a cascade. Another 1.5-miles later, you'll reach the junction for **Lower Cathedral Lakes**. To see this larger of the two lakes, take a .6-mile spur trail to the right, following a stream to its shore. **Upper Cathedral Lake** is another .75-mile up the trail from this junction, along the stream that runs between the two lakes. Cathedral Pass—between Tresidder and Echo peaks—is about a half-mile farther south on the trail.

More Stuff: One loop hike continues through Sunrise High Sierra Camp and Sunrise Lakes, and then out to Highway 120 at Tenaya Lake. This hike is about 14 miles. From Sunrise you can also pick up the John Muir Trail and continue into Yosemite Valley—a journey of about 22 miles. Tuolumne day-hikers may also consider the nearly 5-mile, round-trip jaunt to Elizabeth Lake. The trailhead is behind the Tuolumne Meadows Campground, accessed via shuttle bus stop number 5. You gain about 900 feet on the way to the glacier-scoop full of water that sits below Unicorn Peak.

69.   TENAYA LAKE   HIKE, FISH

WHAT'S BEST: Scale Half Dome's famous sidekick without driving into Yosemite Valley. Trekkers can put this one on the A-list.

PARK: From the Yosemite National Park east entrance, go about 17 mi. to Tenaya Lake. Park at the west end of lake. At 8,150 ft. **Map:** Tenaya Lake

HIKE: Sunrise Lakes, 7.5 mi., 1,250 ft., Clouds Rest, 14.5 mi., 1,990 ft.

The trail **for both hikes** begins south from the lake, crossing Tenaya Creek. You'll swerve through forest, cross the streams which drain the Sunrise Lakes, and begin a series of switchbacks. To your right will be the great wall of granite that forms the Tenaya Creek drainage—you approach Clouds Rest from the backside of this wall. About 2.75 miles from the trailhead, turn left, or east, at a junction for **Sunrise Lakes**. The three lakes are laid out in a triangle a mile from the junction. *More Stuff:* The meadows of Sunrise High Sierra Camp are about 1.5 miles farther east of the lakes.

TENAYA LAKE

To reach **Clouds Rest**, continue southward from the Sunrise junction, as the trail drops a little into a rumpled topography of forest and stream. After almost 3 miles of this, you'll come to another trail junction at the edge of the steep drainage of Sunrise Creek—go to the right. The backside of Clouds Rest looms above as you ascend to its summit over the next 1.5 miles. Clouds Rest, which tends to collect cloud shreds from the valley, is a .25-mile long, 15-foot wide granite spine. Half Dome is about 2.5 air miles to the southwest. At 9,926 feet, it is the highest among the peaks that ring Yosemite Valley—more than 1,000 feet higher than Half Dome.

FISH: Float tubers and shore casters test their luck in **Tenaya Lake**. Who knows what you'll catch, but the surrounding granite walls are mesmerizing.

70.   OLMSTEAD POINT   HIKE

WHAT'S BEST: You can see Half Dome and Yosemite Valley at this scenic turn-out. A moderate day hike takes you to a seldom-scaled dome—with a front-row seat overlooking the valley.

PARK: Take Hwy. 120 west of the Tioga Rd. entrance to the park. Continue to the turnout on the left, about 19 miles from the entrance station. At 8,200 ft. **Maps:** Yosemite Falls, Tenaya Lake

HIKE: Olmstead Point to Mount Watkins, 7.25 mi., 600 ft.

Olmstead Point gives Tioga Road visitors their first glimpse at fabled Yosemite Valley. Although you're still about 2 hours away by car, the hike to **Mount Watkins** will get you close enough to hear tour buses far below on calm days. To get started, take the trail that runs west, or to the right from the parking area; the easiest way to find it is to walk along the road past a granite hump (watch for cars) and then go down to your left. The trail squiggles up a forested ridge parallel to the road for about .5-mile, and then curves south. The lush forests of the Hidden Lake zone preclude views for the first 2 miles. Then you pop out and climb, while down to your left will be a creek drainage for one of Tenaya Creek's feeders.

You will top out to a flat area, as the trail goes right, away from the creek drainage. Continue a short distance through the flat, granite sand area and then depart the trail—to your left. (The trail continues down Snow Falls to Yosemite Valley.) Though not signed, the route to Mount Watkins is easy to follow. Just keep working your way up through the forest. The actual 8,500-foot summit will be in a sparsely forested, flat oval. To get to the front-row seats, keep going over the top of the giant cue ball. Trees disappear, except for a few knarled beauties. The going will start to get steep, and you'll find some rocky viewing perches. The great wall of Clouds Rest rises 1.5 miles to the south, across the chasm of Tenaya Creek. The Pywiack Cascade is upstream in the granite bowl. Half Dome is 2

miles south of Mount Watkins, and 200 feet higher. *Be Aware:* Prepare for sun exposure and bring plenty of water on this hike. The open granite dome is a cooker.

71. MAY LAKE   HIKE, FISH

WHAT'S BEST: Walk to a serene lake and High Sierra Camp, or get on top of a four-star peak. You'll be in the center of it all—literally.

PARK: From the Yosemite east entrance, go about 21 mi. to 3.5 mi. west of Tenaya Lake. Turn right toward May Lake and drive another 2 mi. to parking at Snow Flat. At 8,800 ft. **Maps:** Tenaya Lake, Yosemite Falls

HIKE: May Lake, 2.5 mi., 475 ft.; Mount Hoffman, 7.5 mi., 2,100 ft.

For both hikes, begin on a gradual, northward climb from the large Snow Flat parking lot. You'll wander up an open, boulder-strewn forest before cresting a low ridge and dropping into May Lake. On the east shore of the lake is one of five High Sierra Camps that encircle the greater Tuolumne Meadows. To some, May Lake is a particular favorite as it affords a faraway feel without having to walk far. Tent-cabin accommodations and a community dining tent are located on the lakeshore. The camps have been operating since the late 1920s.

Mount Hoffman is not visible behind the peak that rises above May Lake's west shore. The well-used trail to Mount Hoffman leaves via the southern shore of the lake—to your left and across Snow Creek. The trail climbs through a series of cataracts and meadows. Bogs of lush green vegetation are accented with dark blue clumps of lupine. It then switchbacks northerly, giving you views of Cathedral Peak and others to the south. Then you reach a sweeping bowl that leads the final six hundred feet to the top—toward your left, or west. The last bit is a doable rock climb, leading to one of the most beautiful vistas in the Sierra. *Note:* Mount Hoffman stands at 10,850 feet and is at the geographic center of Yosemite National Park. *Be Aware:* Although well-used, the trail is not signed or marked on many maps. Bring a topo map and stay on the trail.

More Stuff: A trail leaves to the right, northward, from May Lake. Glen Aulin is about 10 miles away. You can take this trail and loop via Murphy Creek to the highway at Tenaya Lake—about 6 miles from May Lake. This hike works nicely if someone in the group wants to drive to pick up the more-energetic hikers.

FISH: Hikers willing to walk in with a fly-casting pole may hook a rainbow trout dinner from the depths of **May Lake**.

72. NORTH DOME   HIKE

WHAT'S BEST: Don't expect company on North Dome, although you're just a swan dive away from the thousands of visitors to Yosemite Valley. Repeat visitors will want to add this dome to their memory bank.

PARK: From the Yosemite east entrance, drive west about 23 miles, past Olmstead Point and the road to May Lake. Look for trailhead parking on the left, 2 miles past the May Lake road. If you get to Porcupine Flat, you've gone a mile too far. At 8,100 ft. **Map:** Yosemite Falls

HIKE: North Dome via Indian Ridge, 10.25 mi., 650 ft.

The trail to **North Dome** is a net downhill from the trailhead, through the mossy-messy fir forest that is typical of the north side of the valley rim. About .25-mile from the roadside trailhead you'll reach a trail/road that runs parallel to the highway—go straight across. You will walk south across the upper Snow Creek drainage. About 2 miles from the trailhead, veer left at another trail junction. (The right-heading trail goes to Yosemite Falls via Lehamite Creek. Also, be sure not to take a left-heading trail that hooks to the east around the north side of Indian Rock to the Snow Falls trail.) Heading south, your trail begins an upward traverse of Indian Rock, for about 1.25 miles. You will then pass a spur trail to the left. (A .5-mile, round-trip leads to a rock arch, through which you can frame up Half Dome!)

From the Indian Rock spur, the trail drops south along the top of Indian Ridge. After 1.5 miles on the ridge, Basket Dome will appear to your left—at a trail junction. Take a .5-mile spur trail to the left at this point, and you'll find yourself on top of North Dome. At 7,542 feet it is not one of Yosemite's giants. From the top you feel tucked into the valley. But you have a central view of the valley (several thousand feet down) with Glacier Point almost straight across. *Be Aware:* You'll probably want to have a park map or topographical map. The terrain is tricky and crossed by several trails.

73. YOSEMITE CREEK

WHAT'S BEST: The power and majesty of Yosemite Falls is one of the world's wonders. Though no cakewalk, the trail down Yosemite Creek to the top is easier than climbing up from the valley floor.

PARK: *For Ten Lakes Basin,* take the Tioga Rd. entrance. About 24 mi. later, you pass Porcupine Flat. Almost 5 mi. later, look for trailhead parking on the right, on the inside of the bend after the road crosses Yosemite Creek. At 7,800 feet. *Note:* An alternate trailhead to Yosemite Falls is on the opposite side of the road. This trail adds 4.25 mi. and 600 ft. of elevation to the hike. *For Upper Yosemite Falls,* continue past the Ten Lakes trailhead. After another 5 mi. (but before White Wolf) turn left toward Yosemite Creek Campground. The road doubles back over a 5-mi. run to the campground. From the Tioga entrance, it's about 40 mi. At 7,200 ft. **Maps:** Upper Yosemite Falls, Ten Lakes

HIKE: Yosemite Falls, 14 mi., 640 ft.; Ten Lakes Pass, 11.5 mi., 1,800 ft.

To maximize your time at **Upper Yosemite Falls**, you'll want to motor from the trailhead. About 1.75 miles from the car, go left at a trail junction. Your route takes you down to Yosemite Creek, which you follow for 5 miles to the top of the falls. (About .75-mile before the top of the falls, a trail to the right, or west, heads several miles to El Capitan.) When you reach the falls, stay on the right side of the creek, not crossing the bridge, and keep walking toward the edge. A path is cut into the rock and leads right to the edge of the thundering white water. A pipe railing along one hairy section will help those with a healthy fear of heights. The creek drops 2,425 feet to the valley in three pitches, making this the tallest falls in North America. *More Stuff:* The bridge upstream of the falls is a powerful vantage point. To get an even better view, continue across the bridge to Yosemite Point. You'll need to tack on 500 vertical feet and another good mile, but the aerial view of the valley is worth it. Sticking into the air off the point is Lost Arrow—the ultimate phallic rock that is a favorite among climbers.

Ten Lakes Pass is up Yosemite Creek from the falls—a foray into some of the most-spectacular of wilderness. The trail follows the creek but well up the slopes from the water. At little more than 2 miles from the trailhead, you'll cross a fork of the creek, and maintain a steady climb north toward Half Moon Meadow. (Avoid a left-forking trail to White Wolf near the creek crossing.) The meadow is about 5 miles from the car. As the trail cranks up to the north, say good-bye to waters bound for Yosemite Falls. From Ten Lakes Pass you look down to 4 or 5 of the larger lakes in the basin, all of which empty northward toward the Tuolumne River and Hetch Hetchy Reservoir. (And thence to the water glasses of San Francisco.) *More Stuff:* Backpackers will want to put this lake zone in their card file for future reference. Hiking down to the first of the lakes will add about 1.5 miles and 700 feet to the round-trip hike. Another hiking extra is near the top of pass. There you'll find a south-heading spur trail to Grant Lakes.

Tahoe

RUBICON POINT, D. L. BLISS STATE PARK

Lake Tahoe holds enough water to deluge the entire state of California more than a foot deep. But not a drop actually gets there. The Tahoe Basin all drains northeast via the Truckee River through Reno and into Pyramid Lake.

Desolation Wilderness, holding dozens of granite lakes above the lake's southwest shore, is one of California's most popular hiking regions. The streams of the Fallen Leaf and upper Emerald Bay portions of Desolation flow into Tahoe. Vikingsholm, a historic estate on the shores of Emerald Bay, is one of the lake's most scenic attractions, and D. L. Bliss State Park features forested shoreline trails and picture-perfect beaches.

Desolation's more westerly portion, around Lake Aloha, empties into Horsetail Falls and the American River, eventually finding salt water in the San Francisco Bay. Echo Lake is the prime gateway for this portion of the wilderness—a boat taxi shaves several miles off the trail. The southern Tahoe Rim is formed by Alpine's bulwark of peaks—Red Lake, Stevens, Thompson, Jobs Sister, and Freel. At 10,881 feet, Freel Peak is the highest point in the Tahoe Basin.

The first European-American making record of seeing Lake Tahoe was General John Fremont in 1844, from atop Stevens Peak or Red Lake Peak—accounts differ—after having come through the East Carson Canyon. Five years later Fremont was back in Washington D.C. as a nominee for President of the United States, and thousands of California-bound gold seekers beheld the vast blue waters.

Many different names were tried for the lake, including Lake Bonpland after Fremont's botanist and Lake Bigler after California's governor. But "Tahoe" stuck. It's the English spelling of the Washoe word, "Dah-Ho," meaning "Big Water." No place name

PONDEROSA PINE

is more appropriate—an oval 22 miles by 12 miles, Tahoe is the largest mountain lake in North America. The Washoe Indians used the sandy south shore of the lake for their summer Gumsaba, or "Big Time," when one of three main tribes gathered and took whitefish in celebration of the season's plenty. During three seasons of the year, the Washoe foraged the Sierra knowing specifically where and when to go given the weather pattern of a particular year. In the winter, they headed down to the piñon pines and hot springs of eastern Alpine.

The Gold Rush emigrants shook the Washoe world. But Tahoe's real awakening didn't happen until 1860 when the Comstock Lode erupted in Virginia City and the lake's fish and timber were greatly depleted. By the turn of the century, the boom days were over. The early 1900s saw huge mansions and lodges around the lakeshore, serviced by lake ferries and the railroad from San Francisco. Tahoe was quite the destination for the leisure class. Some of these mansions have been preserved at Tallac Historic and Sugar Pine Point State Park. The Gatekeeper's Museum in Tahoe City hosts wide-ranging exhibits on the lake's history.

By the 1960s and 70s, tourism developed into casinos and full-on growth, which threatened the clarity of the lake's waters. But the formation of the Tahoe Regional Planning Agency and League to Save Lake Tahoe have been successful in curbing growth and improving water quality. Unfortunately, recent studies have shown much lake pollution is airborne, coming in over the Sierra from northern California.

Although Tahoe is quite developed, it still offers easy access to exceptional backcountry and water-sport recreation. The Tahoe Rim Trail encircles the crest on the lake basin, accessible via several trailheads. Tahoe City and Kingsbury Grade have four starting

SUGAR PINE POINT STATE PARK

points popular among hikers and mountain cyclists on the TRT. At lake level, Nevada Beach, Sand Harbor, and Chimney Beach all have fine-sand beaches buffeting Tahoe's gin-clear waters. The Lake still reigns, to paraphrase Mark Twain, as surely among the fairest pictures the whole earth affords.

GLENBROOK PIER, NEVADA BEACH, VIKINGSHOLM

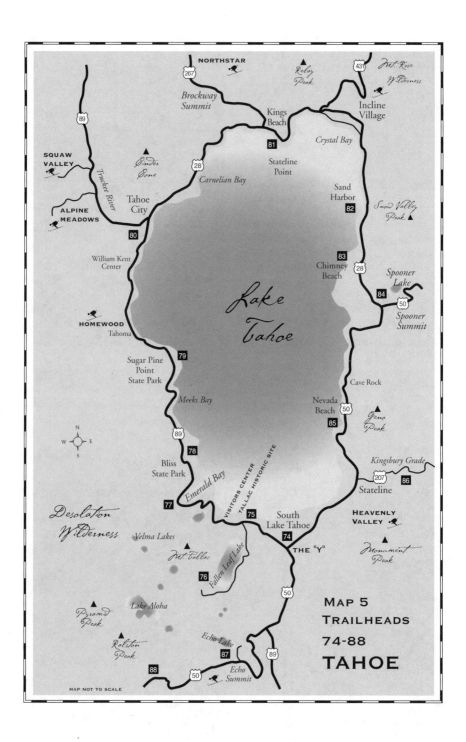

NORTHSTAR

267

Brockway
Summit

431 Mt. Rose
Wilderness

Relay
Peak

Kings
Beach

Incline
Village

81

Crystal Bay

89

SQUAW
VALLEY

Cinder
Cone

28

Stateline
Point

Sand
Harbor

82

Snow Valley
Peak

Truckee River

Carnelian Bay

ALPINE
MEADOWS

Tahoe
City

80

Lake
Tahoe

83

Chimney
Beach

28

Spooner
Lake

84

50

William Kent
Center

Spooner
Summit

HOMEWOOD

Tahoma

Sugar Pine
Point
State Park

79

Cave Rock

Meeks Bay

Nevada
Beach

50

Geno
Peak

N
W   E
S

89

85

78

Kingsbury Grade

Bliss
State Park

207

86

Desolation
Wilderness

77

Emerald Bay

VISITORS CENTER
TALLAC HISTORIC SITE

75

Stateline

South
Lake Tahoe

HEAVENLY
VALLEY

Velma Lakes

74

Mt. Tallac

76

Fallen Leaf Lake

THE "Y"

Monument
Peak

Pyramid
Peak

Lake Aloha

50

MAP 5
TRAILHEADS
74-88
TAHOE

Ralston
Peak

Echo Lake

87

89

88

50

Echo
Summit

MAP NOT TO SCALE

TRAILHEADS

HIKE :   DAY HIKES AND LONGER TREKS
BIKE :   MOUNTAIN AND ROAD BIKE TRIPS
SKI :   CROSS COUNTRY SKIING AND SNOWSHOEING
FISH :   LAKE, STREAM, AND RIVER FISHING

74-88

TH = TRAILHEAD, FS = FOREST SERVICE ROAD, NUMBERED
All hiking distances in parentheses are ROUND TRIP, unless noted for car-shuttles.
Elevation gains of 100 feet or more are noted. Maps listed are USGS topographical,
7.5 series. See Resource Links for recommendations for other optional trail maps

74. TRUCKEE MARSH   HIKE, BIKE, FISH

WHAT'S BEST: Birdwatch and take in vistas of Big Blue on this wide-open stroll to a sandy beach.

PARK: From the "Y," turn right on Hwy. 50 (Lake Tahoe Blvd.) Go about 2 miles and turn left, or north, on Tahoe Keys Blvd. Go 1 mi. and turn right on Venice Dr. Park at trailhead across from marina. At 6,200 ft. **Map:** Emerald Bay

HIKE: Truckee Marsh Beach, 1.75 mi., no elevation.

Walk the **Truckee Marsh**—where the Truckee River spreads out among willows as it fills Lake Tahoe—and keep an eye out for waterfowl, blue heron, and eagles. This short walk is perfect for sunset or sunrise. You walk along the marsh for a half-mile to the lakeshore, where you can wade the sandy shore for a quarter-mile or so in either direction. This stroll is a locals' favorite, and particularly popular among leashed pups.

BIKE: Ride out to the water, or take roads through **Tahoe Keys** houses, skirting the lakeshore, and come out on Highway 89 to pick up the bike path to Kiva Beach. To reach the bike path, take Venice Drive to the left from Tahoe Keys Boulevard. Continue to 15th Street and take a left again.

FISH: In Lake Tahoe are huge fish swimming in waters up to several hundred feet deep. Boat fishermen take off from **Tahoe Keys Marina.**

75. TALLAC BEACHES

WHAT'S BEST: Take a tour of the preserved mansions from Tahoe's golden years, and then amble on a beach walk looking for golden eagles as the peaks of the Sierra soar in the background. Summer swims and fall-color strolls will be just the ticket.

PARK: From the "Y" at South Lake Tahoe, jct. Hwys. 50/89, take Hwy. 89 north about 4 mi., passing Camp Richardson. Turn right at Tallac Historic Site sign and then veer left to the Kiva Beach lot. At 6,200 feet. **Map:** Emerald Bay

HIKE: Kiva and Baldwin beach, Lake Tahoe Visitor Center, and Tallac Historic Site, up to 4 mi., no elevation.

This 1.5-mile lakeshore is the perfect spot to get acquainted with Tahoe, or for locals to entertain guests. From the parking area, take one of the trails to the lake and the pine-shaded sand of **Kiva Beach**. For the nature and view walk, go left at the water on a short walk to Baldwin Beach, a spit of sand separating Lake Tahoe from the Taylor Creek marsh. The slack waters inland are eagle habitat and migratory waters for rainbow trout. The warm, shallow water of Tahoe here is ideal for swimming, and the view of Mount Tallac is inspiring. *Local lore:* Melting snow on the east face Mt. Tallac forms a "cross" in the late spring and summer. Washoe legend says if this cross melts through in any section before July—when their summer Gumsaba, or "Big Time" takes place— a harsh winter will follow.

BALDWIN BEACH, TALLAC HISTORIC SITE

Head east from the parking along a footpath to the **Tallac Historic Site**. This a first-class park preserving the mansions of the late 1800s. Included are the remnants of Lucky Baldwin's Tallac House and Tallac Casino, and the grounds of the Pope and Valhalla estates. Peek through the windows of the restored cottages for a view of what it was like to be a summer guest. The Tallac site hosts a number of events, including the Washoe Tribe summer gathering and several art festivals.

The **Lake Tahoe Visitors Center** is a .5-mile or less walk westward, or left, from the Kiva lot through lodgepole pine (or drive on Highway 89 to the next turnoff). Inside are several exhibits, as well as well as staff eager to give you the skinny on hiking at the lake and into Desolation Wilderness. Leading from the center is a self-guided tour of aspen-laden Taylor Creek. Follow the signs to a building that houses an underwater viewing area of the stream's several species of fish. Children will love it. Big fat trout pose for photographs behind glass in a submerged streambed diorama.

More Stuff: Pope Beach lies east of Kiva, to the right as you face the water. You can walk there from Kiva Beach, about a mile along the shore. *Note:* In between the Forest Service beaches is a strip of private property. It's okay to walk as long as you stay on the beach. By car, the parking for this popular strand of sand is reached via a road between Kiva Beach and Camp Richardson. A nearby dock provides means to walk over some of the lake's clear waters. A lakeside restaurant is a bonus at this beachgoer's hangout.

BIKE: Bike trails extend from before **Richardsons Bay** through the **Tallac Historic Site**, continuing to where the road twists and climbs toward Emerald Bay. The area is made for exploring by bike. Don't fret if you forgot the wheels: The Mountain Sports Center, a bike rental company, is located across from Camp Richardson Resort.

76.   FALLEN LEAF LAKE   HIKE, BIKE, SKI, FISH

WHAT'S BEST: You could film a summer-camp movie at this spectacular lake, replete with activities for the lazy and the energetic. While away hours at Fallen Leaf or take a trek into Desolation Wilderness.

PARK: *From the "Y" at South Lake Tahoe,* jct. Hwys. 50/89, take Hwy. 89 for about 5 mi. to the Fallen Leaf Lake turnoff, on the left. Go in 5 mi., passing the Fallen Leaf Landing. Keep left where the road goes right to Stanford Camp and wind up the last 1.5 mi. to a paved trailhead parking area. At 6,700 ft. *For Angora Lake,* park near the lake at the entrance to Stanford Camp road. See the hike description for a way to drive closer to this lake. **Maps:** Rockbound Valley, Emerald Bay

HIKE: Glen Alpine Falls, 1.75 mi., 200 ft.; Grass Lake, 5.5 mi., 800 ft.; Susie Lake, 8.5 mi., 1,100 ft.; Gilmore Lake, 9 mi., 1700 ft.; Mt. Tallac, 12.5 mi., 3,000 ft.; Dicks Pass, 13 mi., 2,500 ft.; Dicks Peak, 15.5 mi. (2 mi. off-trail), 3,300 ft.; Triangle Lake, 5.75 mi., 1,300 ft.; Echo Peak, 6.75 mi., 2,100 ft.; Angora Lakes, 3.5 mi., 900 ft.

Fallen Leaf Lake is the jumping off point for many spectacular day hikes into Desolation Wilderness. For local advice and to stock up on tasty goodies and essentials for your backpack, you'll want to drop in at the Fallen Leaf Landing store. From the large trailhead parking area, fill out your free day-use permit and head up the cobble road. On an uphill swing, you'll pass the cascade and rustic structures at **Glen Alpine Falls**— the glass-and-rock beauty was designed by Bernard Maybeck. The trail to **Grass Lake,** a worthy destination, is a left fork, about .5-mile after Glen Alpine. To get to **Susie Lake**, pass the Grass Lake fork, continue 1 mile, and take a fork to the left (west). Susie will give camera buffs an itchy finger.

To **Gilmore Lake**, bypass the trail to Susie Lake and pass another left toward Half Moon Lake. Follow signs to a trail that switchbacks up and northerly. Gilmore sits in a large basin below Mt. Tallac. From Gilmore Lake, **Mt. Tallac** is a 1.5-mile, 1,300-foot scamper through a zone rich in flowers. At the top are penthouse vistas of Big Blue—perhaps the best among the many excellent views-from-the-top in the basin. *More Stuff:* Hikers with sturdy knees can make Mt. Tallac a loop by taking the Cathedral Lake trail back to Fallen Leaf—the trail takes off to the east, beginning .25-mile from the south of the peak. The hike to pavement at Stanford Camp is almost 2 miles shorter, but then you need some kind soul to drive you the almost 2 miles back to the trailhead. There is a third variation on the Mt. Tallac climb: Driving on Highway 89, about a mile past Fallen Leaf Road and turn left on Tallac Trailhead Road. This trail makes Tallac about a 9-mile round-trip hike. You connect with the loop hike trail at Cathedral Lake and zigzag up the face of the mountain.

Dicks Pass is a hawk's eye view of the many lakes of the Velma Lakes Basin above Emerald Bay. The pass is achieved by taking the trail that forks to the left, less than .25-mile south on your approach to Gilmore Lake. To **Dicks Peak**, an exhausting but rewarding day hike, leave the trail at Dicks Pass, heading due west up the steep shoulder of the mountain. Keep going until you run out of up.

The trail to **Triangle Lake** takes off to the left, on the east side of Lily Lake just as you leave the trailhead parking. Slack water and brush can make it hard to find—stay to the east of the cabins. You climb steeply through boulders and bush, below the solemn east face of Indian Rock. The trail pops out at a flat, open saddle from where a short trail jogs north to tiny Triangle Lake. To **Echo Peak**—which affords a spot-on look at Echo Lakes—walk east from the saddle, making sure to stay clear of brush on the peak's south face.

Be Aware: With so many options, trails can be confusing in Desolation Wilderness, so follow signs and stay on trails. Off-trail walking is made difficult by small rocks, rock sub-formations, and pesky brush. The wilderness is a backpacker's paradise, made less so only by its popularity. But pretty lake basins provide many campsites. Your permit will specify a camping zone within the wilderness, a policy that disperses campers evenly.

To **Angora Lakes** take a trail beginning on the south side of the creek at the junction of the Stanford Camp Road. Angora Lakes are postcard-quality, with summer cabins and steep walls rising on three sides. You can drive

DESOLATION WILDERNESS, VELMA LAKES

closer to the lakes, but it's a roundabout route: Coming in, about 2 miles from the highway, turn left on Tahoe Mountain Road. Take your first right, on Angora Ridge Road. The road continues 3 miles to trailhead parking a quarter-mile from the lake.

BIKE: The scenic **road to Fallen Leaf** is a dicey ride, due to traffic on summer weekends. Before the Fallen Leaf Road narrows, you can veer right along the lake's southern shore through Fallen Leaf Campground. Crossing Taylor Creek, you'll connect with Cathedral Road, which continues along the west shore.

SKI: Park at the highway and ski in on the Fallen Leaf Road through the (closed) campground to **Fallen Leaf Lake**. A second road skirts partway on the lake's western shore. The lake in winter is a sight you'll never forget, at least until dementia sets in.

FISH: **Gilmore Lake**, with a variety of fish that include Kamloops, big browns, and mackinaw, is a favorite lake among hike-in fishermen. **Cathedral Lake**, a short but steep hike from the west shore of Fallen Leaf, is one of the more accessible places to try for golden trout. Paddle out in **Fallen Leaf Lake** and you've got the cover shot for an REI catalogue.

WHAT'S BEST: Take a family stroll to the Vikingsholm castle and the cascades at Tahoe's bay to behold. Or strap on the boots for a multi-lake hike into a granite basin of Desolation Wilderness. Emerald Bay is one of Tahoe's marquee attractions.

PARK: *From the "Y" at South Lake Tahoe,* jct. Hwys. 50/89, take Hwy. 89 about 9 mi. to Emerald Bay. For Vikingsholm, use the lot that is less than .25-mi. past Eagle Falls, on right. *For the lake hikes,* park on the left at the Eagle Falls trailhead; this is a fee area, although there are about a dozen free spots on the highway. *For Granite Lake,* park at the Bay View Campground, 1 mi. east (before) Eagle Falls parking. *For Eagle Point,* park at Eagle Point Campground, 1.5 mi. east of (before)Eagle Falls. At 6,600 ft. *Note:* Highway 89 is normally closed at Emerald Bay during winter months. The road gets hammered with landslides and was wiped out by major events in 1955, 1980, and 1982. **Maps:** Rockbound Valley, Emerald Bay

HIKE: Vikingsholm and Eagle Falls, 1.75 mi., 550 ft.; Emerald Point, 3.75 mi., 400 ft.; Lake hikes: Upper Eagle Falls, .5-mi., 200 ft.; Dicks Lake, Fontanillis Lake, and Velma Lakes loop, 11.5 mi., 1,900 ft.; Granite Lake, 1.75 mi., 800 ft.; Eagle Point, 1.25 mi., 200 ft.

On prime summer days, the Emerald Bay parking lot is usually jammed. People gather for the fab view at the Emerald Bay Overlook, granite mounds at the edge of the cliff. For the hikes, take the wide road to the left at the overlook, down to water level. **Vikingsholm,** a Norse-inspired castle-home is now restored as a park. It sits on the sandy shore of Emerald Bay at one of the Sierra's most beautiful spots. It was built as a summer home by Lora Josephine Knight in 1929. If you're lucky, the front door will be hosted by Helen Henry Smith, who has spent much of her life on the grounds and has written a monograph on the subject. Tours are offered during the summer. Fannette Island, capped by a teahouse, sits offshore like a mini-magic kingdom. *Note:* A small fee is charged to tour Vikingsholm's interior.

To **Eagle Falls,** take the trail to the right as you face the water at the castle. The path winds through large conifers and up to a railed viewing area. This lovely cataract less visited and more striking than its sister falls at the entrance to the Velma Lakes Basin. To **Emerald Point,** which is the west side of the mouth of Emerald Bay, walk to the left as you face the water. Cabins border a shoreline trail. As the trail hooks left, or north, toward D. L. Bliss State Park, traipse right to the tip of Emerald Point.

For the **lakes loop hike,** (into Desolation) beginning at the Eagle Falls parking, start up the rocky path. The footbridge at **Upper Eagle Falls** is a Kodak moment, and history buffs will enjoy the interpretive signs along the way. From here, serious trek-

EMERALD BAY

kers begin the ascent into a prime portion of the Desolation Wilderness. Within the first mile, you'll stairstep by Eagle Lake. **Dicks Lake** is reached after climbing a rocky ramp and navigating a couple different drainages. About 5 miles into the hike, make sure not to go left toward Dicks Pass. The lake is .25-mile straight ahead from this junction. To reach **Fontanillis Lake**, follow the trail, and the drainage, to the right from Dicks Lake. The ameba-shaped Fontanillis is .25-mile away. Set beneath vertical walls, this puppy is the pick of the litter in the lake basin.

For **Middle Velma Lake**, continue northerly through a forested ridge from Fontanillis Lake. The trail loops within range, but not quite to **Middle and Lower Velma lakes**. To get to those two lakes, jump off the main trail. Desolation Wilderness yawns fetchingly to the west. From the trail junction near Middle Velma Lake, the trail drops down into the valley (passing a spur trail to Upper Velma Lake) and rejoins the trail you walked in on after 1.25 miles. *More Stuff:* From Fontanillis Lake, you can take a shortcut and shave almost 2 miles from the loop hike. Follow the lake's drainage as it sheets out over granite on its way to Upper Velma Lake. Pick your way down and bear right to rejoin the trail.

To **Granite Lake** from the Bay View parking area, take the trail from the back end of the campground. You will switchback at the outset, and then climb less steeply until reaching the small but scenic lake. *Note:* This trail meets up with the trail headed toward Dicks Lake from Eagle Falls.

Eagle Point forms the east side of the opening to Emerald Bay. Parking at the campground may be difficult on summer days, and a day-use fee may apply. The short walk is down to a dramatic perch above the bay. You can take a trail or follow roads through the campground. *More Stuff:* Beginning near the campfire center in the campground, the Rubicon Trail traverses the cliff-side inland to Vikingsholm—a 1.5 mile walk with big views of the bay.

FISH: The **Velma Lakes Basin** is made for hikers who want to carry the pole and shore-cast at a variety pack of lakes. The Velmas are your best bet. Down in **Emerald Bay**, try the pier on the west shore, near the 20-site boat camp.

78. D. L. BLISS STATE PARK   HIKE, FISH

WHAT'S BEST: The name is your likely state of mind as you saunter beaches and trails along one of Tahoe's few wild stretches of forested shore.

PARK: From South Tahoe, take Hwy. 89 up the west side of the lake. After Emerald Bay, turn right into the state park. Continue about a mile and keep right at the check-in station for campsites 1-20. Park in the small lot a short distance after the station. *Notes:* To drive to Calawee Cove: Continue through all the campgrounds and turn right. A day-use fee may be charged. Park areas are closed during the winter. **Map:** Emerald Bay

HIKE: Lighthouse-Rubicon Trail loop, 1.5 mi., 240 ft.; Rubicon Trail to: Emerald Point, 4mi., 320 ft., and Vikingsholm, 7 mi., 340 ft.

On the **Lighthouse-Calawee Cove loop**, you'll pass what's left of the old beacon above the lake. The Bliss family donated 744 acres to the state in 1929. Facing the water at the parking area, go left on the Lighthouse Trail. You'll pass the structure and drop down to the inviting sand beach at Calawee Cove. Rubicon Point is to the right at the cove, marking the south tip of Meeks Bay. From the promontory, you normally can see 75 feet deep into clear waters. To complete the loop from the cove, take the Rubicon Trail south along the shore back to trailhead parking.

Tree-huggers should be happy on the **Rubicon Trail to Emerald Point**, through a veritable Tahoe Sierra arboretum. Keep your eyes and nose peeled for sugar pines, ponderosa, red and white firs, Jeffrey pine, cedar, and juniper. In the lush zones, you may spot cottonwoods, alders, aspen, and dogwood. Ah, bliss. For both hikes, take the trail south, to the right as you face the water. The trail climbs around the toe of Emerald Point, the west side of the entrance to the Emerald Bay. You'll have to drop off the main trail to get to the tippy-tip. To continue to Vikingsholm, just stay with the Rubicon Trail. The final section of trail is along the beach and shoreline.

More Stuff: For a drive-by peek at the upper end of the park, take a spin on the .5-mile Balancing Rock nature trail. To get there, pass the main entrance to Bliss and park 1.5 miles later at a gated service road on the right. You'll have to walk down the road a quarter mile to get to the trailhead.

FISH: Drive to **Rubicon Point** to try for some of the freshest fish on the planet. Mooring buoys are set up for boats, but many anglers shore-cast. Access is via the Calawee Cove parking area, near campsites 141-168.

79. SUGAR PINE POINT STATE PARK
HIKE, BIKE, SKI, FISH

RUBICON TRAIL, D.L BLISS STATE PARK

WHAT'S BEST: The supreme beauty of the forested lakeshore is complimented by stately grounds of one of Tahoe's finest mansions. Roam around and relax. More energetic hikers and cyclists can head for the wilderness via a gentle creek trail inland.

PARK: Take Hwy. 89 north from Emerald Bay for about 9 mi., or south from Tahoe City for about 11 mi. *For the Dolder Nature Trail-Ehrman Mansion stroll,* turn toward the lake at the entrance station and park near the mansion. *For the General Creek hikes,* turn away from the lake and use parking at the far end of the campground. *Notes:* A day use fee may be charged. Areas closed in winter. **Maps:** Meeks Bay, Homewood

HIKE: Dolder Nature Trail-Ehrman Mansion stroll, 2.25 mi.; General Creek Trail to: Lily Pond loop, 4.75 mi., 240 ft., Lost Lake, 12.5 mi., 1,300 ft.

EHRMAN MANSION GROUNDS, SUGAR PINE POINT STATE PARK

With 2,000-plus acres and 1.5-miles of sandy beaches and forested shoreline, Sugar Pine Point is one of Tahoe's centerpieces. The **Dolder Nature Trail** is to the north from the parking area. Aside from viewing some of the park's signature sugar pines (noted by their foot-long cones), the trail passes the highest elevation lighthouse in North America. You'll want to pick your own route for the **Ehrman Mansion stroll**, perhaps starting with the Nature Center located in the old generation plant, followed by a tour of the mansion and its museum. The Queen Anne Victorian is perhaps the finest example of Tahoe's turn-of-the-century estates. Finish your stroll with a walk along the beach and onto the pier. On the north end of the wheelchair path you'll find the hand-hewn log cabin of "General" William Phillips, who was granted 160 acres here in 1860. Right time, right place, that guy. His homestead spared this area from logging that occurred elsewhere.

The **General Creek Trail** runs for miles inland, a gradual uphill beside the creek and its banks of mixed-conifer forests. In the fall, aspen, cottonwoods, and several shrub species will provide color. A range of wildflowers will accent summertime jaunts. For little **Lily Lake**, look for a spur trail on the right about 2 miles into the hike. To reach **Lost Lake** (and its neighbor, Duck Lake) continue up the trail, leaving the state park. About 2.5 miles from the Lily Lake junction, a spur trail leads south and up to the lakes. *More Stuff:* You can use the General Creek Trail to reach the Tahoe Rim Trail-Pacific Crest Trail junction, which is about 6 miles in

EHRMAN MANSION, MEEKS BAY

from the campground. Pass the Lost Lake junction, and then go left when you hit the McKinney-Rubicon OHV Trail that joins the TRT-PCT at Richardson Lake.

BIKE: The paved **West Shore Bike Trail** extends north from the park to Tahoe City, a premier sight-seeing ride. For more taxing rides into wilder country, cyclists have very good options. Ride a loop starting the **General Creek Trail**, past the Lost Lake junction. Go right on FS14N54 which takes you to the **McKinney Rubicon OHV Trail**. This route goes past a series of lakes and reaches the lake at Tahoma, just north of Sugar Pine Point. Riding the paved trail back to the park completes a moderate-to-difficult loop of about 14 miles. *Be Aware:* Watch for pedestrians on the park trails.

Mountain cyclists can take a leisurely loop beginning just south of Sugar Pine, at **Meeks Bay**. At the north end of the bay, ride inland on FS14N42 for less than 2 miles. Then take a trail to the left that connects with FS14N44 back to the south end of Meeks Bay, completing an oval around the margins of Meeks Creek.

SKI: Sugar Pine Point's **General Creek** and **Meeks Bay** are both very good cross-country ski areas. See the biking section for descriptions. Skiers also skate the **McKinney Rubicon OHV Tail**, which you can access via McKinney Rubicon Springs Road, off Highway 89 in Tahoma-Chambers. This area gets a lot of snow and not much sun.

FISH: Serious anglers like to troll the 300-foot-deep ledges offshore **Sugar Pine Point** for big Mackinaw trout and kokanee salmon. Shallower-depth trolling will yield rainbows. Although there is a fishing pier at the state park, shore casters will have their best luck at the mouth of **General Creek** and at the mouth of **Meeks Creek**, a couple miles south of the park. Homesick coast dwellers will appreciate the nautical vibe at the Meeks Bay harbor.

80. TAHOE CITY HIKE, BIKE, SKI, FISH

WHAT'S BEST: Dozens of Sierran waterways feed Big Blue, but only one provides an exit—the Truckee River at Tahoe City. Take lakeside strolls of museums and shops. Cyclists can try some of the best paths at Tahoe.

PARK: Take Hwy. 89, 11 mi. north from Emerald Bay; or take Hwy. 28, 11 mi. west from Incline Village. Park just south of the jct. of Hwys. 89 and 28 at the paved Truckee River Access Lot. At 6,200 ft. *For the Tahoe State Recreation Area,* park at the east end of Tahoe City, at the Boatworks Shopping Mall on Sierra Terrace Rd. **Map:** Tahoe City

HIKE: Truckee River stroll, about .75-mi.; Tahoe Rim Trail to Page Meadows, 5.5 mi., 750 ft.; Tahoe State Recreation Area, .5-mi.

On the **Truckee River stroll**, your first stop should be the dam (Fanny Bridge), where Highway 89 crosses over the river. Normally, huge trout pose just below the railing. Lake Tahoe is surrounded by mountains—the rim—except for this one outflow, where the water escapes toward Reno and then Pyramid Lake. From the dam, veer right into the alpine gardenscape that is William B. Layton Park. On the grounds is the Gatekeeper's Museum, which houses an impressive historic collection, including memorabilia from the Tahoe Tavern Resort and S. S. Tahoe. The Marion Steinbach collection of Native American basketry is one of the best in the world. Complete your stroll by continuing down Tahoe Tavern Road to a Forest Service beach.

To take the pleasant hike on the **Tahoe Rim Trail to Page Meadow**, begin on the bike path on the south bank of the river. Then turn right on a gravel Forest Service Road; after .25-mile you reach the dirt path. Depending on the season, wildflowers or fall color will add zest to this hike. You begin uphill through trees, gaining most of the elevation on the first part of the hike. At Page Meadows several ponds dot an expanse of greenery. *More Stuff:* To take the TRT north, drive toward Truckee on Highway 89 for a short distance and turn right on Fairway Drive. The trailhead is on your left, after only one-tenth mile. The trail ascends steadily through a who's-who of conifers. You'll get some great views of the lake. Cinder Cone is about 7 miles round-trip and 1,100 feet up, if you care to suck some mountain air.

To take a short walk on the long pier of the **Tahoe State Recreation Area**, veer left as you face the shopping center. You'll find a short path and stairs down to one of the lake's sublime viewing spots. Enjoy your lunch. *More Stuff:* The recreation area is a nub of Burton Creek State Park that extends inland. To get there, continue east on Highway 89 a short distance, hang a left on Rocky Ridge Road, and follow it up through a subdivision.

BIKE: Whether you want to dink around or really push the pedals, Tahoe City offers some excellent choices. Perhaps the best for leisure-time riders is the paved path on the north side of the **Truckee River to Squaw Valley**. This ride is about 15 miles, if you include a pedal around the resort that hosted the 1960 Olympics. From the river access parking, you can also jump on the paved **West Shore Bike Trail**. The path follows the highway and lakeshore south about 9 miles to Sugar Pine Point State Park. A nice 10-mile round-tripper is to William Kent Campground and picnic area, or to the Sunnyside Lodge Restaurant just south of it. You can also explore east of Tahoe City by taking a path from Commons Beach just east of the river. It continues several miles past town, to Lake Forest and Dollar Point.

Dirt riders can take the **Tahoe Rim Trail**, both **north and south**—as described in the hiking section. After Page Meadows, the trail becomes a road for a while before making the jump to the Granite Chief Wilderness. (No bikes in wilderness areas.) Going north on the TRT is a climb of about 1,400 feet over 8 miles to Painted Rock. From there it's 11 miles to Brockway Summit. Or, you can make it a loop ride from Painted

Rock by coming back down on FS16N71 or FS16N53—dirt roads that drop back to Tahoe City. Then grab a brewskie at one of the many restaurants.

SKI: Big dumps of snow provide Nordic skiers with choices. **Blackwood Canyon Sno-Park**, one of the better, is 4 miles south of Tahoe City on Highway 89. Also excellent is the **Tahoe Rim Trail to Page Meadow**, one of the hikes listed above. Small **Granlibakken** resort a mile south of Tahoe City offers tracks for cross-country skiers, as does **Squaw Valley**—go 5 miles toward Truckee on Highway 89 and turn left. If the snow is ample, try the roads of **Burton Creek State Park**, perhaps the sleeper choice for skiers. Access the park via Rocky Ridge Road just east of the Boatworks mall.

FISH: The pier **Tahoe State Recreation Area** is made for whiling away some quality time with pole in hand. Farther up the road—turn right on **Lake Forest Road** as you go east on Highway 28—fishermen with craft can access the lake at a state boat ramp.

81.   KINGS BEACH   HIKE, BIKE, FISH

WHAT'S BEST: Meander on a long beach walk or stroll to a seldom-visited lookout. Or step out on the Rim Trail toward the Mt. Rose Wilderness.

PARK: To Kings Beach, near the state line, take Hwy. 50 or Hwy. 89 to Hwy. 28, which runs along the north shore. Park at the Kings Beach State Recreation Area, just west of Hwy. 267. At 6,200 ft. *For the Tahoe Rim Trail,* drive up Hwy. 267. About .5-mile from Brockway Summit, look on the right for a pullout for FS16N56. At 7,000 ft. *For the Stateline Lookout,* go east on Hwy. 28 from Kings Beach. Just east of the casinos, turn left on Reservoir Dr. Pass Wassou Rd. and then turn right on Lake View Ave. Continuing up .5-mi. and park at a gate for Stateline Lookout Rd. At 6,700 ft. **Maps:** Kings Beach, Martis Peak

HIKE: Kings Beach stroll, up to 2 mi.; Tahoe Rim Trail to: Martis Peak Lookout, 9.5 mi., 1,750 ft., or Mt. Baldy, 14 mi., 2,250 ft; Stateline Lookout, 1.25 mi., 320 ft.

Old-time resort cabins and some choice eateries are strung along the lakeshore at **Kings Beach**. The beach area is a hangout for visitors, who migrate among several small beaches and boat docks. The most popular is the farthest east, the Kings Beach State Recreation Area. Then head up the beach to the west, or to the right, as you face the water. You'll come to Secline Beach, the North Tahoe Beach Center, Moon Dunes Beach, and (just around the rounded point) Atagam Beach. This is a people-watching stroll. *Be Aware:* Portions of private property separate beaches; stay within the high-water line and you'll be fine.

The trail climbs from outside the car on the **Tahoe Rim Trail** at Brockway Summit. This section of the TRT, which connects to the Mt. Rose Highway about 19 miles away, is known both for its wildflower meadows and vistas of Tahoe and the northern Sierra. Geologists will note volcanic origins. To reach the **Martis Peak Lookout**, you ascend through mixed-evergreens. After about 4.5 miles, a spur trail leads north to the lookout, about a .5-mile away at an elevations of 8,742 feet. Windswept **Mt. Baldy**, elevation 9,271 feet, is nearly 2 miles farther on the TRT. You cross the state boundary on the ascent and the Mt. Rose Wilderness boundary is about .25-mile east of the summit. *Be Aware:* Bring plenty of water and prepare for wind and sun exposure.

More Stuff: Relay Peak, rising to 10,338 feet is the giant of the north Tahoe Basin. To reach it most easily (9 miles, round-trip, 1,500 feet) start at the Tahoe Meadows trailhead on the Mt. Rose Highway 431. Parking is near a small concrete building, .25-mile southwest of the Mt. Rose Summit.

Because it is a semi-pain to get to, relatively few people catch the view from the **Stateline Lookout**. From the parking, you make a gradual climb around the knobs and reach an interpretive trail at the lookout. You cross the state boundary midway on the walk. About 800 feet below, Stateline Point protrudes, pointing down the 22 miles of Big Blue. From this vantage, the sun reflects off the water, giving you a double sunrise and sunset.

BIKE: The **Brockway Summit** trailhead is a good launch pad for cyclists on the **Tahoe Rim Trail**. Headed easterly, you can burn all the way to **Mt. Baldy** and the Mt. Rose Wilderness boundary. At the Martis Peak junction, you can take FS16N54 to the right and weave a semi-loop into the ride. Headed west on the **TRT** you can pedal 19 miles to **Tahoe City**—a net downhill of 800 feet, although you ride up-and-down five- to seven-hundred feet is several places. A variety of Forest Service Roads make this a premier area for adventurous cyclists.

FISH: Two boat ramps at **Kings Beach** stand ready for deep-water. About 3 miles to the west is the **Sierra Boat Ramp**, at Carnelian Bay. Some of the lake's finest motor cruisers are moored here—worth a gander.

82.   SAND HARBOR   HIKE, BIKE

WHAT'S BEST: Many consider this the most exquisite among Tahoe's many fine beaches. In the summer, substitute pines for palms and your eyes would be thinking Hawaii.

PARK: Take Hwy. 50 north from the "Y" and Statleline. Turn left at Spooner Summit on Hwy. 28. Sand Harbor State Recreation Area is on the left, about 8 mi. down a grade. Or, go east on Hwy. 28 for 5 mi. beyond Incline Village. At 6,200 ft. *Note:* A parking fee is charged. Arrive early (before 10 a.m.) on summer weekends to insure a spot. **Map:** Marlette Lake

HIKE: **Sand Harbor stroll, up to 1 mi.**

Sand Harbor is the crown jewel of the 14,000-acre Lake Tahoe Nevada State Park, by far the largest in the basin. You may wish to begin by keeping left as you enter and parking near the picnic area. Long Sand Harbor Beach will extend to your left. Head to the right on a boardwalk that passes the stage area for the park's wildly popular Shakespeare festival that makes midsummer nights a dream. The route continues around Sand Point, whose boulders and benches provide many a contemplative nook.

Then you'll round the point into the dreamy crescent of sand that is Sand Harbor, with its large pavilion. The north point of the harbor is another A-plus sitting zone, and the park extends for about a mile farther up the shore, if you feel like walking. With many submerged granite boulders and little rock islands, the harbor is the prime put-in for swimmers. Although Sand Harbor hums in the summer, don't overlook the off-seasons. *More Stuff:* Though not a secret among locals, little Hidden Beach doesn't see the masses—there's not enough parking. Look for a turnout 2 miles north of Sand Harbor, where Tunnel Creek enters the lake. The beach is a mile south of where Lakeshore Boulevard joins the highway.

BIKE: **Tunnel Creek Road** is where the popular **Flume Trail** drops down to lake level. Nobody will stop you from riding up, but most people come down from Marlette Lake; see TH84. Though the road originates at Ponderosa Ranch, cyclists can access it 2 miles north of Sand Harbor, across the highway from Hidden Beach. It's 1,600 feet up to the lake, over a distance of 7 miles.

An easier ride is the **Incline Village Bike Trail**, along fancy lakeshore residences and through town. For parking, take a left on Lakeshore Boulevard, 3 miles north of Sand Harbor. The path begins within .25-mile. You can ride a couple miles on flat ground and then double back to take a path up the hill to town. Two beaches—Incline and then Burnt Cedar—provide scenic rest stops, and the Hyatt Regency is worth a look.

83. CHIMNEY BEACH   HIKE

WHAT'S BEST: Droves of sunbathers seek this undeveloped coast on prime summer days, but you can always find a spot to call your own.

PARK: From Spooner Summit, take Hwy. 28 for about 5 mi. toward Incline Village; or take Hwy. 28 about 2 mi. up the hill from Sand Harbor. *Two National Forest parking lots:* One is on the lake side of the road, just south of the boundary between Washoe and Carson City counties. The second, larger lot is less than .5-mi. north, across the county line and on the mountain side of the road. **Map:** Marlette Lake

HIKE: Chimney Beach-Secret Harbor, up to 3.25 mi., 400 ft.

BIG BLUE

Since **Chimney Beach** and **Secret Harbor** were favorite nudie sunbather haunts years before the official parking lots were put in, a number of half-assed trails were forged down the forested hillside. Try to avoid these, as erosion is a problem. From the north-end parking, take a .5-mile long path that cuts down to Chimney Beach, which is at the north end of the shore. You will indeed find the remains of a chimney, what's left of an estate. From there head south, or left, as you face the water. Secret Harbor is nearly a mile away. You'll be on a shoreline trail that dips and climbs between the water and the forested, granitic landforms that separate the coves. On the homeward leg of the hike, you have the option of taking a road that is farther up the hillside and parallels the shore. Boaters as well as hikers frequent this coastline. Big submerged boulders and sandy beaches, make it an excellent choice for a swimming, with visibility up to 100 feet. But don't overlook Chimney Beach in the spring and fall, when you have the place virtually to yourself.

84. SPOONER LAKE   HIKE, BIKE, SKI

WHAT'S BEST: Though not on the tourist circuit, locals head to Spooner Lake for four-season, muscle-powered fun.

PARK: Take Hwy. 50 to its junction with Hwy. 28 at Spooner Summit. *For Spooner Lake,* go .75-mi. toward Incline Village from the junction and turn into developed parking for the lake. At 7,000 ft. *For the Tahoe Rim Trail hikes,* go east of the highway for .5-mi.; the trail crosses the highway with trailhead parking on both sides. At 7,150 ft. *Be Aware:* Watch for high-speed traffic on Hwy. 50. **Map:** Marlette Lake

HIKE: Spooner Lake shore, 1.5 mi.; Spooner Lake to: Marlette Lake, 9.5 mi., 825 ft., or Tahoe Rim Trail loop, 8.5 mi., 1,300 ft.; Tahoe Rim Trail North to Snow Valley Peak, 12.5 mi., 2,100 ft.; Tahoe Rim Trail South to: Duane Bliss Peak, 7.25 mi., 1,500 ft., or South Camp Peak vista, 10.25 mi., 1,650 ft.

Set in sprawling meadowlands and surrounded by Jeffrey pine and aspen, **Spooner Lake** begs an easy stroll. The margins of the shore support a variety of Sierran flora, and quiet hikers are bound to see wildlife in the air and on the ground. Spooner Lake is the southern end of Lake Tahoe Nevada State Park, which spreads north to nearly Incline Village.

For the longer hikes to **Marlette Lake** and **the Tahoe Rim Trail loop**, start out on North Canyon Road, which is to the left as you face the water at the parking area. The easily graded road is well suited for group hikes. It follows a creek to the mile-long oval that is **Marlette Lake**—a source of water for Carson City to the east. You may see an occasional vehicle on the road, since those-in-the-know have gate keys. The **Tahoe Rim Trail loop** begins about 2.75 miles from the trailhead (and before the lake). Go right at North Camp on a connector trail. This 1.5 mile segment climbs about 600 feet and hits the TRT. Hang a right through the forest back to Spooner; you need to drop off the trail to the right before getting to the highway. *More Stuff:* You can make a longer loop hike, and take in the lake, by continuing on North Canyon Road. A second connector trail is about a mile beyond the first and joins the TRT at Snow Peak; this loop is 11.5 miles.

The **Tahoe Rim Trail North** from Spooner summit twists through open Jeffrey pine forest that reveals occasional views of both the Carson Valley and Lake Tahoe Basin. The bare rock of **Snow Valley Peak**, elevation 9,214 feet, is the highest point around for many miles. The peak is a king-of-the-world spot, but you can find view spots on the trail without doing the peak.

From Spooner Summit, the **Tahoe Rim Trail South** ascends into the Carson Range through mixed-conifers, mostly Jeffrey pine. At a small meadow not far in, keep an eye out for aspen that are carved by 19th-century Basque sheepherders. To scale **Duane Bliss Peak** look for a spur trail on your left—after passing a junction with FS14N32B that is 2.75 miles from the trailhead. From the 8,658-foot summit you're looking down on Jacks Valley to the east and on Glenbrook Bay on the Tahoe side. At the **South Camp Peak vista**, the TRT reaches its high point between Spooner and Kingsbury Grade. You might have to button up the windbreaker on the traverse up the peak's volcanic slopes. Tahoe spreads to the north and south like an inland sea. *More Stuff:* Genoa Peak is less than a mile away, and 300 feet up from the vista. At 9,150 feet, it is the tallest in this part of the Carson Range. To stand there, go south on the TRT and take a left-forking dirt road. *Be Aware:* Bring plenty of water. Since it follows a ridge, the TRT is stingy with water.

BIKE: Cyclists have been pedaling from **Spooner Lake** since before Spandex. A winning ride is the **Flume Trail to Lake Tahoe**. Head to Marlette via the North Canyon Road and keep left at the lake. After 1.5 miles, the route becomes the Flume Trail; continue for 4.5 miles and turn left on Tunnel Creek Road for the roll to lake level. This ride is 13.5 miles to Hidden Beach, 2 miles north of Sand Harbor. *Note:* A shuttle van (no reservations required) will take you back to Spooner during the summer.

Or, skip the car-shuttle and take a great **loop ride around Marlette Lake**. From Spooner Lake, follow North Canyon Road and keep right at the lake; you hit the TRT after 7 miles and 1,200 feet. Then go left on the TRT, climbing another few hundred feet over 2.75 miles. The trail then drops over 2.5 miles and joins Tunnel Creek Road. Go left for .5-mile, and go left again at the Flume Trail. Enjoy Tahoe Views back to Marlette and Spooner. This ride is some 23 miles, with 1,700 feet of net gain.

SKI: Although the Sierra tends to suck the snow from Pacific storms, depriving the Carson Range to its east, **Spooner Lake** can be an excellent locale for cross-country skiers. You can ski around the lake, or head up **North Canyon Road**, which provides a moderate thrill on its downhill return. The lake region sparkles when it's sunny, and is also a good choice during snowfall—with little threat of getting lost or of an avalanche.

85. NEVADA BEACH
HIKE

WHAT'S BEST: Try this park for swimming, star gazing, and long beach walks. Tahoe looks like an ocean in the Alps from this pine-buffered run of sand.

PARK: From Hwy. 50 at the Round Hill Shopping Center, turn left (west) toward on Elks Point Rd.—1.5 mi. north of the jct. of Hwy. 50 and Kingsbury Grade, Hwy. 207. Fee parking inside park and limited street parking outside. At 6,200 ft. **Map:** South Lake Tahoe

HIKE: Nevada Beach 1 to 3 mi., no elevation.

At **Nevada Beach**, large Jeffrey pines spaced in granite sand lead to the blue waters of Tahoe and an in-your-face look across the width of the lake to Mt. Tallac and the Sierran Crest. The walk north is short, ending at Elk Point, the boathouse at Marla Bay. The walk south passes several docks, along the golf course and beyond the Edgewood Country Club. In all seasons but summer, Nevada Beach is used by few people. *Note:* Signs notwithstanding, it's okay is to walk the shoreline, as long as you stay at water's edge.

More Stuff: Zephyr Cove, with its period lodge and public beach, is a few miles north of Nevada Beach on Highway 50. This is also where you can take a paddle wheeler across the lake to Emerald Bay. Another Tahoe highlight, Cave Rock, once a sacred burial site for Washoe, is about 5 miles north of Nevada Beach. The highway is bored through the rift of an ancient volcano. On its south side is a road down to Cave Rock State Recreation Area—the easiest place to dip a toe in the lake if you're driving the east shore.

86. TAHOE RIM TRAIL AT KINGSBURY
HIKE, BIKE, SKI

WHAT'S BEST: Get high in the Carson Range on some of the Tahoe Basin's lonely trails.

PARK: From Hwy. 50 at Stateline just north of the casinos, go east on Kingsbury Grade, Hwy. 207. This highway also connects with Hwy. 395. *For Kingsbury Grade North*, from just west of the summit, turn north on North Benjamin, which becomes Andria Dr. Continue 2 mi. to roadside parking at road's end. At 7,800 ft. *For Kingsbury Grade South*, at the summit turn south on Tramway Dr. and continue for 1.5 mi. Look for trailhead parking at the south end of the Heavenly Stagecoach parking lot. At 7,500 ft. **Maps:** Glenbrook, South Lake Tahoe

HIKE: Kingsbury Grade-Tahoe Rim Trail North to: Castle Rock, 1.25 mi., 150 ft., or Genoa Peak, 12.75 mi., 1,375 ft. Kingsbury Grade-TRT South to: East Peak Lake, 7 mi., 650 ft., or Monument Pass 10.25 mi., 1,300 ft.

It is testament to the hard work of the Tahoe Rim Trail Association and a cooperative spirit in the community that the trail was established in this region of the ski resort and lake view homes. Beginning at **Kingsbury Grade North** the road to **Castle Rock** is almost an immediate left from the trailhead. You wind out on FS13N80 to the craggy formation and its penthouse look at the lake. The TRT to **Genoa Peak** continues along the upper reaches of a forested network of streams, but don't count on water on the trail. At 5.75 miles from the trailhead, the trail crosses FS14N33. Jog right on this dirt track, and then go left on FSN32, which runs beside the TRT. The trail to Genoa Peak is a right-hand spur. From the peak, at 9,150 feet, you get a big look into the Carson Valley, as well as a photo op of the big blue sheet to the west.

From **Kingsbury Grade South**, the TRT travels the east side of the Carson Range, so don't plan on a view of Tahoe. East Sierra newcomers will find the steep panoramas a welcome surprise. The trail squiggles through a forest of behemoth red fir and western white pine (with 6-inch long cones) during its opening segment. These magnificent life forms escaped the sawyers' blades during the logging boom of the late 1800s that supplied the Comstock Lode. For **East Peak**

CAVE ROCK, NEVADA BEACH

Lake, look for a road to the right, about 3.25 miles from the trailhead. Set below its namesake mountain just to the west, the little lake is sure water on an otherwise dry run of the TRT. A road S-turns to the top of the 9,591-foot peak, beginning at the western shore. **Monument Pass**, at 8,820 feet, is a crease below the vertical wall of Monument Peak, rising another 1,250 feet due west. This is one rough piece of country. A road leads from just below the pass to South Lake Tahoe, via the Cold Creek drainage. To the east, the land drops about 4,000 feet over 2 horizontal miles. *More Stuff:* It's 3.75 miles farther on the TRT to Star Lake.

BIKE: Adventure bikers gleefully ride from Kingsbury Grade North on **Genoa Peak Road** to **Spooner Summit**. This road with a view, a.k.a. FS14N32, covers some 14 miles through the Carson Range. This is no pussy-pedal, but you don't have to be a pro. You'll do about 1,000 feet of climbing on the way. Make sure to veer right on FS14N32B on the north end of the ride, .5-mile after the road crosses the TRT near Duane Bliss Peak. You can also pump from Kingsbury Grade North on a **loop ride to Genoa Peak**. About 5 miles from the trailhead, veer left from the road onto FS14N33— and then make an immediate left on the **Tahoe Rim Trail** for the homeward leg.

SKI: **Heavenly Valley**, at Kingsbury south, is one of the world's top resorts.

87.   ECHO LAKES   HIKE, SKI, FISH

WHAT'S BEST: This summer-cabin resort is the entrance to a land of lakes and polished granite. For Sierra newcomers, it may be love at first sight.

PARK: Take Echo Lakes-Berkeley Camp Rd. off Hwy. 50, 4 mi. west of jct. Hwys. 89/50 in Meyers. About a mile west of Echo Summit. Drive in 2.5 mi. to the marina lot, or park at the overflow higher up. At 7,400 ft. *For the car-shuttle,* park at Horsetail Falls, TH88. **Maps:** Echo Lake (primary), Pyramid Peak

HIKE: **Lake Aloha, Desolation Wilderness, 14.5 mi., 750 ft.; Pyramid Peak, 16 mi. (6 mi. off-trail), 2,400 ft.; Horsetail Falls car-shuttle, 10 mi., 1,000 ft.**

The walk to **Lake Aloha** can be shortened by 4 or 5 miles—and made more fun—by taking the boat taxi from the marina at Lower Echo Lake. The taxi shuttles hikers to Upper Echo Lake. The trail from lower Echo runs along the north shore behind cabins of Echo Lakes and then becomes a rocky ramp all the way to Aloha. The popular path is part of both the Pacific Crest Trail and the Tahoe Rim Trail. The sprawling Lake Aloha is Desolation's signature lake, set in a vast granite basin below a wall of peaks that push 10,000 feet. You'll find many little coves with rock islands.

More Stuff: Many short side trips are possible on the PCT to Lake Aloha within a quarter-mile of the trail are a number of lakes: Ralston Lake, Tamarack Lake, Lake

ECHO SUMMIT

LeConte, Triangle Lake, Lake of the Woods, Lake Margery, and Lake Lucille. Triangle Lake is farther off the trail, on the way to Fallen Leaf Lake, TH76. A hike from Echo Lakes to Fallen Leaf via Triangle Lake 4.5-mile car shuttle, utilizing the boat taxi. Driving between the two trailheads almost takes longer.

For Echo Lake to Horsetail car-shuttle, take a trail toward Lake of the Woods, about a mile before reaching Lake Aloha—very near a spur trail to Lake Margery. You'll reach the lake after a half-mile. This trail continues along the east shore of the lake and loops west to little Ropi Lake, 1.5 miles away. Follow the drainage south from the lake, along some pond-sized lakes, and you'll reach Horestail Falls. The trail drops down Pyramid Creek to the trailhead at Twin Bridges.

To scale **Pyramid Peak**, the sentinel of the Tahoe Sierra and American River drainage, leave the trail, heading due west, just as you get to the south end of Lake Aloha. The peak will be in full view. Make your way through the numerous small lakes, keeping Pyramid to your right, or north. Start to climb, still heading west, until Pyramid is directly north, and climb that shoulder—the peak's south face—to the top.

SKI: The road into Echo Lakes is a 4- or 5-mile round-trip run. Echo Lakes are quite a sight in winter, frozen and buried in snow. **Echo Lakes** is a **Sno-Park**, as is **Echo Summit**, on the south side of the road, just west of the summit. The drive up here can be rough in winter conditions, especially considering the traffic. You can count on plenty of snow late in the year.

FISH: Desolation Wilderness is stocked with virtually all mountain trout: golden, rainbow, brown, brook, mackinaw, and cutthroat. In the **area of Lake Aloha**, some good bets for hike-in fishermen are **Tamarack Lake, Lake Lucille, Lake Margery and Heather Lake.** In **Echo Lakes,** with a boat ramp accessible by car, you can also catch fat Kokanee Salmon, a species planted in the 1940s.

ECHO LAKE SPILLWAY

88.   HORSETAIL FALLS
HIKE

WHAT'S BEST: This white-water falls is the back door to Desolation Wilderness. Ralston Peak is highly underrated.

PARK: At trailhead parking, just east of Twin Bridges on Hwy. 50, 7 mi. west of Echo Summit. At 6,000 ft. *For Ralston Peak*, park at Camp Sacramento, about 6 mi. west of Echo Summit on Hwy. 50. At 6,550 ft. **Maps:** Pyramid Peak, Echo Lake

HIKE: Horsetail Falls top and Avalanche Lake, 4 mi., 1,300 ft.; Lake of the Woods, 8 mi., 1,900 ft.; Lake Aloha, 10 mi., 2,000 ft. Ralston Peak, 8.25 mi., 2,750 ft.

Horsetail Falls, the spewing of Pyramid Creek as it drains the lakes of Desolation Valley, is a short and breathtaking hike. At the top is **Avalanche Lake**, one of more than a dozen lakes and lakelets that dot the mile-square granite zone southwest of lake Aloha—an interesting area to explore. To Lake of the Woods, take a trail heading northwest from Avalanche Lake. The Aloha trail runs along the north shore of Lake of the Woods, which you can take and then loop back for the descent of Horsetail Falls.

Considering the scenic payoff, the hike to **Ralston Peak** is a bargain. The trail begins on the north side of the highway, and is a steep slog up the east canyon that is the Pyramid Creek drainage. You enter Desolation Wilderness in forest about 1.5 miles into the hike. You won't see much until the journey is almost complete: After 3.5 miles you reach a spur trail to the right, heading up the last .5-mile to the 9,235-foot summit. The lakes of the wilderness lay to the north like a board game, and Pyramid Peak rises 1.5 miles to the northwest—as the eagle flies.

ECHO LAKE AND DESOLATION WILDERNESS

Driving Tours

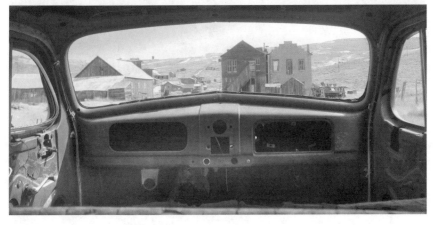

EMIGRANT HIGH COUNTRY

WHAT'S BEST: You'll retrace portions of the Emigrant Trail, Pony Express route, and Snowshoe Thompson's tracks into the high valleys of the Carson Pass. Alpine scenery and natural beauty abound. **DRIVE TIME:** Approximately 2 to 3 hours. **ROADS:** Two-lane state scenic highways and byways with little traffic. Some optional dirt roads, with four-wheel drive recommended. **BEST TIME:** Autumn is ideal, when the campgrounds have closed and fall color is out. Summer also very good—try late afternoon for sunset views. Snow will make roads chancy in winter.

START AT WOODFORDS, JCT. HWYS. 88/89.

At this junction in 1847, Samuel Brannan renamed a sacred Washoe falls that gushed from a mountain high above after himself. Brannan Springs became a way station for Mormon emigrants, the first settlement in the Utah Territory, which included lands now called Nevada. The Gold Rush thwarted the Mormon's westward ho, and by the time the Pony Express stop was established here in 1864, the place was known as Careys Mill, after John Carey who ran a lumber mill. Carey moved on when business for the Comstock Lode got slow, but left behind his name on the mountain above town—Cary Peak, as the surveyors chose to spell it. In 1869, Daniel Woodford set up what he called the Sign of the Elephant Inn—a term making reference to mirages seen by wagon-weary emigrants. People liked the inn so much they renamed the town after him.

Woodfords, subject to canyon winds, has suffered through five devastating fires, most recently in 1989. Fire has destroyed structures, but people have remained: The Mountain Garden Bed and Breakfast is operated by Linda Merrill, whose relatives have been here since Willis P. Merrill opened a trading post in 1854. Next door to the B&B is Woodfords Station, where you might start out the tour with some of its famous chili at the counter, and keep an ear open for some local goings-on while you're at it.

CONTINUE WEST ON HWY. 88/89 UP WOODFORDS CANYON.

During emigrant years, wagons by the thousands went up Woodfords Canyon, known then as Rocky Canyon or Big Canyon. One wagoneer, having crossed the entire country, wrote in his diary, "This Kanyon beats all we have ever seen ... We had to cut the wagon in half and use it like a cart." Halfway up the canyon is Snowshoe Springs, named for Snowshoe Thompson who, during his 20 years crossing the Sierra alone in winter on skis, would hole up in a secret cave on the north side of the canyon.

After topping Woodfords Canyon you'll see Sorensen's Resort, first established in 1928. It is one of the oldest continuously operated resorts in the Sierra. For the last twenty-plus years, the resort has been under the care of Patty and John Brissenden, who have done much to promote low-impact tourism and to preserve the scenic resources of the region. The resort today offers a wide-range of events and workshops, including photography, stargazing, fly-fishing, and history walks. The Norway House at Sorensen's was imported piece-by-piece from its native land. Sorensen's is a gathering place for mountain lovers, both local and from around the globe. You'll want to check out the book and gift store, and kick back with a beverage or meal on the resort's aspen-shaded deck.

CONTINUE WEST OF PICKETTS JCT. ON HWY. 88. CONTINUE ABOUT 3 MI. AND TURN LEFT BLUE LAKES RD.

Just west of Picketts Junction is the Hope Valley Wildlife Area, where you can get out and take a short stroll to the West Carson River. Or park at one of several turnouts and walk a short distance out into the heart of Hope Valley—many rate this place as tops in all the Sierra.

Note: Blue Lakes Road is paved for the 10 miles to Lower Blue Lake. This loop portion of the tour off Highway 88 includes about 6 additional miles of unpaved road. If you don't want to drive unpaved road (or have a passenger vehicle) go in 10 miles until pavement ends and double back. Then continue west on Highway 88 to Red Lake, which is 2 miles east of Carson Pass.

Blue Lakes Road, first called Border Ruffian Pass Road, was in the Silver-boom days of the 1870s the major north-south route from the Carson Valley and Tahoe to Ebbetts Pass and Sonora. But Hope, Faith and Charity valleys (which you pass through on Blue Lakes Road) were named before then. Some say the names derived from a group of Mormons returning to Utah after a tragedy (at Tragedy Springs) and who were buoyed by the beauty and ease of passage they encountered on the way down. Others say the valleys were named by a group of Masons who were racing a group of Odd Fellows to establish a charter in California in 1860. The Odd Fellows went over Carson Pass. The Masons took the route through three valleys, naming them with growing confidence on their way to Murphys Camp. Sadly, history does not record who won.

In the 1880s, Faith Valley was a dairy, where dairyman Harrison Berry is credited with the introduction to California of the square churn with baffles. Berry claimed the wild grasses of Faith and Charity valleys made for better-tasting butter than he got out of the cows back in his Midwestern home state. The method he developed for churning butter became the way it was done throughout the West.

SORENSEN'S CABIN, WEST CARSON RIVER

CONTINUE TO BLUE LAKES.

EL DORADO INFORMATION CENTER

Blue Lakes is now a popular campground for families and fishermen. At Blue Lakes in the late 1800s a race track operated during the summers near the mining towns of the day, Summit City and Harmonial City. Blue Lakes, just a few miles from Ebbetts Pass, was a crossroads for miners headed to various mining camps and way stations. Drive along the east shore of both lakes and the road will take you over Forestdale Divide and back out to the lower end of Red Lake on Highway 88. The road is nicely graded and safe, but one narrow downhill stretch near the end may give flatlanders sweaty palms. The divide separates runoff headed for the Pacific from that which is bound for the Great Basin.

CONTINUE TO RED LAKE AND HWY. 88.

The unpaved road on the south side of Red Lake is the old emigrant stage route. (Some in your party may wish to walk up to Carson Pass, if you have a driver willing to meet the hikers there.) At the west end of Red Lake, just below the Carson Pass, is the scarred rocky face that symbolizes the pluck and perseverance of emigrants. Look for the marks of wagon wheels left behind on

JUNIPER ON CARSON PASS

CARSON PASS

"Devils Ladder" as they hoisted their loads the last yards of a 1,000-mile journey. Donner Pass lives in infamy, but historical diaries suggest emigrants faced Devils Ladder with greater trepidation.

Near here, not coincidentally, in the late 1850s John Studebaker opened a tire-setting shop with $68 capital. At this wagon-busting location, Studebaker didn't have many idle days—nor many customers who were in a position to quibble over price. He parlayed his earnings from that enterprise to establish the Studebaker Automobile Company when he returned to Indiana.

CONTINUE WEST ON HWY. 88 TO CARSON PASS.

Then-Captain John C. Fremont named this pass in honor of his scout, Kit Carson, when they passed through in 1844. (Fremont went on to be a general and a presidential candidate.) From Stevens Peak—or near it—just north of the pass, Fremont and his party were the first Europeans to note the existence of Lake Tahoe. Local Washoe people guided the expedition to the pass. A Snowshoe Thompson monument is at the Carson Pass turnout, although the pass was seldom on his route when crossing the mountains. The Emigrant Trail followed what is now Highway 88 for about another 20 miles, until west of Silver Lake, where it diagonals northwest toward Placerville. The interpretive center at the pass offers souvenirs and a wide-selection of books. The center's docents are well-versed on local trail conditions and history. *Note:* A day-use fee is charged for parking.

TURN LEFT ON WOODS LAKE RD., ONE-HALF MI. WEST OF CARSON PASS. DRIVE TO LAKE AND COME BACK OUT TO HWY. 88.

Woods lake is a cozy, forested lake, but not without its towering peaks. Lost Cabin Mine is a short walk from the picnic ground. Bring mosquito repellant in the summer. If you're ready for a picnic, this is the place.

CONTINUE WEST ON HWY. 88 TO CAPLES LAKE.

James "Doc" Caples and family passed this way emigrating to California in 1849. They couldn't forget the place and came back within a couple years, building a block timber home that was visited by travelers for decades. Then two lakes—Twin Lakes—were here, separated by a narrow strip of rock. The two lakes were made one and named for Caples after the dam was put in; ironically the raised lake level submerged Doc's home site.

TURN LEFT ON KIRKWOOD RD., 1 MI. WEST OF CAPLES LAKE.

Kirkwood is a world-class ski resort boasting the highest base elevation and deepest average snowfall among California resorts. The resort is also hopping in the summer, with mountain bike rentals and other outdoor adventures. On the way back, check out the old Kirkwood Inn. By taking a walk around its bar you will have been in three counties: Amador, El Dorado and Alpine. Nearby is Kirkwood Cross Country, managed by Alpine's world champion, multi-sport wonder Debbie Waldear.

CONTINUE WEST ON HWY. 88 TO SILVER LAKE

Just west of Kirkwood, the highway climbs over the precipitous Carson Spur, where eagles soar and avalanches present a danger during winter storms. A few miles past the spur is Silver Lake. Volcanic cliffs rises nearly 2,000-feet above an idyllic lakeshore dotted with rustic cabins. Kit Carson Lodge will fill the bill for a romantic dinner, and its gift shop offers both the whimsical and practical. At sunset the lake casts the aura of an Illuminist painting.

ICE FISHING ON CAPLES LAKE

Tour Two
WASHOE COUNTRY AND ALPINE VALLEYS

WHAT'S BEST: Take a spin through the Washoe wintering grounds, Snowshoe Thompson's home site, Markleeville, and valleys reminiscent of the Alps. Most visitors don't see what lies just off the main roads around Markleeville. **DRIVE TIME:** From 1.5 to 2 hours, depending on stops. **ROADS:** Quiet county roads and unpaved roads passable in passenger vehicles. **BEST TIME:** This is a four-season tour, although winter storms often close back roads.

START AT DIAMOND VALLEY RD., A HALF-MILE SOUTH OF WOODFORDS ON HWY. 89/4. DRIVE PAST THE SCHOOL INTO DIAMOND VALLEY.

In the late 1800s, Diamond Valley—named for its shape as seen from above—was the site of six or seven homesteads and several sawmills, all servicing Virginia City 50 miles to the north. The eastern Sierra's first irrigation ditches were constructed here by Snowshoe Thompson and Washoe Indians, taking water from the West Carson at Woodfords.

Midway through the valley, where Indian Creek crosses under the road and on its south side, is Snowshoe's home site. He died here in 1876 of an undetermined illness at forty-nine. Some say it was appendicitis and others say it was pneumonia; he had been too ill to walk and had to resort to seeding his fields from horseback. Local lore says that he pointed as he lay dying toward a secret silver mine near Silver Peak. A marker commemorates the site, unless vandals have taken it again. Regardless, the important view is not of his house, but of where he built it. Look in a circle. From this spot Thompson, most-accomplished among mountaineers, had access to six routes through the Sierra. Silver Peak, along with saw-toothed Raymond Peak, loom to the south. That giant knob in the east is Hawkins Peak.

TURN RIGHT AT INDIAN CREEK RD., UNPAVED, AT EAST END OF DIAMOND VALLEY. CONTINUE PAST INDIAN CREEK RESERVOIR.

Among these volcanic outcroppings and piñons, the Washoe wintered for centuries, trapping rabbits in droves in the sagebrush and harvesting nuts from the squat, grayish pines. Arrowheads, made with obsidian from the Mono Lake area, and grinding rocks are common in this area. If you find Washoe artifacts, or other objects from bygone pioneer days, please leave them behind. The Washoe way of life was altered forever in a few short years when the piñons were cut during wood drives to service the Comstock Lode—the river was filled with up to 150,000 cords, wood six-feet deep for several miles, floating north. Dutch Valley, just south of Diamond Valley, is a major community for today's Washoe Tribe of California and Nevada. The tribe has about 1,600 members in the two states, up from a low of 300 in the late 1800s. Prior to Europeans coming in 1850, the tribe's population was about 5,000, living on 1.5 million acres with Lake Tahoe as the center of their world.

ABOUT 2 MI. PAST INDIAN CREEK RESERVOIR, TURN RIGHT ON PAVED AIRPORT RD. STOP AT CURTZ LAKE.

At Curtz Lake are three, short self-guided nature study trails: a vegetative trail, a soil-geology trail, and an aquatic trail. Signs identify the plants, which include most of those indigenous to

WASHOE GRINDING ROCK, BASKET WEAVER SUSIE

the piñon pine belt. In the fall the trees are laden with pinenuts, which are found in the cones. They can be eaten right from the cone, if the birds and squirrels don't beat you to them, or oven roasted at a low temperature for a short time.

CONTINUE DOWN AIRPORT RD. TURN LEFT ON HWY. 89/4, DRIVE TO MARKLEEVILLE. CONTINUE THROUGH TOWN.

In 1861, Jacob J. Marklee recorded 160 acres that became the town site. Other than that, his claim to fame was operating a toll ferry across the Middle Fork of the Carson River (now Markleeville Creek) and being shot dead by one H.W. Tuttle in 1864. Tuttle was acquitted after arguing self-defense.

The Alpine Visitors Center is on the right as you enter town—the small structure belies the enormity of information inside. The Wolf Creek Restaurant, at the town's only intersection, was renovated and renamed in 2002, much to the chagrin of many visitors who lament the loss of the former pool bar with brassieres pinned to the ceiling. It was formerly the Alpine Hotel and Cutthroat Saloon—named for the fish, not the activity. Regardless of name changes, this is the original structure built in 1862 in Silver Mountain City and moved here in 1885. It's previous names were Fisk Hotel and Hot Springs Hotel. The Markleeville General Store, which is across the street and next to the courthouse, is more than a century old, unusual since these wood-frame buildings of the Old West have often burned. This is the best place to pick up supplies, and don't overlook the curio shop in the back.

PASS THE COURTHOUSE AND TURN RIGHT ON LARAMIE ST.

The granite block courthouse dates from 1928, built over the home site of the unfortunate Jacob Marklee. In 1864, Silver Mountain City was voted the county seat. Markleeville had a population of about 2,600, with more than 15,000 other residents scattered in local mining districts. A telegraph line was strung to town from Genoa, Nevada. During the Civil War, an armory with a company of Union troops was stationed here. In 1875, when silver was demonetized, an exodus took place, dropping the area-wide population to around 1,000, a majority of whom voted to make Markleeville the county seat.

CARY PEAK; RUDDEN'S MARKLEEVILLE STORE

CONTINUE PAST THE LIBRARY TO HOT SPRINGS RD. JOG RIGHT AND THEN TURN LEFT AND UP THE HILL.

The granite-block Library, twin to the courthouse, is a welcoming place; stop by to visit and get the local lowdown. Perched with a view of town, Alpine County Museum and Historical Complex is the site of Old Webster School, historic jail, and museum. The grounds are a great picnic spot. The museum holds a noteworthy collection of artifacts, photographs and documents. The complex has received statewide recognition as one of the Sierra's best.

BACKTRACK DOWN THE HILL AND CONTINUE WEST ON HOT SPRINGS RD.

On the right as leave town is Villa Gigli, where Ruggero and Gina Gigli offer authentic Italian cuisine, original artwork, and homespun hospitality. Featured in *Bon Appetit* magazine, the restaurant is open only on weekends and draws diners from all around. Stop in to make reservations for a memorable evening—a Markleeville classic.

GO 2 MI. TURN LEFT ON PLEASANT VALLEY RD., CONTINUE 3 MI. INTO PLEASANT VALLEY, ABOUT 2 MI. UNPAVED.

Set below Raymond Peak and fringed with cottonwoods, conifers, and groves of aspen, Pleasant Valley combines the alpine with the bucolic. Aspen, even those growing in the most remote of hanging valleys throughout Alpine County, are often inscripted with the artful carvings of Basque sheepherders. The valley's display of fall color is an event worth seeing as are the trees in summer leaf when the slightest breeze starts their leaves "quaking" in the sunlight.

Pleasant Valley was the probable route of Captain Joseph Walker on his expedition of 1833, though his records are not as detailed as those of Fremont, who ventured through here 11 years later. During the silver boom a few decades later, Pleasant Valley was the main route to high mining towns, like Summit City and Silver Mountain City on Ebbetts Pass. On the south side of Pleasant Valley is Raymond Canyon, site in the late 1800s of Raymond City, large enough to have a drug store and saloon. Rural legend tells of a cave in this area, where Raymond City's last miners stored belongings one year—and never returned to get them. Don't count on finding it, no one else has.

GO BACK TO HOT SPRINGS RD. TURN LEFT, DRIVE 4 MI. TO GROVER HOT SPRINGS STATE PARK.

It is not difficult to imagine why the Washoe gathered in Hot Springs Valley for generation upon generation. Fremont's expedition encountered the amiable people there in 1844, and several Washoe guided a group to what was later named Carson Pass. Some locals doubt this version of the story, reasoning that the meeting took place in Pleasant Valley, since the verbose Fremont did not mention hot springs in his diary.

In 1854, John Hawkins, a rancher and farmer, took up squatters' rights in Hot Springs Meadow. In 1878 the Grover family purchased the land from Hawkins, and ran a dairy. The Grovers later opened a resort in concert with the Hot Springs Hotel (which was the renamed Fisk Hotel) in Markleeville. The property twice changed hands in the 1900s: its old-growth pines and cedars were cut, and then, in 1959, it was sold to California State Division of Parks and Beaches. The structure near today's pool facility dates back to around 1900.

Grover's natural mineral waters, which are cooled to just above 100 degrees before being piped into the pool, draw visitors from throughout the West, many of whom boast of the water's curative powers. Some people actually drink it, though this is not commonly recommended. The facility, which includes a cold pool, is open year around with the exception of Christmas, Thanksgiving and New Year's. The campground is open all year.

PHOTO COURTESY ALPINE COUNTY MUSEUM

THE OFT-NAMED FISK HOTEL, NOW WOLF CREEK RESTAURANT

TOUR THREE
HISTORIC MINING DISTRICTS

WHAT'S BEST: Glimpse into Mogul and Monitor Mining Districts, and the Dixon Mine in the alpine valley of Wolf Creek. Then head east past Chalmers Mansion and Silver Mountain City to the ski resort village of Bear Valley, one of the Sierra's best kept secrets. **DRIVE TIME:** About 3 or 4 hours from Markleeville. **ROADS:** Scenic state highways and unpaved roads, some with four-wheel drive recommended. **BEST TIME:** Forget about this one in winter and spring. Snow blocked. Try mid-summer and plan for a dinner out or picnic in Bear Valley at the end of the day. Mid-autumn will be the choice time for leaf peepers.

START AT MARKLEEVILLE, GO SOUTH ON HWY 89/4. TURN LEFT ON HWY. 89 TOWARD MONITOR PASS.

At the turnoff to Monitor Pass stood the town of Mt. Bullion. Across the river is evidence of a mining tunnel dating back to the 1860s. A post office was set up here in 1869, called "Bullionia," but it didn't stop the town from vanishing by 1873.

CONTINUE UP HWY 89 FOR 2 MI. TURN LEFT ON LOOPE CANYON RD., FS190. *Note:* This begins 8 miles off road. If you'd rather drive pavement, continue on Hwy. 89 for 4 mi. to the Leviathan Mine Rd., which is 2 miles above Heenan Lake.

At this turnoff, where you will see evidence of recent mine workings, was the town of Monitor—later named Loope. Telegraph and Wells Fargo offices were established here in 1865. With a population of 2,500 in 1864, Monitor finished a close third in the voting to become county seat. The town was abandoned in 1888, but begun anew in 1898, when a Dr. Loope arrived representing Eastern investors. This attempt to rekindle mining was not successful, due to faltering backers and poor ore, and not helped at all by fires and floodwaters. Climbing up from the highway through the old Mogul Mining District, you'll pass a left turn to a recently worked Cal/Silver Mine, and then Curtz Mine and Morningstar Mine. Use extreme caution at mine sites and heed private property signs.

CONTINUE ON FS190, TAKING RIGHT FORKS WHEN OPTIONS ARISE. THEN TURN RIGHT ON LEVIATHAN MINE RD., FS052. DRIVE BACK OUT TO HWY. 89, AND TURN LEFT ON HWY. 89 TO MONITOR PASS.

On the south side of Monitor Pass are some roads dipping into the upper Monitor District, and also leading to the Dump Canyon route of the camel trains. Just east of the pass is the road to Leviathan Peak, and the relatively short hike to the magnificent view from the peak's lookout station. Aspen groves on the open slopes of Monitor add fiery splotches of color in the fall.

TURN BACK TOWARD MARKLEEVILLE. CONTINUE TO HEENAN LAKE.

Note the poster-quality view at the historical marker in the aspens as you come west on Monitor. Heenan Lake, which now is the only Lahontan Cutthroat breeding stock lake in California, was in the late 1800s the entrance to the lower Monitor District mines in Lexington and Monitor canyons. Bagley Valley ranch, with its Vaquero Camp, predated the miners in the region.

CONTINUE DOWN TO HIGHWAY 89. TURN LEFT AT HWY. 4 TO WOLF CREEK RD. DRIVE IN 6 MI., 2 MI. UNPAVED, AND FOLLOW SIGNS TO DIXON MINE.

The campground at Centerville, at the turnoff on Highway 4, was once the mining town of the same name. The main road to Bodie, near Bridgeport, came through here and into Wolf Creek and Silver King Valley. Dixon Mine, below the southern end of Wolf Creek Meadow, is of more recent lineage. It is set dramatically in the river canyon, with workings on both sides of the river. Before leaving Wolf Creek, you may wish to take the unpaved road south through the meadow. The road ends at a major trailhead for the Carson-Iceberg Wilderness.

DRIVE BACK TO HWY. 4, TURN LEFT, GOING WEST ON HWY. 4.

Chalmers Mansion is marked by the tall brick smokestack that was once used in connection with a nearby silver ore reduction plant. Lord Chalmers, an Englishman, came to Alpine in 1867 to develop mining property on behalf of investors in London. He first worked the Mt. Bullion and Monitor districts, but in 1870 purchased mines near Silver Mountain City. By 1880 London investors had poured in thousands more dollars, allowing Chalmers and his new bride, former housekeeper Mrs. Laughton, to live well. But no rich strike materialized. In 1885 Chalmers returned to London to raise more money, but died instead. Mrs. Chalmers and the couple's child became destitute and moved to San Francisco.

Scossa Cow Camp, the picturesque ranch house and corral just up the road, is a working concern. Snowshoe Thompson's widow, Agnes, married into the Scossa family around 1880. West of Scossa Camp, is the site of Silver Mountain City, Alpine's county seat from 1864 to 1875. Scandinavian miners first settled here in 1858, naming it Konesberg (various spellings). Snowshoe Thompson bested some of his fellow Norsemen in a ski contest here at "jump rock." This was the first known ski competition in the United States. By 1863 the Silver Mountain District town had 50 or 60 buildings, some 15,000 people, and 300 mining claims. The richest of the claims was in IXL Canyon.

Scossa Cow Camp, Chalmers Mansion

MONO COUNTY COURTHOUSE, BRIDGEPORT

CONTINUE WEST TO EBBETTS PASS ON HWY. 4.

The first European man known to cross the Sierra, Jedediah Smith, did so here in 1827. But the route was named for Major John Ebbetts who crossed in 1849 leading a group from the Knickerbocker Exploring Company of New York. This route may well have become the first railroad crossing of the Sierra. In 1853, Major Ebbetts was retained by the Atlantic and Pacific Railroad Company to survey and begin. But early in 1854 Ebbetts drowned on Petaluma Creek near San Francisco when his steamer ship blew up. West of Ebbetts Pass is the trail leading north to Border Ruffian Flat, once a hideout for the fabled Murietta Gang.

CONTINUE DOWN HWY. 4 ANOTHER 14 MI. TO LAKE ALPINE AND BEAR VALLEY.

Bear Valley is a major ski resort and home to many of Alpine's best cultural events, including, Reggae on the Mountain Spring Break, High Sierra Music Festival, and Bear Valley Music Festival. You can combine a swim in Lake Alpine or bike ride around the village with viewing a first-class performance of *La Boheme* held under a circus-sized tent in the tall cool pines. You'll want to see the walk-in fireplace at Bear Valley Lodge. For provisions and camping stuff, try the Bear Valley General Store, Bear Valley Adventure Company, or Bear Valley Sports Shop. Nose around. You'll probably want to come back. Today's recreational and cultural pursuits are in contrast to the area's history as an out-of-the-way place. Bear Valley was home to the last grizzly bear spotted in California. It was also a remote way station on Big Tree Road operated by Harvey Blood, and, after that, the region was used as a getaway for Alpine's renegade recluse, Monty Wolf.

TOUR FOUR
BODIE, MONO LAKE, AND RURAL NEVADA

WHAT'S BEST: Visit the ghost town of Bodie, the statuesque tufas of Mono Lake, the waterfowl havens of Bridgeport and Topaz Lakes along the east side of the Sweetwater Mountains through rural Nevada. Most Sierra visitors are surprised to see the open country that lies just over the crest from Lake Tahoe. **DRIVE TIME:** About 6 or 7 hours. *Note:* This tour ends at Mono Lake, which is below the east entrance to Yosemite National Park. To see the Tuolumne Meadows in the park's high country, you can drive east on Tioga Road, which will add an hour or two to the day. **ROADS:** State scenic highways, with traffic in the summertime. Some unpaved driving, but okay for passenger cars. **BEST TIME:** Depending on weather conditions, this is a four-season driving tour, with the exception noted immediately below. Optimum time is mid-to-late summer, to take advantage of the longer days. Tioga Road into Yosemite is closed during the winter and spring.

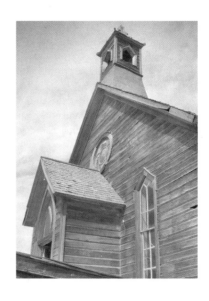

START AT MARKLEEVILLE, TAKE HWY. 89 OVER MONITOR PASS TO THE JCT. WITH HWY. 395. TURN RIGHT, OR SOUTH, AND CONTINUE THROUGH COLEVILLE, WALKER, AND THE WALKER RIVER CAN-YON. *Note:* If Monitor Pass is closed, take Hwy. 88 to Gardnerville and proceed south on Hwy. 395.

The Walker River Canyon was the route of Captain Joseph Walker, whose expedition in 1833 was the first known exploration of the Sierra—some ten years before Fremont. His poorly documented route continued northwest through portions of Alpine County near Markleeville. This rugged canyon was cataclysmically altered by the New Year's Day flood of 1998, which straightened out some bends and turned forests into gravel bars.

CONTINUE SOUTH ON HWY. 395 TO BRIDGEPORT.

Bridgeport is the Big City for recreational tourists in the summer, with several good American

BODIE

fare restaurants. Ken's Sporting Goods, painted barn red, is the best outdoorsman's store in the East Sierra. The town hosts several good eating places, but to grasp the true cow-country ambience, try the Sportsman, across the street from Ken's. Bridgeport is the spot to replenish picnic supplies or grab a frosty cone after a long day of hiking.

The late 1800s was Bridgeport's boom period. Known then as the logging town of Big Meadows, Bridgeport supplied Aurora and Bodie with some 50,000 cords of wood, as well as millions of board feet of lumber. Bridgeport is big views, cattle grazing ranchlands, and wide open spaces. A back road to Bodie, Aurora Canyon Road, leaves east from Bridgeport, near Bridgeport Lake. Bridgeport's courthouse, still a working building, was built in 1880, after it was learned that Aurora was in Nevada and therefore could not be the county seat.

CONTINUE SOUTH ON HWY. 395. TURN LEFT 7 MI. SOUTH OF BRIDGE-PORT ON BODIE RD., DRIVE IN 13 MILES TO BODIE STATE PARK.

Gold was discovered here in 1859 by Mr. Bodie, who died in a blizzard a few months later. The silver discovery at the Comstock Lode drew resources and attention, while a series of mining ventures failed here over the ensuing years, including one by Leland Stanford. In 1877, an accidental cave-in at Standard Mine revealed a rich quartz ledge. Another rush was on. During the next dozen years, Bodie's heyday, some $30 million in gold and silver was mined, equaling about $700 million in today's values. Some 12,000 miners roamed the hills and town, which claimed the wildest streets and worst weather in the West. Bodie State Historical Park preserves much of the mining town virtually intact, as if people just walked away.

LEAVE BODIE SOUTH ON GRADED COTTONWOOD CANYON RD., GO 12 MI., TURN RIGHT ON HWY. 167, GO WEST SEVERAL MILES AND TURN LEFT ON CEMETERY RD. TO THE COUNTY PARK AT MONO LAKE. *Note:* Cottonwood Canyon may be closed during the winter; if so, backtrack to the highway and continue south.

A short walk leads to some of the tufa towers, calcium carbonate growths caused by a chemical reaction between minerals in the lake and underwater springs. Mono, which has no outlet, is mineral-rich. It was some 600-feet deeper when glacier melt filled it, and before water from major creeks was diverted to Southern California. Due to efforts of the Mono Lake Committee and other conservationists, this diversion has largely ceased and the lake level is rising. At least a million water birds visit Mono, many drawn by its population of brine shrimp.

CONTINUE WEST ON HWY. 167 TO HWY. 395, TURN LEFT AND GO 3 MI. TURN LEFT AT MONO LAKE VISITORS CENTER.

The visitors center, itself a sight to see perched above the west shore of the lake, has a very good bookstore and several natural history presentations. The back patio of the center is a spectacular viewing area. Interpretive trails lead to the lakeshore.

TUFAS EMERGE AS LAKE LEVEL DROPS

CONTINUE SOUTH TO LEE VINING.

Lee Vining buzzes with Yosemite tourists during the summer. The must-stop for visitors is the Mono Lake Committee offices in the center of town. If you're hungry, you'll have several choices, but the best is just south of Lee Vining at the bottom of Tioga Road—the deceptively named Tioga Gas Mart. Inside you'll find gourmet deli treats as well as an array of gifts, books, and souvenirs.

BACKTRACK NORTH ON HWY. 395 OVER CONWAY SUMMIT TO BRIDGEPORT. VEER RIGHT ON HWY. 182, SWEETWATER RD.

Bridgeport Lake is a popular fishing lake, and also a major rest stop and wintering ground for migrating waterfowl. In the old days, cordwood for the mines was floated across the lake. Departing the lake, the road takes you up the east side of the Sweetwater Mountains. The Sweetwaters, underrated fly-fishing and hiking country, are visible to the southeast from many Alpine peaks and are sometimes mistaken for the White Mountains because of their granite slopes.

CONTINUE—HWY 182 BECOMES HWY. 338 IN NEVADA—TO WELLINGTON.

Wellington is at the southern end of Smith Valley, which, along with Mason Valley in Yerington, is a farming greenbelt stuck between the Pine Nut Range and the Great Basin. The bar and restaurant in Wellington, a well-known watering hole, draws people from Reno and Carson City who are looking to revisit the hospitality of old Nevada.

TURN LEFT OR WEST ON HWY. 207 TO HWY. 395.

At Highway 395, you can jog left a few miles to Topaz Lake. The large lake is popular among water skiers and boat fishermen, and its southern shore marshes are a landing zone for waterfowl and other birds. Topaz Lake Lodge is a lively casino known for its lake view and seafood buffet.

CONTINUE NORTH ON 395 THROUGH MINDEN-GARDNERVILLE, TO JCT. HWY. 88. GO SOUTH ON HWY. 88 TO RETURN TO MARKLEEVILLE.

Sharkey's Casino in Gardnerville is something of a landmark, with its western and boxing memorabilia and 20-pound prime rib dinners. Although the place has recently changed hands, the old-time flavor remains. Live band music can be heard every Friday and Saturday night. Along the main drag in Gardnerville you'll also see a couple of Basque restaurants where five-course meals are served family style and picon punch is the recommended aperitif. Midway in town is the Carson Valley Historical Society, where every history buff will want to take a peek.

TOUR FIVE
CARSON WAY STATIONS TO THE COMSTOCK LODE

WHAT'S BEST: Travel along the old way-station route, through Nevada's oldest town to the railroad and mining museums in Carson City. Finish up in honky-tonk Virginia City, the

CARSON VALLEY

capital of the Comstock. Much of the history of San Francisco derives from the events that took place along this tour. **DRIVE TIME:** Varies greatly depending on stops, from 3 to 7 hours, from Woodfords. **ROADS:** Scenic state highways and some divided highway with traffic. Suburban congestion in Carson City. **BEST TIME:** This tour is ideal for a spring getaway, when much of the Sierra is closed due to snow. This also might be a wintertime choice, to be combined with a more mundane shopping trip in Carson City.

START AT WOODFORDS AND GO EAST ON HWY. 88. GO 3 MILES, AND TURN LEFT AT BOTTOM OF HILL. THEN TURN RIGHT, IMMEDIATELY. CONTINUE NORTH AS FREDERICKSBURG RD. BECOMES FOOTHILL RD.

Ironically, the first emigrants to chronicle this route were eastbound. In 1848, several hundred Mormon soldiers who had been recruited to fight in the Mexican-American war returned from Southern California, seeking a route better than over the north side of Tahoe, which crossed the Truckee River too many times. They came through Hope Valley, then unnamed, and proceeded north along the west edge of the Carson Valley before turning east for Salt Lake. A few years later, west-bound Mormon emigrants returned seeking to establish Brigham Young's empire in California. But travelers to the Gold Rush, and later the Comstock Lode, came into conflict with the Mormons. Remote lands became not so remote. From 1850 to 1857, the Carson Valley saw bitter disputes between Mormons and non-Mormon settlers competing for business.

As you drive Foothill Road north, keep on the lookout for historical markers. You'll see one for Thomas and Elzy Knott, millwrights from the Midwest whose far-sighted businesses were cut short by conflicts with the Mormons; handsome Elzy Knott was shot dead while playing poker. Another marker commemorates Lucky Bill Thorrington, an associate of the Knotts who ran a way station. Thorrington was convicted of horse thievery, in a Mormon tribunal, and hung. Snowshoe Thompson worked with the Knotts and Thorrington. Aside from markers, look for old poplar trees, which are signs of former emigrant homesteads.

CONTINUE PAST KINGSBURY GRADE.

Walley's Hot Springs Resort dates from 1862, its mineral waters having warmed guests ranging from Ulysses S. Grant and Mark Twain, to Clark Gable and a number of modern entertainers who come over Kingsbury after headlining at Tahoe's casinos. A number of pools varying in temperature overlook the valley.

CONTINUE TO GENOA.

Established in 1851 and first called Mormon Station, Genoa is Nevada's oldest permanent settlement. Mormon Station Historic State Monument features a restoration of the original trading post, with a number of artifacts, including a pair of Snowshoe Thompson's oaken skis—then called snowshoes. The park and stockade, normally a quiet picnic spot, comes alive on the Fourth of July during Genoa's annual, free concert. Across the street from the park in a historic building is the Genoa Courthouse Museum, and a walk around Genoa's back streets will reveal a number of other historic buildings, including the oldest bar in Nevada.

As you leave Genoa, look for the community cemetery to visit the memorials of the valley's pioneers, including that of Snowshoe Thompson, his wife, Agnes, and son, who died at age 11. Next to Snowshoe's grave, look for a crude granite marker, roughly inscripted "Bill," which may be the grave of Lucky Bill Thorrington, whose body was secreted away by friends after his execution.

CONTINUE NORTH AS ROUTE BECOMES JACKS VALLEY RD. THE ROAD TURNS EAST AND MEETS HWY. 395. TURN LEFT INTO CARSON CITY.

The open serenity of the Jacks Valley Wildlife Area ends at Highway 395, where the big-box shopping malls typical of much of modern America have been built. Carson City is a fairly busy crossroads. But you'll find many tucked-away gems worthy of a vacation stop. Across from Fairview Street you'll see the large complex for the Nevada State Railroad Museum, which features a number of engines and cars, mostly from the Virginia & Truckee Railroad, the short line that serviced the Comstock Lode. The large grounds are encircled by a track on which visitors can take a ride during the summer.

A mile or two north of the railroad complex, just past the silver-domed state capitol building, is the Nevada State Museum, one of the finest in the West. Natural and human history are both exhibited, from prehistoric times to the late 1800s. The museum building originated as a U.S. Mint, coining the famous Carson City silver dollars. Massive steel shutters still remain as does the original press which occasionally mints commemorative coins. The museum's gold mine replica is a kid's favorite. You'll also find exhibits displaying a range of historical artifacts, including Dat-So-La-Lee baskets, cowboy gear, gaming memorabilia, and prehistoric skeletons of a mammoth and giant ichthysaurous—a dinosaur fish that swam when Nevada was under the sea. A children's museum is located across the street, a few blocks north.

The State Capitol Building houses the Governor's office and various other departments of state government. Large shade trees make the surrounding gardens a quiet respite on hot summer days. Be sure to visit the small museum on the second floor. Other buildings in the complex include the handsome Supreme Court Library and newly renovated State Legislature building. West of these structures is the historical district of Carson City, many blocks square.

CONTINUE NORTH ON CARSON ST., TURN RIGHT ON HWY. 50, EAST. CONTINUE EAST, TURN LEFT, OR NORTH, ON HWY. 342 TO VIRGINIA CITY.

Gold was discovered here in 1850, but at that time only a few miners prospected, most choosing instead the richer placers of the Mother Lode in California. To this day, the Comstock Lode is the richest deposit of minerals ever discovered. During the first ten years of the strike, San Francisco doubled in size to nearly 400,000 people, at a time when the population of Los Angeles was less than 5,000. The ore from the Comstock built the city.

In spite of fires, Virginia City remains preserved as a lively tourist attraction, with old buildings, mining works, cemeteries, and miles of underground shafts—as well as private museums, curio shops, bars, snack stands, and bawdy restaurants. The Virginia & Truckee Railroad runs a short trip, and there are several old mansions and tours of original businesses, such as one of the *Territorial Enterprise*, where Mark Twain wrote as a young man under the tutelage of Dan DeQuille. Virginia City's camel races, which take place in mid-September, are symbolic of the wide-open, eclectic nature of the place. Most of the attractions are in an eight-block radius of the downtown area.

TO RETURN FROM VIRGINA CITY: JUST NORTH OF VIRGINIA CITY, TURN RIGHT ON SIX MILE CANYON RD., HWY. 79. FOLLOW THE ROAD TO HWY. 50, TURN RIGHT, RETURN TO HWY 395 AT CARSON CITY.

GENERAL ULYSSES S. GRANT (5TH FROM LEFT) IN VIRGINIA CITY

As you head back through the desert to Carson City, look for Sutro Tunnel on the right, an engineering marvel. The tunnel was bored through the base of the mountains to drain water that had infiltrated the miles of Comstock shafts. For his efforts, engineer and civic leader Adolph Sutro earned a ton of money, enough to build San Francisco's spectacular turn-of-the-century attractions.

Tour Six
LAKE TAHOE CIRCLE

WHAT'S BEST: Nature, nightlife, and cultural heritage combine on this drive around the 72-mile shore of the largest alpine lake in North America. The Big Blue loop is one of the most scenic drives in the world. **DRIVE TIME:** Approximately 4 to 5 hours, from Hope Valley. **ROADS:** The lake is almost always in view from the two-lane state highways that encircle it. **BEST TIME:** Autumn is lovely at the lake, and you'll enjoy relative serenity. During the summer, bring along a swimsuit, and stay to enjoy a dinner out.

START AT PICKETTS JCT. HWYS. 88/89 IN HOPE VALLEY. DRIVE LUTHER PASS INTO MEYERS.

You get to pick from among three tales of how Luther Pass was named: for Ira M. Luther who operated a sawmill in Carson Valley in the early 1860s; or for Mr. Luther of Sacramento, the first to cross in a wagon in 1854; or for young Lieutenant Luther, in the command of Colonel Albert Sydney Johnson, an army engineer making improvements to the toll road in 1857, who was run out of town for being a Confederate sympathizer. Regardless, when you top Luther Pass, you enter the Tahoe Basin, into which more than 60 streams and creeks flow, but only one flows out—the Truckee River at Tahoe City.

TURN RIGHT ON HWY. 89/50 AT MEYERS.

Yanks Station here was a renowned watering hole and way station. Christmas Valley, a forested section along the Truckee River, is in the shadow of Echo Summit and gets the heaviest snowfall in the basin at lake level.

CONTINUE TO THE "Y," JCT. HWY. 89/50 AND TURN RIGHT ON HWY. 50 TOWARD STATELINE.

You'll pass through some of Tahoe's urban development that was in part a result of popularity brought about by the 1960 Olympics in Squaw Valley. In recent years, however, due to a bi-state Tahoe Regional Planning Agency, beautification efforts have been made, greatly enhancing the area. The marina for the Tahoe Queen, one of the lake's two paddle-wheel steamers, is on Ski Run Boulevard. For the ski-high view of the lake, try the recently opened Heavenly Valley gondola that picks people up at street level—located on the California side just as you reach the casinos. For another tasty view spot, try the top of Harrah's at Stateline, where a gourmet buffet is served.

CONTINUE PAST KINGSBURY GRADE, HWY. 207.

Kingsbury is the road over Daggett Pass, the most direct way back to Alpine County from Stateline. Perched at the top is the north entrance to Heavenly Valley Ski Resort, rated among the world's best. To see Nevada Beach, one of the best places to appreciate Lake Tahoe, turn toward the lake at Round Hill Shopping Center, a few miles north of Kingsbury. The beach stretches from the Edgewood Golf Course, noted for its nationally televised celebrity golf tournament, to the south end of Marla Bay. Campers can spread their tents under tall pines, install their folding chairs, and relax with a commanding view of the lake and the west shore peaks.

Farther north on Highway 50, around the next few bends, is Zephyr Cove with its old lodge restaurant, good swimming beach, and the M.S. Dixie—another Tahoe paddle wheeler, which travels across to Emerald Bay. Past Zephyr Cove is Cave Rock, perhaps the best boat launch and a good picnic spot. The highway is bored through a rift of an ancient volcano. Just as Highway 50 turns east and climbs from the lake is a private road down to Glenbrook, open to visitors. Glenbrook has short lakeside walks with good fall color. This area was the center of the logging business in the late 1800s, when Tahoe was being used for timber and fish to feed the Comstock.

AT SPOONER SUMMIT, TURN LEFT ON HWY. 28. CONTINUE TOWARD INCLINE VILLAGE

A few miles beyond Spooner Lake—which is a recommended fall color walk, and a popular cross-country ski area—you'll come to the improved parking area for Chimney Beach. This beach, as well as Secret Beach and some unnamed spots, are a hike down of a few hundred feet.

SAND HARBOR

You'll find a number of sandy coves with large granite boulders submerged in turquoise water. The sun can be very intense at this high elevation; the strongest level of sunblock is *de rigueur*.

CONTINUE ON HWY. 28.

At the bottom of the grade, you come to Sand Harbor. Part of Nevada Lake Tahoe State Park, this a beautiful swimming beach and home to Tahoe's summer Shakespeare festival. Between Sand Harbor and Incline Village, you have a chance to visit the Ponderosa Ranch from TV's Bonanza. Hoss, Pa, and Little Joe may be gone, but the home fires still burn at the ranch. Beyond Incline Village Ski Resort is Stateline north, home to smaller, old-style casinos, where you can usually feed the family for under two bucks each if you go for the special. The Cal Neva was the notorious hangout for Frank Sinatra and the Rat Pack.

CONTINUE TO TAHOE CITY ON HWY. 28.

You'll drive through Kings Beach and Tahoe Vista, with their lakeside cabins and motels, and then into Carnelian Bay, where the marina features some classic vintage inboards—worth a walk-around. Tahoe City will be the best stop for shopping and strolling. Both its main drag and lakeshore feature art galleries, fine restaurants, and hip outdoor gear shops. August is traditionally the month to escape the city and holiday at "The Lake." Behind the Boatworks Shopping Mall is a state park with a pier that will take you as far as you're going to get onto the lake on foot. From the end of the dock you can view the north shore's "double sunrise"—one sun that rises over the mountains and the other which is reflected off the lake.

TURN LEFT, SOUTH, AT HWY. 89 TOWARD HOMEWOOD.

At this junction—on Fanny Bridge—be sure to check out the Truckee River spillway, Tahoe's only drainage. Huge trout loiter here for tourists. Nearby is William B. Layton Park, a pleasant picnic spot, and Gatekeeper's Museum with a notable collection of Tahoe memorabilia and Indian basketry. This zone is also excellent to explore on mountain bikes, as paved bike trails lead in both directions along the lakeshore as well as north on Highway 89 toward Squaw Valley along the Truckee River. Family rafting down the Truckee is also popular.

CONTINUE SOUTH ON 89 TOWARD SOUTH LAKE TAHOE.

This stretch of Highway 89 includes the William Kent Visitors Center and Sunnyside Restaurant, two spots to enjoy the lake in different ways. Farther down, just north of Meeks Bay, is Sugar Pine Point State Park, featuring the Ehrman Mansion, an example of the opulent summer homes that were built in the early 1900s, Tahoe's golden years. Old estates, and some new ones, dot the shoreline along this westerly coast. South of Meeks Bay, with its large campground and picturesque sailboat harbor, the road leaves the lake for several miles.

Then you come to D. L. Bliss State Park. Bliss offers some short trails at the sheer lakeshore and good picnic spots. Just beyond the entrance to Bliss, are two or three turnouts with lake views. South of here you wind down to Emerald Bay, the setting for Vikingsholm. Even if you don't have time for the short walk down to castle on the bay, be sure to pull in for a view—the *crème de la crème* among Tahoe's finest.

CONTINUE ON HWY. 89.

After Emerald Bay, Highway 89 winds down to lake level at Kiva Beach, the Tallac Historic Site, and Pope Beach. Be sure to see the underwater stream viewing area located at the visitors center near Kiva Beach. (The visitors center is also the best place at the lake to get recreational and natural history information.) The Tallac Historic Site is another winner for the family, featuring a half-dozen preserved mansions and a long stretch of beach.

Side Trip: Across the highway from Kiva Beach is the 5-mile-long road to Fallen Leaf Lake, a whole other universe of scenic beauty. The best place to enjoy a beverage or snack is the marina at Fallen Leaf Store. You may also want to nose around Stanford Camp, which is just around the lakeshore. A number of trails from the lake lead into the Desolation Wilderness.

A short distance beyond Kiva Beach on Highway 89 is Camp Richardson, which hosts a wide-range of summertime fun, including bike rentals. Its lodge and restaurant are a favorite destination among Tahoe visitors, especially in fall during its Renaissance Faire. Having made the Big Blue loop, it's time to ask that age-old question: Where do we eat? You have many choices: See page 230 for help.

SOD ROOF AT VIKINGSHOLM, CAMP RICHARDSON

Alpine's
COMMON PLANTS
& ANIMALS
TREES

HIGHER ELEVATION
Mountain Hemlock (droopy tops)
Whitebark Pine
Red Fir

MID AND LOWER ELEVATION
Jeffrey Pine (vanilla smell)
White Fir (shade and north slope)
Lodgepole Pine (mistakenly called Tamarack)
Piñon Pine (Great Basin, pinenuts a Washo staple)
Yellow Pine (also Ponderosa, Jeffrey's west-slope cousin)
Sierra Juniper (slow growing, most old-growths)
Incense Cedar (wet places, first choice of pioneer loggers)
Western White Pine (also Silver Pine, narrow, six-inch cones)
Sugar Pine (huge cones, rare on east slope, crest)

DECIDUOUS
Aspen (red, orange, yellow in fall, tree-carver's and beavers' favorite)
Alder (in wet places, bush-like)
Cottonwood (low elevation, a sign of water)

FLOWERS

ALL HABITATS
Lupine
Violets

WET HABITATS
Columbine
Shooting Star
Tiger Lilly
Douglas Iris
Corn Lily
Rein Orchid
Buttercup
Monkey Flower
Evening Primrose
Swamp Onion
Cow Parsnip
Delphinium

MOIST HABITATS
Death Camas
Cinquefoil
Wild Rose
Aster
Blue Dicks
Larkspur
Sierra Primrose
Red Heather
White Heather
Ithuriel's Spears
Snow Plant

DRY HABITATS
Pride of the Mountains
Mule Ear
Paintbrush (many varieties)
Phlox
Yarrow
Mariposa Lily
Scarlet Gilia
Fireweed
Flax
Stickseed
Prickly Poppy
Sulfur Plant
Green Gentian

BIRDS

CRITTERS

Nesting in Alpine
All Season
Bald Eagle
Golden Eagle
Red-Tailed Hawk
Great Horned Owl
California Quail
Clark's Nutcracker
Stellar's Jay
Piñon Jay
American Dipper
Robin
White-headed Woodpecker
Canada Goose
Water Ouzel

Mule Dear
Black Bear
Coyote
Bobcat
Mountain Lion
Marmot
California Ground Squirrel
Golden Mantle
   Ground Squirrel
Gray Squirrel (in trees)
Chipmunk
Short-tailed Weasel
Badger
Red and Grey Fox
Beaver (introduced)

Cottontail
Jackrabbit
Raccoon
Porcupine

Mostly Summer
Blue Grouse
Turkey Vulture
Common Merganser
American Kestrel
Spotted Sandpiper
Common Nighthawk
Calliope Hummingbird
Cliff Swallow
Barn Swallow
Mountain Bluebird
Red-winged Blackbird
Brewer's Blackbird
Western Tanager
Purple Finch

GEAR

Never take new boots out of the box and start hiking … Break in new boots by wearing them around the house and while driving … Get boots with Gore-Tex lining … Boots should feel good to stand in right off the bat … Minority opinion: External frame packs are better than internal frame for backpacking: they have more compartments, can be leaned against something and leaned on, allow air circulation on your back, and you can tie things to the frame … Butane canister stoves are easier to use than liquid gas stoves … For warmth, layer clothes, starting with polyester or silk, then down and fleece, and Gore-Tex or equivalent … Use a Thermarest pad … Pack with a tent or shelter … Hiking poles are a third leg … Throw in the backpack: garbage bags, Ziplocks, athletic tape, paper clip … A collapsible water bottle gives you flexibility in selecting camp site … Sunscreen, sunglasses, hat … Always bring food, water, and extra clothes when day hiking … Light gloves are a good idea in summer … Test stove and put up tent before leaving home … Buy a larger stuff sack than the one the tent comes in … Use synthetic sleeping bag … Carry Swiss Army knife and a flashlight … Socks: blend of acrylic, wool, stretch nylon … Golden Rule of backpacking: Take everything you need and not one thing more.

CAMP TIPS

All the usuals about not spoiling or camping near water sources … Hang stuff to dry on limbs … To break a limb for firewood, drop a big rock rather than use Kung Fu move … Camping too close to water invites mosquitoes and dew … Use wet sand to wash dishes away from stream … Don't build fires where wood is scarce … Never leave a rock fire ring that you built … Wilderness is about enjoyment, not roughing it …

Don't camp downwind from a dead tree ... Bury waste; burn t.p. ... Never sleep in a tent with someone who had black beans for dinner ... Take off sweaty clothes and put on dry first thing in camp ... Other uses for hiking poles: camp billiards, fencing, weenie roasts ... Only the finest resort hotel rivals the finest campsite.

MISHAPS AND HOW TO AVOID THEM

A dog is a bear's worst friend ... Never be the tallest thing around when lightning is around ... If you see lightning in the distance, get down from the ridge ... If you can smell a forest fire you are in its path ... Carry DEET mosquito repellant and don't forget to put it on clothes ... Drinking hot liquid will warm you quicker than a fire ... The only cure for altitude sickness is lower altitude ... Ibuprofen ... Cross rivers at widest spots, not in white water or smooth fast water ... Use a stick or pole to cross river ... Don't cross water deeper than your crotch ... On loose rock slopes, groups stay close together and not directly down-slope from each other ... Stretch before, during and after hikes ... When cold, eat food ... Hiking poles save knees and ankles ... Tell someone where you're going ... Unstrap your pack when crossing a creek ... Most hypothermia happens in summer ... Fight back against a mountain lion ... Bears are dangerous if you see cubs ... You can't outrun a bear, but you might outrun the other guy ... In lightning, avoid water, high ground, metal gear and tallest trees ... Snowshoe Thompson's hypothermia prevention technique: dance on a big rock all night ... It's easier to prevent blisters and dehydration than to cure ... When cold, the first thing to cover is your head.

TRAIL TIPS

In hot weather, dip your hat or bandana in a stream and put on head ... At noon, the sun is due south ... The top of the shadow of a vertical stick, over time, traces a line from west to east ... Moss grows on all sides of trees ... Get oriented the moment you get lost, retrace footsteps ... Mark your path off-trail as you go with little piles of rocks ... When lost, relax, don't panic, drink water ... Watch your watch to gauge your distance; know when half your time is used up ... Start early ... Sun intensity increases 5% for every 1,000 feet elevation ... You need a topographical map to walk long distances cross country ... Don't cross trail junctures until entire group has gathered ... Never cross manzanita ... Zen of hiking: A trail is the most direct path of least resistance ... Shortcuts can take twice as long; know the terrain and where you're going before heading off-trail ... stay on trails in Yosemite and other popular spots.

CROSS COUNTRY SKIING

Use track skis with Teflon lubricant ... Layer clothes and avoid sweating ... Just because you're not sweating doesn't mean you don't need water ... Bring nuts, dried fruit, chocolate ... Extra power bars ... Extra dry socks ... Know how to build a snow cave. . . Don't ski below a snow laden cornice ... Or on top of one ... Check your pockets for missing objects after you've taken a face plant . . . Wear sunscreen ... Wrap duct tape around your ski pole to be used for repairs ... Use caution crossing snow bridges.

FOOD AND DRINK

Eat before you're hungry … Filter or boil drinking water … Drink before you're thirsty … Drink a lot of water … Hiking food is any without water in it … Drink a lot of water … You can buy most backpacking food in a supermarket … Eat several snacks during day, not one big lunch … The Complete John Muir Camp Cookbook: stale bread and stream water … Throw in extra trail mix or jerky … Bring iodine to treat water if pump breaks … Drink a lot of water … Never put a banana or pear in a knapsack … Indulgence is okay if you're willing to carry the load.

FEET

Your feet are your car … Cut your toenails before a hike … Soaking feet, or any appendage, in cold water will cure soreness and sprains … Bring Band Aids, moleskin, athletic tape, Neosporin … If shoes give you a blister twice, don't take them on your next hike … Take care of blister before it's a blister … Wash your socks everyday … It's hard to cross a river in bare feet; bring Tevas … Soak tired feet at lunch … Squeeze Vitamin E capsules on blisters or burns … Warming wet shoes next to the fire is a recipe for burnt sole … Don't sleep with socks on you've hiked in, they'll make your feet colder … Tao of mountain climbing: Virtue is a person with two feet who gets to the top of the hill.

WALKING

Never walk downhill with your hands in your pockets … Slow and steady wins the race … The shortest distance between two points is around … Fall up the mountain by leaning uphill, pushing off back foot, falling forward … Coming downhill, fall on your butt, not your face … Avoid walking in the heat of the day … Place feet on flat spots … If you don't know where you are, stay on trail … Stay on trail anyway … Groups never lose sight of each other, especially the slowest and fastest persons … Following deer will lead you to brush … North facing slopes lead to snow … Carry no more than one-third body weight … Never rest so long that you are tired when you start again … Tightening your stomach when you walk makes you light on your feet.

DISCLAIMER

By following the directions and engaging in the activities suggested in this book you may be bitten, burned, buoyed, bummed-out, broken, buffed, bent, befriended, bewildered, enlightened, injured, elated, energized, unnerved, lost, discovered, loved, lonely, betwixt and between. The authors and publisher can take neither credit nor blame for any of it, but sincerely do wish you the happiest of trails. Think of this book as you would any other piece of outdoor gear: It will help you do what you want to do, but it depends solely upon you to supply responsible judgement and common sense. Please obey all regulations; see *Resource Links* for a list of agencies that oversee public lands.

MARKLEEVILLE DEATH RIDE

One summer morning in 1974, Woodfords cyclist Wayne Martin got on his ten-speed and led a few out-of-town friends on a little ride. That evening—after pedaling for 129 miles and climbing more than 16,000 feet—one of Martin's friends protested, "That was a death ride!"

Today it is The Death Ride, one of California's premier cycling events. Since those cult beginnings, some 50,000 cyclists have made the grueling ride, gutting it up and down five mountain passes in one day.

In the early days, The Death Ride was a race, with a predawn shotgun blast heralding a simultaneous start for all riders. But in 1986, with more than 1,000 cyclists in an all-out contest for the best time, the California Highway Patrol determined that the ride might literally live up to its name if things weren't toned down a bit. Since then, the race has been changed to a tour, with staggered starts and options to ride fewer than five passes. There's even a website, www.deathride.com.

The Death Ride is limited to 2,500 avid riders. Currently, the course covers Monitor Pass, over and back, and then up and down Ebbetts, Carson and Luther passes. A barbecue celebration is held at Turtle Rock Park after the tour, which lasts at least until the last bent-over cyclist makes it back. Counting families and friends who join the contestants, the county population more than quadruples on the July weekend.

ALPINE EVENTS

Contact Alpine County Chamber
of Commerce, 530-694-2475

New Year's Eve ~ Torchlight Parade, Kirkwood
March ~ Snowshoe Thompson Family Ski
Spring Break ~ Reggae on the Mountain, Bear Valley
Spring Break ~ Kirkwood Jamming Party
Memorial Day ~ Masters Road Race, Bear Valley
Late March ~ Extreme Ski Competition, Kirkwood
Summer ~ Friends of Hope Valley Music Festival
July 4 ~ High Sierra Music Festival, Bear Valley
Second weekend of July ~ Markleeville Death Ride
July through August ~ Bear Valley Music Festival
Late August ~ Bear Valley Fat Tire Fest
Labor Day weekend ~ Bear Valley Triathlon
Mid-September ~ Kirkwood Rodeo
Late September ~ Octoberfest, Bear Valley
Late September ~ Woodfords Community Fair
Halloween ~ Markleeville Childrens' Parade
Fall ~ Watercolor Workshops, Sorensen's
Thanksgiving ~ Sorensen's Thanksgiving Feast
Winter ~ Sled Dog Races, Hope Valley

Glossary to Understanding Alpine Culture & Customs

Waving: When passing another car, raise two fingers off steering wheel; applies especially when passing deputy.

Fashion footwear: Winter, Sorels; summer, none.

Non-library information centers: Markleeville Post Office, Sorensen's Resort, Woodfords Station (mornings only), Markleeville Store

Sign of Spring: Turns from too damn cold to too damn hot

Sign of Summer: Snow shovels are off the porches

Sound of Fall: Wood splitter

Sign of Winter: Cat sleeps with dog

Peak Commute Traffic: Tahoe to Kirkwood, 9 a.m., Kirkwood to Tahoe 5 p.m., winter only.

Critical Mass: Line forms at Grover Hot Springs.

Proper attire: Never wear a suit in Markleeville, attorneys exempted.

Human Migration Pattern: Memorial Day, incoming; Labor Day, out-going.

Capital offense: Littering

Violent Crime: Dumpster diving bears

Pedestrian Warning: Look both ways before sleeping in the street.

Star-studded Event: Meteor shower

Alpine Fact Sheet

Temperatures
Highs: record 98°, summer average 85°, winter average 44°
Lows: record -22°, summer average 53°, winter average 23°

Precipitation
Average annual rainfall, 21 inches
Record snowfall, Tamarack Lake, 73.5 feet

Average annual snowfall, 7.5 feet
Average snowfall, Kirkwood, 30 feet

Elevations
Markleeville, 5,500 feet
Grover Hot Springs, 6,000 feet
Woodfords, 5,700 feet
Hope Valley, 7,000 feet
Kirkwood, 7,800 feet
Bear Valley, 7,100 feet
Highest, Sonora Peak, 11,462 feet
Lowest, Fredericksburg, 4,800 feet

Population: 1,200
Campsites: 650

Acreage
Alpine County is nearly a half-million acres, and 96 percent of it is public land. The sizes of the Wilderness Areas which are partly in, or close to, Alpine County are:

Carson Iceberg 160,871 acres
Emigrant 112,277 acres
Desolation 63,745 acres
Mokelumne 105,163 acres
Hoover 48,601 acres
Ansel Adams 15,933 acres

Yosemite Fact Sheet

Yosemite National Park was established in 1890, the nation's second, following Yellowstone. Much of the park area was set aside for protection in 1864. The complex geology—plate shifts, volcanic, glacial—dates back 500 million years. Some 10,000 years ago, the park was buried in ice. Yosemite covers 1,169 square miles, the same size as Rhode Island; about 94 percent of the park is wilderness, unlike Rhode Island.

ELEVATION: The park ranges from 2,000 to 13,000 feet
Yosemite Valley is just below 4,000 feet. Tuolumne Meadows is 8,600 feet. Tioga Pass, the park's east entrance, is the highest auto pass in California, at 9,945 feet.

MILES OF ROADS: 200
Both Yosemite Valley and Tuolumne are serviced by free shuttle buses during the extended summer. Tioga Road, Highway 120, through Tuolumne Meadows is open during the extended summer.

MILES OF TRAIL: 800
Throw in 20 miles of bicycle paths, 27 vehicle bridges, and 90 footbridges.

RAINFALL (INCLUDING MOISTURE IN SNOWPACK): Yosemite Valley, 37.2 inches
November through March sees 5 to 6 inches of rain on average. During the driest months—June through September—less than an inch falls. The valley sees an average of 29 inches of snow. The high country gets ten times that —snow can fall during any month at high elevations, but generally doesn't start until October. In March, the pack usually begins to recede.

HOT MONTHS, YOSEMITE VALLEY: June and July, average high 90 degrees
Early fall and late spring sees average highs the mid-70s and low 80s. Late fall and early spring hovers in the high 50s and 60s. Winter highs are in the high 40s. Count on temps 10 to 15 degrees cooler in Tuolumne. Morning can be near freezing during the summer.

ANNUAL VISITORS: 3.6 million; in the wilderness overnight, 50,000
That's about 9,800 visitors per day; or one employee for every 3.8 visitors, if you're counting.

NUMBER OF CAMPSITES: 1,521, in the park, for a maximum of 9,400 people.
In Tuolumne Meadows and Big Oak Flat are 843 campsites that will sleep 5,182 people—that's 55 percent of the total camping.

NUMBER OF LODGING ROOMS & CABINS: 1,517. *At Tuolumne Lodge and the High Sierra Camps are 125 tent cabins, or 8 percent of the total lodging.*

CENTER OF THE PARK: Mt. Hoffman, 10,850 feet.

HIGHEST POINT IN THE PARK: Mt. Lyell, 13,114 feet

BIGGEST LIVING THING: Giant Sequoias
Related to the redwood, these Sierra beauties are taller and more slender than their coastal cousins. Sequoias are king among life forms when it comes to size-volume, growing to 300 feet with diameters of up to 35 feet. With old growths averaging around 2,500 years old, the sequoias are second-fiddle in age only to bristlecone pine. Mariposa Grove's Grizzly giant (south of the valley) is daddy at 2,700 years old. In the park, trees will be found at three groves: Mariposa, Tuolumne, and Merced.

TALLEST WATERFALL IN NORTH AMERICA: Yosemite Falls, 2,425 feet.
Yosemite Falls drops in three pitches, 1,430 feet in Upper Fall, 675 feet in Middle Cascade, and 320 feet in Lower Fall. Yosemite Valley also receives 8 other waterfalls of 300 feet or more, including Sentinel at 2,000 feet, Horsetail at 1,000 feet, Ribbon at 1,612 feet, Bridalveil at 620 feet, and Nevada at 594 feet. You'll run out of fingers and toes counting falls and cascades in the backcountry. Some of the largest are near Glen Aulin, including Waterwheel and California falls.

Tahoe Fact Sheet

Sitting at an elevation of 6,229 feet, Tahoe is 22 miles long and 12 miles wide. The 72 mile shoreline takes in 193 square miles; to walk the surrounding mountains on the Tahoe Rim Trail, plan on covering 165 miles. It's also known as The Lake and Big Blue. Tahoe comes from the Washoe word "DAH-ho," meaning "Big Water." For sure. The lake's water would deluge the entire state to a depth of almost about 14 inches. It is the biggest alpine lake in North America.

Rural legend says the depth of the lake has never been measured, but that's fiction. Average depth is 989 feet, and the deepest spot is 1,645 feet. That puts the lake bottom several hundred feet below the Carson Valley, which is over the mountains to the east. Rural legend claims this big hole was created by a collapse of a volcano; not true. Although there was volcanic activity in the north lake basin, Tahoe was formed by the rise and fall of earthquake faults 24 million years ago, and by subsequent glacial scouring.

Annual Number of clear days: 240; partly cloudy, 67; cloudy, 29.
Clearest months are July and August (27 days average); Cloudy months are January and February (13 days average). Your chances, year around, of seeing the sun at Tahoe are about 85 percent.

Hot Months: July, August, September (average, 79 degrees)
Record high is 94 degrees, in August. The dry air makes it comfortable, but the high altitude gives the heat a much greater intensity. The yearly average high is 56 degrees.

Cold Months: January, February (average high, 38 degrees; low, 17 degrees)
The record low is –15 degrees in January. The volume of the lake keeps temperatures higher than areas nearby, such as Truckee and Hope Valley. The yearly low temperature average is 29 degrees.

Rain (including moisture in snowpack): Yearly average, 31 inches.
Most moisture comes in January, with 6.1 inches. The driest month is July, which receives less than a quarter-inch on average.

Average Yearly Snowfall: At lake level, 10 feet; on the rim, 25 to 42 feet.
Some 18 ski resorts are near Tahoe, along with 20 Sno-Parks and Nordic ski areas. Nearly 9,000 acres are in ski resorts. You can drop 3,600 feet over 5.5 miles at Heavenly.

Average surface temperature, summer: 67 degrees
Shallow beaches, such as Baldwin, have temps into the 70s. The surface never freezes; at 1,500 feet below the surface the temperature is 37 degrees. Emerald Bay occasionally freezes, most recently in 1989.

Water Evaporation, per day: *1.4 million tons, enough for 3.5 million people. The evaporation drops the lake level only one-tenth inch.*

Purity: *You could see a white Frisbee 75 feet below the surface. It is 99.7 percent pure, the same as distilled water. Pure as the driven snow. Thank the League to Save Lake Tahoe and the Tahoe Regional Planning Agency.*

Highest point on Tahoe Rim: Freel Peak, Alpine County, 10,881 feet.; lowest: Lake level, Truckee River in Tahoe City. *The lake is fed by about 65 streams, but only the Truckee River provides an escape. Some 30 peaks of 9,000 feet or higher comprise the rim of the Tahoe basin.*

Trailblazer
KIDS

Families exploring the great outdoors create memories for life—those dazzling starry skies, toasting marshmellows over a campfire, sitting on top of the world in a field of wildflowers. Or how about skiing under a full moon on snow that sparkles like jewels, making snow angels, or taking a dunk in nature's swimming hole? In the Alpine Sierra the best things in life *are* free, or at least only require a modest admission fee. In a few years, the kids will be snagging your *Trailbazer* and heading out on their own.

TH = TRAILHEAD, DT = DRIVING TOUR. CHECK THE TEXT FOR DESCRIPTIONS AND LOOK IN RESOURCE LINKS FOR PHONE NUMBERS.

PLACES THAT MAKE HISTORY FUN—

Sorensen's Resort, TH22, page 61
Sorensen's offers seasonal specials, such as Emigrant Trail walks, star-gazing, water color lessons, ski tours—give them a call to see what's on tap.
Alpine Museum and Historical Complex, Markleeville, DT2, page 184
"Lock 'em up" in the old jail or take a seat in the one-room school.
Bodie State Historical Park, Bridgeport, TH58, page 122
Looks like folks just walked away from this old ghost town—and they did! Bodie is the real deal.
Tallac Historic Site, South Tahoe, TH75, page 153
Big old mansions surround the spacious grounds. Snacks are nearby, at Camp Richardson.

Vikingsholm Castle, Emerald Bay, TH77, page 156
A walk down to the bay leads to a Norseman's stone castle with sod roofs. You can walk on to a pier or to a waterfall afterwards.
Ehrman Mansion, West Tahoe, TH79, page 161
Sugar Pine Point's mansion may be the lake's most impressive. Baby stroller friendly paths. The beach and pier are great for a picnic.
Gatekeeper's Museum, Tahoe City, TH80, page 163
William Layton Park is set right on the lake, and next to Fanny Bridge where huge trout loll around for the cameras. Indian baskets and old memorabilia are unique.
Ponderosa Ranch, Incline Village, DT6, page 197
Okay, so maybe Little Joe and Hoss weren't historical figures, but the intact set from the famous TV show is old enough to qualify.
Nevada Museum and Railroad Museum, Carson City, DT5, page 193
Feel the Old West with a ride on a restored train, or know what it's like get into and old gold mine.
Mormon Station and Virginia City, DT5, pages 193 and 194
See the recreated old fort that was Nevada's first settlement, then check out the buzzing honky-tonk that was the richest town in the West. Ice cream and fudge for the kids, a shot of red eye for the folks.

BOAT RIDES—

Tahoe Queen, South Tahoe; M.S. Dixie, Zephyr Cove
These paddle wheelers take you across Big Blue. See Recreational Activities in Resource Links.
Saddlebag Lake Boat Taxi, Yosemite, TH62, page 163
Make it a round-trip or take a tour of some of the 20 lakes that are in the neighborhood.
Echo Lake Boat Taxi, west from Tahoe, TH87, page 172
Walk back along the lake, or take a hike into Desolation Wilderness and catch the boat back.

FAMILY NATURE HIKES—

Frog Lake, TH4, page 36
Wildflowers in June and July and big-time Sierra vistas.
Hope Valley, TH20, page 58
Everybody can spread out, fish, swim, and stroll.
Carson River vista, TH30, page 77
You'd never guess that this volcanic river canyon awaits.
Grover Falls, Markleeville, TH33, page 81
A level walk through the forest leads to pools and a waterfall.
Dorothy Lake, TH40, page 90
This mini-hike has all the elements of a High Sierra trek.
Green Lake, TH57, page 93
Mid-level hike gets you to a big lake in the Hoover Wilderness.
Middle Gaylor Lake, Yosemite, TH64, page 136
Get out of the car right after entering the park and walk to this wildflower lake.
Truckee Marsh, South Tahoe, TH74, page 145
Combine a beach picnic with short walk. Birds and locals like this path, which sees few tourists.
Rubicon Trail, West Tahoe, TH78, page 78
Pick your length of hike on this Bliss State Park trail that is cut into granite walls in places. Beaches and forest accent big lake view.
Spooner Lake, North Tahoe, TH84, page 168
Pines and aspen surround this pretty lake. Roam around and count the different birds and critters.

LET'S GO SWIMMIN'—

American River Potholes, TH8, page 43
If you don't want to walk to these granite tubs, take the plunge in Silver Lake, which is right across the highway.
Roger's Rock, TH20, page 59
A pool in the river on a short hike in Hope Valley.
Grover Hot Springs, TH33, page 80
Hike to the waterfall and follow with a soak or swim.
Virginia Lakes, TH59, page 129
Take a boat out and find a place for a picnic.
Tuolumne River, TH66, page 136
Wading and rafting in late summer.
Baldwin Beach, TH75, page 152
Shallow water is warmer than most of Tahoe. Bring your own shade for this strip of sand.
Fallen Leaf Lake, TH76, page 154
This resort lake near Big Blue has boat rentals and a place to get treats when the diving is done.
Calawee Cove, TH78, page 158
From the big sand beach is an excellent coastal trail at Bliss State Park.
Kings Beach, TH81, page 164
You have your choice of several beaches and lots of walk-to eateries and tourist stores.
Sand Harbor, TH82, page 165
Arrive early in the summer. Two big beaches with submerged rocks make for a fantasy swimfest.

LET'S GO SWIMMIN'—CONT'D
Nevada Beach, TH85, page 170

Tall pines and a huge run of sand will suit all beachgoers. View across the lake at the Sierra is prime.

SKY HIGH RIDES—

Both Heavenly Valley and Squaw Valley ski resorts have gondola rides that operate in the summer. They're not cheap, but the payoff is big. Get off at the top for a summer picnic. See Recreational Activities in Resource Links.

VACATION VISITORS CENTERS—

Mono Basin Scenic Area, TH61, page 132

An architectural beauty sits with a stunning view of Mono Lake. The movie theater is tops. Walks to the fanciful tufas, an old volcanic crater, and an obsidian crater will supply geological curiosities.

Tuolumne Meadows, TH66 and TH68, pages 138 and 140

The center, set in a historic building is chock full. Across the highway is a walk into the meadows to Soda Springs and Parsons Lodge. Check out the stable for horse rides and grab a cone at Tuolumne Store, down the road.

Lake Tahoe Basin, TH75, page 152

The big deal is the short walk to Taylor Creek stream profile, an underwater look at native fish. Beaches are nearby, as are the mansions of Tallac Historic site. Down the road, bike rentals are available at Camp Richardson.

TIME FOR A PICNIC OR A REST STOP—

Trailblazer *is full of places in nature where you can sit a spell and enjoy a meal in the outdoors. Here are a few suggestions, close to the car; not all have facilities.*

Schneider Cow Camp, TH5, page 40

A short walk leads to an old barn, a nice place to settle in.

Silver Lake, TH10, page 44

Check out the doings at Kit Carson Lodge, then have lunch there or find a place along the classic lakeshore.

Woods Lake, TH14, page 50

This little lake has a fairy tale picnic grounds.

Wolf Creek Meadow, TH38, page 66

Turn left when you get down there and find a spot along the creek at the bridge.

Pacific Valley, TH44, page 97

Takes a little walking, but you can find many places along the creek amid flowers and a view of surrounding peaks. Lake Alpine, just down the highway, is a roadside choice.

Buckeye Creek, TH55, page 117.

The campground is a scenic and out-of-the-way spot to kick back for a few hours. Ditto for Green Creek on page 121, which is a drive in from the highway. Relax and unwind.

Lembert Dome, TH67, page 139

Look up at the dome, surrounded by Tuolumne Meadows.

Tenaya Lake, TH69, page 141

Ansel Adams loved this polished granite lakeshore. Down the road, get a view of Yosemite Valley with your lunch, on top of one of the big rocks at Olmstead Point, page 142.

Fallen Leaf Lake, TH76, page 153

Pick up lunch when you get there and settle in amid the activity at the marina.

Sugar Pine Point State Park, TH79, page 159

The pier and mansion, plus the beach and trails, will make for a full day.

Tahoe State Recreation Area, TH80, page 163
Here's a pier and beach, right behind the shopping center. Pick up lunch in Tahoe City and take a moment at this quick getaway.
Sand Harbor, TH82, page 165
Pick a day in the off season to pull in at this world-class beach.
Spooner Lake, TH84, page 168
You're high up from Tahoe here, and away from other parks— the perfect place to pull in for a picnic in the quaking aspen.

SHORT HIKES TO TOP OF THE WORLD—
Elephants Back, TH4, page 39
An adventure for big kids..
Leviathan Peak, TH48, page 103
The lookout station on the top adds more interest to this stand-alone giant.
Leavitt Lake Pass, TH52, page 115
This perch isn't a peak, but it feels like one. The drive in and ramp to the top will make this feel like an achievement.
Lembert Dome, TH67, page 139
Your kids may get hooked for life on Yosemite.
Mt. Watkins, TH70, page 142
This is a longer hike (7 miles) but it's easy walking and you get to a point right above Yosemite Valley. This dome is a treasure.
Stateline Lookout, TH81, page 165
Not many visitors know about this one.
Castle Rock, TH86, page 163
This is just a hop off the Tahoe Rim Trail at Kingsbury Grade. Some family members can take a longer walk.

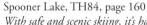

SKI TRIPS—
Kirkwood Cross Country, TH12, page 48
Get expert advice for beginners on some of the Sierra's best snow.
Hope Valley-Willow Creek, TH20, page 59; TH24, page 66
Follow Snowshoe Thompson's tracks into the forest or on a moonlight skate. Nearby Hope Valley Outdoor Center will fix you up with equipment and hot cocoa.
Hangmans Bridge, TH34, page 82
When the snow is right you can follow a level, scenic ski with a soak at Grover Hot Springs.
Bear Valley, TH45, page 99
You have a lot of choices. Bear Valley Cross Country will get you started.
Fallen Leaf Lake, TH76, page 153
Park at the highway and ski into the lake, or on the trails at Tahoe. The open, level spots are also a natural for moonlight runs.
Sugar Pine Point, TH79, page 159
The park has some level paths for families. At Tahoe City, just up the highway, are several ski resorts with tracks for beginners; see page 164.
Spooner Lake, TH84, page 160
With safe and scenic skiing, it's hard to keep this state park off the list. Beginners can ski around the lake, and more advanced skiers can head up the trail.

Resource Links

HOPE VALLEY CAMPGROUND

RESOURCE LINKS

VISITOR INFORMATION
Alpine County Chamber & Visitors Center, 530-694-2475
Amador County Chamber of Commerce, 209-223-0350
Carson City Convention and Visitors Bureau, 800-638-2321, 775-687-7410
Carson Valley Visitor Authority, 800-727-7677
Eastern Sierra Interagency Visitors Center, 760-876-6222
Incline Village-Crystal Bay, 800-468-2463
Tahoe-Douglas Visitor Center, 775-588-4591
Lake Tahoe Visitors Authority, 800-288-2463. 530-544-5050
Mono Basin Scenic Area Visitors Center, 760-647-3044, 873-2408
Mono County Visitor Information, Lee Vining, 800-845-7922
Nevada Commission on Tourism, 775-687-4322
South Lake Tahoe Chamber of Commerce, 530-541-5255
Tahoe Rim Trail Association, 775-298-0012
Tuolumne County Visitors Bureau, 800-446-1333
Virginia City Chamber of Commerce, 775-847-0311
Virginia City Tourism Authority, 775-847-7500
Yosemite National Park, 209-372-0200
Yosemite Sierra Visitors Bureau, 559-683-4636

CONSERVATION AND PRESERVATION GROUPS
Alpine County Historical Society, Markleeville, 530-694-2317
Calaveras County Historical Society, San Andreas, 209-754-1058
California Wilderness Coalition, 530-758-0380
Carson River Watershed, 775-887-7450
Carson Valley Cultural Center, Gardnerville, 775-782-2555
Friends of Hope Valley, Box 431, Markleeville, CA 96120
Kit Carson Mountain Men, Jackson, 209-223-1695
Lake Tahoe, Heritage Resource Manager, 530-573-2652
League to Save Lake Tahoe, 530-541-5388, 584-1660
Mono County Historical Society, Bridgeport, Box 417, CA, 93517
Mono Lake Committee, Lee Vining, 760-647-6595
Nevada Historical Society, Reno, 775-688-1191
North Tahoe Historical Society, Tahoe City, 530-583-1763
Pacific Crest Trail Association, Sacramento, 916-349-2109
Sierra Club, Berkeley, 510-848-0800
Sierra Nevada Alliance, South Tahoe, 530-542-4546
South Tahoe Historical Society, 530-541-5458
Tahoe Heritage Foundation, 530-544-7383
Tahoe Rim Trail Association, Incline Village, 775-298-0012
Washoe Tribe Archive and Cultural Center, 775-888-0936
Yosemite Association, 209-379-2646

MUSEUMS, NATURAL HISTORY & CULTURAL ATTRACTIONS

ALPINE COUNTY, CARSON VALLEY—
Alpine County Museum, Markleeville, 530-694-2317
Alpine County Arts Commission, 530-694-2787
Bear Valley Music Festival, 800-458-1618, 209-753-2574
Brewery Arts Center, Carson City, 775-883-1976
Bowers Mansion, Carson City, 775-849-1825
Carson Valley Museum, Gardnerville, 775-782-2555
Fourth Ward School Museum, Virginia City, 775-847-0975
Genoa Courthouse Museum, 775-782-4325
Mackay Mansion, Virginia City, 775-847-5208
Mormon Station, Genoa, 775-782-2590
Nevada Children's Museum, Carson City, 775-884-2226
Nevada State Capitol, 775-687-5030
Nevada State Museum & Mint, Carson City, 775-687-4810
Nevada State Railroad Museum, Carson City, 775-687-6953
Storey County Courthouse, Virginia City, 775-847-0968
Territorial Enterprise, Virginia City, 775-847-7950
The Castle, Virginia City, 775-847-0275
Way It Was Museum, Virginia City, 775-847-0766

EAST SIERRA, YOSEMITE—
Bodie State Historic Park, 760-647-6445
Mono Basin Area Visitors Center, Lee Vining, 760-647-3044
Mono Basin Historical Society & Museum, 760-647-6461
Mono Lake Committee, Lee Vining, 760-647-6595
Mono County Museum, Bridgeport, 760-932-5281

BODIE CEMETERY

LAKE TAHOE—
Ehrman Mansion, Sugar Pine Point,
530-525-7982
Gatekeepers Museum, Tahoe City,
530-583-1762
Heavenly Gondola, 775-586-7000
Lake Tahoe Shakespeare Festival,
Sand Harbor, 800-747-4697
Ponderosa Ranch, Incline Village,
775-831-0691
South Lake Tahoe Museum, 530-541-5458
Squaw Valley Cable Car, 530-583-6955
Tallac Historic Site, 530-543-2694, 544-3029
Vikingsholm Castle, 530-525-7277

SUPPLEMENTAL MAPS

Trailblazer's maps and descriptions are enough to get you down the road and trail. But to get the big picture, and for backcountry hiking and longer bike rides, you may wish to pick up a supplemental map. An area-wide road map will be most useful, and it will probably include campgrounds and public boundaries. Rand McNally is a good source, as is AAA.

Trailblazer country is covered by 65 USGS quadrangle maps, as well as some 30 other driving and trail maps—an unmanageable stack if you were to consult them all. Listed below are the best; pick the ones that suits your needs. Purchase information is included; many of the maps are also available at visitor centers and ranger district offices in the area.

USGS Quadrangles, 7.5 series, 1-888-ASK-USGS. For mountaineering and backcountry hikes, you should have a quad. Use a larger map for the big picture and then select a quad to focus in. An index map, which shows the quads for California, is available from the USGS. The downside to these maps is that you can walk off them in a day. (The old 15 series topos showed a mile per square, an area four times as large on the same size map.)

Toiyabe National Forest, Carson Ranger District, 1-888-ASK-USGS, 775-882-2766. Printed on two sides, this map covers the largest area, including all of Lake Tahoe and the northern Carson Range and south through Markleeville to Sonora Pass. Of course, hiking detail is sacrificed. Shows all the public lands (color-coded) and includes highways and Forest Service Roads. Shows campgrounds and trailheads. Get this for the big picture. Also very useful for adventure cyclists who want to chart a course.

Toiyabe National Forest, Bridgeport Ranger District, 1-888-ASK-USGS, 760-932-7070. Ditto the above description for the Carson District. One side begins at Sonora Pass and extends to Mono Lake. Side two is less useful, as is depicts the desert and military lands of southwest Nevada.

A Guide to the Mokelumne Wilderness, 1-888-ASK-USGS, , 530-694-2475. A waterproof 15 series topo that shows the Mokelumne Wilderness (from Carson Pass in the north to Ebbetts in the south), as wells as El Dorado and Toiyabe national forests at Carson Pass and west of Markleeville. Includes a northern piece of the Carson-Iceberg. Nice graphics, shows trailheads. Good all-sport map.

Carson-Iceberg Wilderness, 1-888-ASK-USGS, 530-694-2475. A 15 series topo that shows all the wilderness—south of Highway 88 and Highway 89 at Monitor Pass, west of Highway 395, and north of Sonora Pass on Highway 108. Fills in between the Mokelumne and Hoover map. Too bad the areas outside the road boundaries are white space rather than more map. A good trail map.

Get Lost in Alpine County, 530-694-2574. Shows the major roads, lakes, peaks and campgrounds—a useful reference for driving and camping.

Hoover Wilderness, 1-888-ASK-USGS, 760-932-7070. This 15 series topo is a winner since it shows not only the Hoover, but also the eastern Emigrant and northern Ansel Adams wilderness areas, and the north high country of Yosemite. It also includes the Toiyabe National Forest on the east side, and a chunk of the Stanislaus and Carson-Iceberg Wilderness on the west. Campgrounds, Forest Service roads, trails, and trailheads delineated. Fills in nicely above Yosemite and south of Markleeville.

Topographic Map of Emigrant Wilderness, Wilderness Press, 1-800-443-7227. Shows trails, roads, campsites of this wilderness. Also shows a piece of northern Yosemite. Much of the area is west of Trailblazer's activities, and the included activities are shown in the Hoover map. Will appeal to backpackers coming in from the west slope.

Yosemite National Park and Vicinity, Wilderness Press, Berkeley, 800-443-7227. This topographical trail map takes in a huge area, from Twin Lakes in Bridgeport in the north to Mammoth in the south. West to east it covers from Yosemite Valley to Mono Lake. Big picture day hikers will like it.

Trail Map of the Yosemite High Country, Tom Harrison Maps, 800-265-9090, 415-456-794. Harrison's usual high quality depicts the greater Tuolumne area, as well as Yosemite Valley. Great graphics. Special appeal to park backpackers. Wish it extended to the north Yosemite border and east to Mono Lake.

Yosemite National Park Trail Tracks, Fern/Horn Endeavors, 970-586-2743. A 3-D picture map that shows all of the trails in the greater Tuolumne area and Yosemite Valley. Not to scale, although specific hiking distances and elevations are included. Makes it easy to understand the terrain, especially if you're not familiar with topo maps.

Ansel Adams Wilderness, 1-888-ASK-USGS. A 15 series topo that shows trails in this wilderness—that is south and east of Yosemite, north of the John Muir Wilderness, and west of June Lakes-Mammoth. This is the place for stark peaks of the steep East Sierra. The appeal is mainly for backpacking.

Lake Tahoe Recreation Map, Tom Harrison Maps, 800-265-9090, 415-456-794, 775-298-0012. Count on Harrison. This is the best all around map for Lake Tahoe hiking and biking. It includes the Tahoe Rim Trail and Desolation Wilderness. Waterproof and easy to read.

South Tahoe Basin Recreation Topo Map, Fine Edge Productions, www.FineEdge.com, 13589 Clayton Lane, Anacortes, WA, 98221. Covers South Tahoe and—a bonus—extends south to the Silver Lake and Blue Lakes area of the Mokelumne Wilderness. It works for hikers, but the special appeal is for mountain biking. Specific bike trips are described.

Tahoe Rim Trail, Tahoe Rim Trail Association, 775-298-0012. The association provides the public with eight fold-out topo maps that combine to cover the whole trail. Unusually well written trail descriptions. Excellent free pubs, but money contributed to the association is money well spent. They get things done.

Tahoe Rim Trail, Take it Outdoors! Trail View Maps, 775-558-2603, 775-298-0012. A must if you plan on doing the whole enchilada; for hikers, bikers, and equestrians. Has area map and elevation strip map, and provides details for camps, water sources, and junctions along the way.

RECREATIONAL OUTFITTERS & ACTIVITIES

MARKLEEVILLE, HOPE VALLEY, KIRKWOOD—
Sorensen's Resort, Hope Valley, 800-423-9949, 539-694-2203
Fly-fishing, history hikes, stargazing, arts, skiing
Alpine Fly Fishing (Pleasant Valley) 530-542-0759
Alta Alpina Cycling (Death Ride co-sponsor) 775-265-7077
Ahwahnee Whitewater, 209-533-1401
Family Mountain Shuttle Service (rafters, etc.) 530-694-2966
Horse Feathers Fly-Fishing, Woodfords, 800-423-9949, 530-694-2399
Hope Valley Outdoor Center (all sports) 800-423=9949, 530-694-2266
Kirkwood Corral, 209-258-4600
Kirkwood Cross Country, 209-258-7248
Kirkwood Ski & Summer Resort, 800-967-7500, 209-258-6000
Horseback, bikes, fishing, golf, lake sports
Kit Carson Lodge, Silver Lake (boat rentals) 209-258-8500
River Rafting (ask at Carson District), 775-882-2766

BEAR VALLEY—
Bear Valley Cross Country and Adventure Co. 209-753-2834
Nordic skiing, kayaking, biking; rentals and tours
Bear Valley Mountain Resort (ski), 209-753-2301
Bear Valley Sports Shop, 209-753-2844
Mountain Adventure Seminars, 209-753-6556
Sierra Nevada Adventure Co., Arnold, 209-795-9310, Sonora, 532-5621

BRIDGEPORT, YOSEMITE
Caldera Kayaks, Lee Vining, 209-935-4942
Hunewell Guest Ranch (packers) 760-932-7710
Ken's Sporting Goods, Bridgeport 760-932-7707
Kountry Korners (trailhead shuttle) 877-656-0756
Leavitt Meadows Pack Station, 530-495-2257
Little Antelope Pack Station, 530-495-2443, 775-782-8977
Nidever Mountain Guide, Lee Vining, 760-648-1188
Troutfitter (fly fishing), 760-924-3676
Virginia Lakes Pack Station, 760-937-0326, 775-867-2591
Willow Springs (fly fish) 760-932-7725
Yosemite Outfitters, Lee Vining, 760-647-6464
Yosemite Valley Activities, 209-372-1220

TAHOE—
Alpine Meadows (downhill), West Shore, 800-949-3296
Anderson's Bike Rental, South Tahoe, 530-541-0500
Camp Richardson Corral, 530-541-3113
Camp Richardson Marina, South Tahoe, 530-542-6570

Clair Tappaan Lodge (cross country), 530-426-3632
Diamond Peak (cross country), Incline, 775-832-1177
Fallen Leaf Store & Marina, 530-541-4671
Flume Trail Shuttle, 775-749-5349
Heavenly Valley Resort (including gondola), 800-243-2836, 775-586-7000
M.S. Dixie (paddle wheel cruise), 775-589-4906
Mountain Sports Center, South Tahoe, (bikes), 530-542-6584
Northstar Nordic Ski Center, 530-562-2475
Royal Gorge, Soda Springs, 1-800-500-3871
Shoreline Bike Shop (rentals), Stateline, 775-588-8777
Sierra at Tahoe, Echo Summit (downhill) 800-288-2463, 530-659-7453
Sierra Ski & Cycle Works, Round Hill Tahoe, 775-541-7505
Ski Homewood (downhill), West Shore 530-525-2992
Spooner Lake Cross Country, 775-749-5349
Squaw Creek Nordic, 530-530-583-6300
Squaw Valley USA (all activities) 530-583-6955, 800-545-4350
Tahoe Cross Country, Tahoe City, 530-583-5475
Tahoe Fly Fishing Outfitters, 530-541-8208
Tahoe Queen (paddle wheel cruise), 530-541-3364
Tahoe Whitewater Tours, Tahoe City, 800-442-7238
Zephyr Cove Stables, 775-588-5664

FISHING

California Department of Fish and Game, 916-355-7040
Nevada Department of Wildlife, 775-465-2242

Fishing Licenses

(partial list; licenses widely available)—
Sorensen's, 1-800-423-9949,
    530-694-2203
Woodfords Station, 530-694-2930
Markleeville General Store, 530-694-2448
Kirkwood General Store, 209-258-7294
Kit Carson Store,
    Silver Lake, 209-258-8500
Carson River Resort, 1-877-694-2229
Lake Alpine Lodge, 209-753-6237
Bear Valley Sports Shop, 209-753-2844
Bear Valley Adventure Co., 209-753-2834
Sportsman, South Tahoe, 530-542-3474
Tahoe Fly Fishing Outfitters,
    530-541-8208
Ken's Sporting Goods,
    Bridgeport 760-932-7707

GIFTS, SPORTING GOODS, AND GENERAL STORES

ALPINE, BEAR VALLEY—

Sorensen's Bookstore & Gifts, Hope Valley 800-423-9949, 530-694-2203
Bear Valley General Store, 209-753-2842
Bear Valley Sports Shop, 209-753-2844
Kirkwood General Store, 209-258-7294
Markleeville (Rudden's) General Store, 530-694-2448
Reno Mountain Sports, Reno, 775-825-2855
Sierra Nevada Adventure Co., Arnold, 209-795-9310, Sonora, 532-5621
Sierra Pines Store, Woodfords, 530-694-2949
Woodfords Gifts & Antiques, 530-694-2935
Villa Gigli Collection, Markleeville, 530-694-2253
Feather's Edge Finery, Bear Valley, 209-753-2013
Bear Valley General Store, 209-753-2842
Kit Carson Store & Gallery, Silver Lake, 209-258-8500

EAST SIERRA, YOSEMITE—

Ansel Adams Gallery, Yosemite Valley, 209-372-4413
Ansel Adams Gallery, Mono Lake, 760-647-6581
Eastern Sierra Trading Post, Bridgeport, 760-932-7231
Ken's Alpine Shop, Bridgeport, 760-932-7707
Three Flags Trading Post, Walker, 530-495-2955
Tioga Gas Mart, Lee Vining, 760-647-1088

TAHOE—

Alpenglow Sports, Tahoe City, 530-583-6917
Boatworks Shopping Mall, North Tahoe, 530-583-1488
Cobblestone Mall, North Tahoe, 530-583-1580
Caesar's Tahoe, Stateline, 775-588-3515
Fallen Leaf Store & Marina, 530-541-4671
Great Outdoor Clothing, South Tahoe, 530-541-0664
Grizzley's Mountain Furnishings, South Tahoe, 530-542-2667
Long's Drugs, South Tahoe, 530-544-1500
Rainbow Mountain, South Tahoe, 541-7470
Shirt Connection, 530-541-7179
Ski Run Marina Village, South Tahoe, 530-542-6287
Sports Ltd., South Tahoe, 530-544-2284
Squaw Creek Mall, Squaw Valley, 530-583-6300
Womensport, Zephyr Cove, 775-586-0066

CAMPING & PUBLIC AGENCIES

Trailblazer's activities take you into seven wilderness areas, a national park, several state parks and county parks, and several national forests. Each of these public lands has slightly different regulations regarding use, which may change from year to year, so you'll want to contact the appropriate agency listed below to make sure you have the most current information. Some campgrounds are open all year, but most are only available from late spring through early fall.

The following rules are among the most important: You need a permit to car camp anywhere or to sleep overnight in the wilderness; Some wilderness areas have fire restrictions, and all prohibit camping near water sources; Vehicles and bicycles are not allowed in wilderness areas; Vehicles must stay on designated roads in designated areas in all national forests; Hunting and fishing are allowed only by permit at certain times; Control your pets in all areas—the Carson Pass area has leash restrictions, and pets are not allowed in Yosemite or on state park trails; Prepare for bears: bear canisters are available for purchase or rent in Yosemite and at many sporting goods stores.

Most of the campgrounds are run by the Forest Service, and facilities vary from none (dry camping) to full showers and picnic tables. Hundreds of campsites are available at Tahoe, in Alpine County, and in the Bridgeport area. Most of the campgrounds have some reserved and some non-reserved sites; some campgrounds are all first-come, first served. The trailhead listings in Trailblazer will give you an idea of what the area is like. Give the appropriate agency a call, and they'll set you up.

COUNTY PARKS
Turtle Rock Park, Markleeville, 530-694-2140
Davis Creek, Washoe Valley, Nevada, 775-849-0684

STATE PARKS

STATEWIDE RESERVATIONS, CALIFORNIA, 800-444-7275
STATEWIDE RESERVATIONS, NEVADA, 775-687-4384, 687-4379
California Information, 800-777-0369
District Office, Tahoma, 530-525-7232
West Shore Tahoe, 530-525-7277, 541-3030, *Emerald Bay, D.L. Bliss, Eagle Point*
Lake Tahoe Nevada, 775-831-0494, *including Sand Harbor, Spooner*
Sugar Pine Point, West Shore Tahoe, 530-525-7982
Tahoe State Recreation, North Shore, 530-583-3074
Grover Hot Springs, Markleeville, 530-694-2248
California Department of Fish & Game, 760-872-1171
Mono Lake Tufa Reserve *(no camping)*, 760-647-6331
Bodie Historical Park *(no camping)*, 760-647-6445

FOREST SERVICE CAMPGROUNDS &
  WILDERNESS PERMITS; *See below for Yosemite permits*

AREA WIDE CAMPING RESERVATIONS, 877-444-6777
Bayview Campground, Emerald Bay, 530-544-5994
Bear Valley Office, 209-795-1381
Bishop Field Office, 760-873-2500, 873-2483
  Ansel Adams, John Muir wilderness areas.
Bridgeport Ranger District, 760-932-7070
  *Hoover, Emigrant, Carson-Iceberg, Mokelumne wilderness areas. Some 20
  campgrounds with nearly 500 sites are in the Bridgeport area. Toiyabe
  National Forest*
Carson Ranger District, Carson City, 775-882-2766
  *Mokelumne and Carson-Iceberg, Mt. Rose wilderness areas. Toiyabe
  National Forest*
El Dorado National Forest, 530-644-6048 (automated)
El Dorado Pacific Station, 530-644-2349
  Desolation Wilderness permits and west side information
El Dorado-Carson Pass (summer) 209-258-8606
Fallen Leaf Campground, 530-544-0426
Lake Tahoe Basin Management Unit, 530-543-2674
  East Desolation and Tahoe information
Lee Vining Ranger District, 760-647-3044
  Inyo National Forest, east of Yosemite camping.
Markleeville, 530-694-2475
  Carson-Iceberg, Mokelumne wilderness areas.
Mono Basin Visitors Center, 760-873-2408
Nevada Beach, Tahoe, 775-588-5562
Sierra National Forest, 559-877-2218, 658-7588
Stanislaus National Forest, Sonora, 209-532-3631, 795-1381
  Emigrant, Mokelumne, Carson-Iceberg. West Sierra camping
Truckee Ranger District, Tahoe National Forest, 530-587-3558
William Kent and Kaspian Campgrounds, West Shore Tahoe, 530-583-3642

YOSEMITE
Wilderness Permits, 209-372-0740
Campgrounds, 800-436-7275
General Campgroud Information, 209-372-4845
Valley Visitors Center, 209-372-0200

BUREAU OF LAND MANAGEMENT
Bishop, 760-872-4881
Carson City, 775-885-6000

PRIVATE & OTHER PUBLIC CAMPGROUNDS

TAHOE—
Camp Richardson, South Tahoe, 800-544-1801
Camp Shelly, South Tahoe, 925-373-5700
Campground by the Lake, South Tahoe, 530-542-6096
Lake Forest, North Tahoe, 530-583-3796
Meeks Bay Resort, 530-525-6946
Zephyr Cove, East Shore, 775-589-4981

BRIDGEPORT AREA—
Lower Twin Lakes, 760-932-7751
Mono Village, 760-932-7071
Doc and Al's, 760-932-7051
Bridgeport Reservoir, 760-932-7001

SUMMARY OF ALPINE COUNTY CAMPGROUNDS
(FS)=Forest Service, (BLM)=Bureau of Land Management

Grover Hot Springs is open all year. Lower-elevation campgrounds are open April or May through October; higher-elevation (above 7,000') open June through September.

With piped water and flush toilets and showers
Grover Hot Springs (State), 76 sites, 5,900'
        (4 mi. west of Markleeville on Hot Springs Road)
Hope Valley Resort (FS/priv), 24 sites, 6,900'
        (1 mi. east of Picketts Jct. on Hwy. 88/89)
Indian Creek Reservoir (BLM), 29 sites, 5,600'
        (4 mi. in Airport Rd., between Markleeville/Woodfords)

With piped water and flush toilets:
Highland Lakes (FS), 35 sites, 8,600'
        (7 mi. in on Highland Lakes Road, west of Ebbetts Pass)
Lake Alpine (FS), 27 sites, 5 walk-in sites, 7,300'
        (near Lake Alpine Lodge, Hwy. 4, west of Ebbetts Pass)
Pine Martin-Silver Valley (FS), 58 sites, 7,400'
        (at east end Lake Alpine, Hwy. 4)
Silver Tip (FS), 25 sites, 7,500'
        (.75-mi. west of Lake Alpine, Hwy. 4)

Turtle Rock Park (county), 28 sites, 6,100'
> (.5-mi. Turtle Rock Rd., between Markleeville/Woodfords)

With piped water and vault toilets:
Bloomfield (FS), 12 sites, 7,900'
> (2 mi. on Highland Lakes Road, west of Ebbetts Pass)

Lower Blue Lake (PG&E), 16 sites, 8,000'
Upper Blue Lake (PG&E), 32 sites, 8,200'
Upper Blue Lake Dam (PG&E), 25 sites, 8,200'
> (10 mi. in on Blue Lakes Road, off Hwy. 88)

Caples Lake (FS), 35 sites, 7,800'
> (west end of Caples Lake on Hwy. 88)

Crystal Springs (FS), 20 sites, 5,800'
> (2 mi. west of Woodfords on Hwy. 88/89)

Hope Valley Campground (FS), 20 sites, 7,200'
> (3 mi. in on Blue Lakes Road, off Hwy. 88)

Kit Carson (FS), 12 sites, 6,600'
> (1 mi. east of Picketts Jct. on Hwy. 88/89)

Markleeville Creek (FS), 10 sites, 5,500'
> (1 mi. south Markleeville on Hwy, 89/4)

Middle Creek (PG&E), 6 sites, 8,200'
> (10 mi. in on Blue Lakes Road, off Hwy. 88)

Silver Creek (FS), 22 sites, 6,800'
> (on Hwy. 4, 7 mi. west jct. Hwy. 4/89)

Snowshoe Springs (FS), 13 sites, 6,100'
> (2 mi. east of Picketts Jct., Hwy. 88/89)

Woods Lake (FS), 25 sites, 8,200'
> (2 mi. on Woods Lake Rd., 1 mi.,
> west Carson Pass)

Stream water and vault toilets or no facilities:
Centerville Flat (FS), 12 sites, 5,900'
> (on Hwy. 4 at Wolf Creek Road turnoff)

Hermit Valley (FS), 6 sites, 7,500'
> (on Hwy. 4 west of Ebbetts Pass)

Mosquito Lake (FS), 9 sites, 8,200'
> (on Hwy. 4, east of Lake Alpine)

Pacific Valley (FS), 6 sites, 7,600'
> (on Hwy. 4 east of Ebbetts Pass)

Camp Richardson Resort, Virginia Lakes Resort, Tuolumne Meadows, Sorensen's Resort

Where To Stay

(P) = PRICEY, $200 AND UP
(M) = MODERATE, $100 TO $200
(C) = CHEAP, UNDER $100

MARKLEEVILLE, HOPE VALLEY, KIRKWOOD—

Sorensen's Resort, Hope Valley (C-P) 800-423-9949, 530-694-2203
  Cabins, larger homes; weddings and groups
Bed, Bike & Bagel, Markleeville (C-M) 530-694-9337
Carson River Resort, Markleeville (C-M) 877-694-1165
Creekside Lodge, Markleeville (M) 530-694-2511
Diamond Valley House, Woodfords (M-P) 800-423-9949
  On five forested acres with stream, sleeps six, pets welcome
J. Marklee Toll Station, Markleeville (C-M) 530-694-2507
Kirkwood Accommodations (M-P) 209-258-8575
Kirkwood Real Estate (M-P) 888-258-8777, 209-593-7767, 800-557-7919
Kirkwood Resort Co. (M-P) 209-258-6000
Kirkwood Vacations (C-M) 800-967-7500, 209-258-7000
Kit Carson Lodge, Silver Lake (M-P) 209-258-8500
Mountain Creek Cabin, Markleeville (M) 530-694-2454
The Mountain & The Garden (B&B), Woodfords (M) 530-694-0012
Woodfords Inn (C) 530-694-2410

BEAR VALLEY—

Base Camp Lodge (C-M) 209-753-6556
Bear Valley Lodge (C-P) 209-753-2327
Bear Valley Real Estate (condo rentals) (M-P) 209-753-2334
Lake Alpine Lodge (C-M) 209-753-6358
Tamarack Lodge (group lodging available) (C-M) 209-753-2080
1859 Historic National Hotel, Jamestown (C-M) 800-894-3446

CARSON VALLEY—

Carson Valley Inn & Casino (M) 800-321-6983, 775-321-6983
Historian Inn, Gardnerville (C) 877-783-9910
Genoa House Inn B&B, Genoa (M) 775-782-7075
The Jensen Mansion (M) 775-782-7644
Walleys Hot Springs, Genoa (C-P) 775-782-8155, 800-628-7831
Wild Rose Inn B&B, Genoa (M) 877-819-4225

East Sierra, Yosemite—

Best Western Lakeview, Lee Vining (C-M) 760-647-6543

Cain House B&B, Bridgeport (C-M) 800-433-2246

Doc and Al's Resort, Bridgeport (C-M) 760-932-7051

Hunewell Guest Ranch, Bridgeport (M) 760-932-7710

Meadowcliff Resort, Coleville (C) 888-333-8132

Reverse Creek Lodge, June Lake (C-M) 800-762-6440

Topaz Lodge & Casino, Topaz Lake (C) 800-962-0732

Tioga Lodge, Mono Lake (M) 760-647-6423

Tioga Pass Resort, at Yosemite boundary (M) 209-372-4471
>   *Includes meals and transportation for skiers; cabins in summer.*

Virginia Lakes Resort (C-M) 760-647-6484

Yosemite High Sierra Camps, 559-253-5674

Yosemite Valley (C-P) 559-252-4848
>   *The Awhahnee, Wawona, Yosemite Lodge, Curry Village*

Yosemite Sierra Visitors Bureau (west side lodging info.) 559-683-4636

Yosemite West Cottages (M) 559-642-2211

Lake Tahoe—

Cal-Neva Lodge & Casino, North Shore (C-M) 775-832-4000

Camp Richardson Resort, South Shore (C-M) 800-544-1801

Doc's Cottages, Stateline (C) 775-588-2264

Hyatt Regency, Incline Village (P) 800-553-3288

Lakeland Village Resort, South Tahoe (C-P) 800-822-5969

Lakeside Inn & Casino, Stateline (C) 800-624-7980

Lazy S Lodge, South Tahoe (C) 800-862-8881

Mayfield House B&B, Tahoe City
    (M-P) 888-518-8898

Marriott's Timber Lodge, South Tahoe
    (M-P) 800-845-5279

Station House Best Western, South Tahoe
    (C) 800-822-5953

Tahoma Meadows B&B, West Shore
    (C-P) 866-525-1553

The Resort at Squaw Creek, Squaw Valley
    (M-P) 800-327-3353

Tahoe Vacation Rental Connection, South Tahoe
    (M-P) 530-542-2777

Zephyr Cove Resort, East Shore
    (M-P) 775-589-4981

Where to Eat

(C) = Cheap or takeout (Less than $10)
(M) = Moderate, Family ($10 to $20)
(P) = Pricey, Special Occasion ($20 and up)

SORENSEN'S CAFE

MARKLEEVILLE, HOPE VALLEY, KIRKWOOD—

Sorensen's Café, Hope Valley (C-M) 800-423-9949, 530-694-2203
Breakfast, lunch, dinner; great wine list; sun deck
Hope Valley Resort (C) 530-694-2266
J. Marklee Toll Station, Markleeville (C-M) 530-694-2507
M's Coffee House, Markleeville (C) 530-694-9337
Kirkwood Inn (C-M) 209-258-7304
Kit Carson Lodge, Silver Lake (M) 209-258-9564
Sierra Pines, Woodfords (C) 530-694-2949
The famous burger really is; they grill the bun.
The Deli, Markleeville (C) 530-694-9595
Villa Gigli, Markleeville (M) 530-694-2253
Summer weekends, organic gourmet Italian; outside dining available
Wolf Creek Restaurant, Markleeville (M) 530-694-2150
In historic Fisk Hotel building
Woodfords Station, Woodfords (C) 530-694-2930
Belly up to the counter; site of annual chili cook-off

BEAR VALLEY—

Headwaters Coffee House (C-M) 209-753-2708
The Grizzly Bar and Grill (C-M) 209-753-2327

CARSON VALLEY—

Carson Valley Inn, Gardnerville (C-P) 800-321-6983, 775-782-9711
J&T Basque Dining Room, Gardnerville (M) 775-782-2074
La Ferme, Genoa (M-P) 775-783-1004
Overland Hotel (Basque) (M) 775-782-2138
Sharkey's Casino, Gardnerville (C-M) 775-782-3133

KIT CARSON RESORT

HAPPY JACK THE CAMPSIDE COOK

EAST SIERRA-YOSEMITE—

Hayes Street Café, Bridgeport (C) 760-932-7141
Latte Da Coffee Café, Lee Vining (C-M) 760-647-6310
Meadowcliff Resort, Coleville (C) 888-333-8132
Mono Inn Restaurant, Lee Vining (M-P) 760-647-6581
Nicely's Restaurant, Lee Vining (C-M) 760-647-6477
Rhino's Bar & Grill, Bridgeport (C-M) 760-932-7345
The Sportsman, Bridgeport (C-M) 760-932-7020
Walker Burger, Walker (C) 530-495-2219
Whoa Nellie Deli, Tioga Gas Mart, Lee Vining (C-M) 760-647-1088

TAHOE—

Brewery at Lake Tahoe, South Shore (C-M) 530-544-2739
Cafe Fiore, South Tahoe (C-M), 530-541-2908
Evan's Gourmet Café, South Tahoe (M-P) 530-542-1990
Fresh Ketch, South Tahoe (M-P) 530-541-5683
Freshie's, South Lake Tahoe, (C-M), 530-542-3630
Forest Buffet, Harrah's, Stateline (M-P) 800-648-3773
Jacksons Beachside Grille, Kings Beach (M) 530-546-3315
Mirabelle French Cuisine, Stateline (M-P) 775-586-1007
Nepheles, South Tahoe (M-P) 530-544-8130
Paradise Grill, North Tahoe (C-M), 775-831-9944
Riva Grill on the Lake, South Tahoe (C-M), 530-542-2600
Scusa!, South Tahoe (M) 530-542-0100
Sprouts Natural Food Café, South Tahoe (C) 530-541-6994
Sunnyside Resort, Tahoe City (M) 530-583-7200
Tahoe Biltmore, North Shore (C-M) 800-245-8667

index

Notes

FOR PUBLISHER-DIRECT SAVINGS TO INDIVIDUALS AND GROUPS, AND
FOR BOOK TRADE ORDERS, PLEASE CONTACT:

DIAMOND VALLEY COMPANY
89 Lower Manzanita Drive
Markleeville, CA 96120

Phone-fax: 530-694-2740
www.trailblazertravelbooks.com
trailblazer@gbis.com

All titles are also available through major book distributors, stores, and websites.
Please contact the publisher with comments and suggestions. We value your
readership.

DIAMOND VALLEY COMPANY S
TRAILBLAZER TRAVEL BOOK SERIES:

ALPINE SIERRA TRAILBLAZER
Where to Hike, Ski, Bike, Fish, Drive from Tahoe to Yosemite
ISBN 0-9670072-6-7

KAUAI TRAILBLAZER
Where to Hike, Snorkel, Bike, Paddle, Surf
ISBN 0-9670072-1-6

*"In layout, design
and content, the
very essence of
what an outdoor
guide should be."*
—Midwest Book Review

GOLDEN GATE TRAILBLAZER
Where to Hike, Stroll, Bike, Jog, Roll
in San Francisco and Marin
ISBN 0-9670072-2-4

MAUI TRAILBLAZER
Where to Hike, Snorkel, Paddle, Surf, Drive
ISBN 0-9670072-4-0

*"The new
outdoor bible."*
—Sundance Quarterly

HAWAII THE BIG ISLAND TRAILBLAZER
Where to Hike, Snorkel, Bike, Surf, Drive
ISBN 0-9670072-5-9

*"Taking you to
the heart and
soul of your
destination."*
—guidetotravelguides.com